Collaborating for Change

Collaborating for Change

A Participatory Action Research Casebook

EDITED BY SUSAN D. GREENBAUM,
GLENN JACOBS, AND PRENTICE ZINN

Rutgers University Press

New Brunswick, Camden, and Newark, New Jersey, and London

Library of Congress Cataloging-in-Publication Data

Names: Greenbaum, Susan D., 1945– editor. | Jacobs, Glenn, 1940– editor. | Zinn, Prentice, 1964– editor.
Title: Collaborating for change : a participatory action research casebook / edited by Susan D. Greenbaum, Glenn Jacobs, and Prentice Zinn.
Description: New Brunswick, New Jersey : Rutgers University Press, [2020] | Includes bibliographical references and index.
Identifiers: LCCN 2019015390 | ISBN 9781978801165 (cloth) | ISBN 9781978801158 (paperback) | ISBN 9781978801172 (epub) | ISBN 9781978801189 (mobi) | ISBN 9781978801196 (pdf)
Subjects: LCSH: Action research—United States—Case studies. | Social change—United States—Case studies. | Social justice—United States—Case studies. | United States—Social conditions—21st century—Case studies.
Classification: LCC H62 .C5656 2020 | DDC 303.48/40973—dc23
LC record available at https://lccn.loc.gov/2019015390

A British Cataloging-in-Publication record for this book is available from the British Library.

∞ The paper used in this publication meets the requirements of the American National Standard for Information Sciences—Permanence of Paper for Printed Library Materials, ANSI Z39.48-1992.

www.rutgersuniversitypress.org

Manufactured in the United States of America

Dedicated to community-based activists struggling to achieve social and economic equality

Contents

Collaborating for Change

1

Introduction

• •

SUSAN D. GREENBAUM

This volume explores the potentials and contradictions of grassroots collaboration with academic researchers. We implicitly critique patronizing neoliberal "service learning" efforts designed to expose students to life "on the other side of the tracks." We explicitly attempt to correct ideas about the presumed cultural and personal shortcomings of poor people, especially those of color, who are often thought to be responsible for their own lack of success. In contrast, we offer stories and analysis of participatory and egalitarian research projects that have bridged class divides and can erase misconceptions about poverty and injustice.

Don't mourn; organize. Joe Hill issued that charge prior to his 1915 execution, falsely convicted of murder but killed for his labor agitation. His message resonates today. Confronting a gathering storm of menacing political forces, we critically need a surge of progressive organizing and effective action. This volume speaks to a part of that task. It is about projects undertaken by activist organizations and academic researchers in the United States who work together to marshal evidence in support of humane policies and progressive change.

Data that are made credible by the professional credentials of researchers form a necessary, if insufficient, condition for achieving policy and political goals. Researchers who work with community-based organizations can provide valuable ammunition, and they can benefit their own scholarship in the process. Of equal importance are possibilities for cross-class alliances that can help remedy fundamental imbalances in power. Despite this potential, forces at all levels may dilute or discourage cooperation. Generalized political resistance to reform and increasingly corporatized university governance often conspire to defeat joined efforts to alter the status quo. Faculty performance metrics, institutional pressures to desist, and various punitive obstacles may hinder faculty from getting involved. Interactional tensions, unfamiliar frames of reference, and cultural differences can make it hard to forge authentic and comfortable partnerships. History has demonstrated the difficulty of this work but also the amazing human achievements it has many times helped bring about.

Our book offers examples of social justice projects that involve explicitly coequal partnerships and deliberate efforts to achieve organizational democracy and societal transformation. All were funded by the Sociological Initiatives Foundation (SIF). The foundation began in 1998, with origins in the journals *Sociological Abstracts* and *Language Learning and Behavior Abstracts* and the radically progressive views of its founders. Proceeds from their sale to Cambridge Scientific Abstracts were placed in an endowment fund from which SIF awards small grants to support collaborative research-driven activism. Priorities are to address problems affecting low-wage workers, immigrants, ethnic and gender minorities, the homeless, and other powerless groups. Also supported are projects for linguistic issues such as language maintenance or revitalization, second-language acquisition, bilingualism, and literacy. Since its inception, SIF has awarded grants to scores of organizations, initiating or augmenting a variety of projects. Several grantees have won substantial and remarkable victories benefitting local communities and society at large. The dividends of these efforts, often bought with temporary setbacks, include valuable lessons for activists, researchers, students, and others interested in progressive social change. Important insights also have been gained from less successful projects, where the obstacles were greater and achievements more modest. Evolving strategies for making change require both kinds of interrogation.

The chapters present varied examples of activist research that is collaborative through all phases of the work (often referred to as participatory action research, or PAR). SIF's emphasis on participatory methods is epistemologically sound, tactically smart, and ethically imperative. PAR helps ensure that research questions are framed and measured appropriately and those affected by likely outcomes have maximum input about, and comprehension of, both results and interpretations. To succeed, activist research must be rigorous enough to withstand skepticism; to be effective, it must reflect and include perspectives that may not be taught in conventional research methods courses. Taking on contested areas of reform greatly amplifies the crucial importance of doing sound and defensible research. Mixed methods and carefully triangulated designs aid in meeting that standard without sacrificing inclusion.

Core benefits in this approach to research include enhancing skills of inquiry for both researchers and community partners and building vital trust and cohesion among actors engaged in the arduous process of effecting social change. Internal dynamics of class, ethnicity, and gender can bedevil such arrangements. Relationships that go sour, or complaints that researchers fail to assist communities where they collect data, are frequent stumbling blocks to establishing effective university-community engagement. Based on both experiences and analyses, several authors present ideas and methods for resolving and overcoming such obstacles. Our volume offers substantive examples across a spectrum of place and purpose, situated in discussions of both theory and method and aimed at readers who are, or wish to be, doing this work. We challenge manipulative neoliberal ideas about community engagement and conventional beliefs that rationalize and sustain the idea that researchers must maintain social distance and functional control to ensure "objectivity."

Objectivity and rigor are not the same, and the reality of the former is open to debate. Few researchers design without expecting, or hoping for, particular outcomes. Researchers and their activist partners who have written these chapters were hoping for justice and expecting change. Their work was intended to expose problems and illuminate issues to change laws, policies, and practices. Rigor in design and implementation are doubly important in such endeavors.

The collaborations described in our book join university researchers and some of the poorest and most badly treated workers in the United States—laborers, restaurant workers, nannies, house cleaners, and dairy and forest workers. Many are immigrants struggling through an era of intense oppression. Others are simply too poor to make ends meet or live indoors. Native Americans fighting to protect their natural resources and cultural heritage are also included, groups who have a freighted history with researchers and a long list of broken promises. This book is about coproducing knowledge, turning it into power, and establishing viable and equitable alliances across divides of class, color, gender, and origin.

Chapters are divided into three parts. Following this introduction, Glenn Jacobs (board chair of SIF) examines the linked issues of methodological rigor and professional credentials in contested political environments and the significance of PAR in achieving valid results and building organizational capacity. We argue that using PAR in these cases yielded better and more accurate research, and the process invigorated organizing and participation among members of the partner groups.

The second part introduces descriptions and narrations about selected projects funded by SIF. Chapters address issues of collaborating openly, fairly, and successfully across wide social distances while challenging power imbalances that both cause and reflect the vast inequities in our society. Stigma and cultural differences are explored in relation to homelessness and the working class. A subtext concerns the strategic use of white privilege and access through social networks. Class Action, a group in Boston, has researched subtle cultural differences incubated in the distances between social classes and wrongly reinterpreted to mean lower-class inferiority. Through varied and creative outreach, Class Action strives to erase misunderstanding and help activists learn valuable lessons from each other. The San Francisco Coalition on Homelessness uses participatory research to fight prejudices against unhoused people in a very expensive housing market and a reputedly liberal political climate but one with cruel measures that vilify and criminalize homelessness. Nobody Leaves Mid-Hudson (NLMH) is an organization that began with the Occupy movement against evictions but was persuaded by the grass roots that unaffordable energy was a higher priority. The partnership that grew out of that process bridged class and ethnic differences between Vassar students and Poughkeepsie neighborhood activists and has grown more durable from consensus building that was directed from the ground.

Labor struggles are the subject of the next and largest part. Chapters vary by geography and job description, but problems are remarkably similar. Identifying and achieving solutions are also similar. It takes both solid evidence and effective organizing to prevail in a political climate that prefers to reject claims of discrimination and unfairness. The bottom layer of the labor market in the United States is rife with corrupt and evil practices. These include wage theft, sexual and physical abuse, dangerous working conditions, insecure and unpredictable income, threats of deportation, and scant legal protections. In chapters about immigrant domestic workers in Boston, immigrant forest workers in Oregon, restaurant workers across the United States, day laborers in Nevada, construction workers in Texas, and immigrant dairy workers in Upstate New York, the wider landscape of labor exploitation is made visible. In each of these cases, research anointed by PhDs was a critical component of a much bigger organizational project. These are not typical semester-long service learning projects. Rather, they involve long-term commitments, delicate negotiation and diplomacy on several sides, and careful strategies based on democratic consensus building. The accuracy and validity of the data that are presented and narrative and qualitative contributions that can make statistics come to life are central concerns. These chapters also echo the importance of participatory research in organizing and awareness building.

The final part focuses on activism related to heritage and language. Erasure of cultural traditions and practices constitute a softer form of genocide. Ability to function in the dominant culture is a critical asset that should be achievable without losing birth culture. A major concern of SIF has been to support projects that combat barriers of language, literacy, and xenophobia, as well as those that actively preserve the linguistic and cultural assets of immigrants and Native Americans. Two chapters in this part, both situated in the northwest, deal with environmental threats and language retention. The Nimiipuu (also known as Nez Perce) are fighting with other groups in Idaho against the incursion of huge oil tankers on their territory. Students and faculty at the Northwest Indian Language Institute at the University of Oregon collaborated with high school teachers and students at the Nixyáawii Community School, who together invented and created digital materials in their native languages for the preschoolers at the Tamalut immersion school. A final note: Most of the contributed chapters have multiple authors, partly due to the collaborative nature of this work. Authors' names are listed alphabetically, and ordering does not reflect relative importance in the project or publication.

2

The Epistemology and Hybridity of Participatory Action Research

• •

What and Whose Truth Is It?

GLENN JACOBS

> Epistemology. The branch of philosophy that studies the nature of knowledge, its presuppositions and foundations, and its extent and validity.
> —*The American Heritage College Dictionary*

> Humanist sociological findings can help push for participatory social arrangements, even to the extent of sweeping revolutionary changes.
> —Alfred McClung Lee, *Sociology for Whom?*

The term *epistemology* conveys the aura of a sequestered preserve of scholars, experts, and technicians. It is associated on the one hand with the language and terminology of abstract philosophy and on the other with the esoteric methodological codes of academic conduct and research design and analysis, both of them associated with the realms of philosophers, experts, and trained scientists whose grasp of how to conduct systematic inquiry is commonly viewed as valid and credible. Moreover, the uncovering of knowledge in scientific work is neither conducted nor written by laypeople and is removed from the subcultures of subaltern groups such as the poor and the homeless and of racial and ethnic minorities as well.

This common view of empirical reality is the nonnegotiable preserve of scientific truth representing a legacy of the Enlightenment and a foundation for extraordinary progress in medicine and technology. That canon represents an ontic distance between the researcher and the objects of research only capable of being understood by the scientific intellect of the researcher. These precepts underlie the related canon of "positivism" composing the "notions of objectivity, expertise, and neutral distance that have long dominated social science," which are derived from the taken-for-granted know-how of the physical sciences (Sandwick et al. 2018, 477). However, what is true for the latter has remained open to challenge and debate by common sense in the realms of the social sciences.

Nearly a century ago, a founder of sociology in the United States, Charles Horton Cooley (1864–1929), set forth a key epistemological distinction between physical and social science and, by extension, quantitative versus qualitative sociology. Cooley saw this distinction as composing the fundamentally different kinds of knowledge of the physical and social sciences, labeling them respectively "spatial" and "social" knowledge, each derived by different research methods. The former uses standardized units of measurement and quantification (i.e., statistical methods) and the latter derives from "sympathetic introspection," or the understanding that ordinary members of society have of themselves and each other based on sympathetic reflection and observation (Cooley 1926; Jacobs 2006, 187–192).

Cooley viewed social knowledge as appropriately studied by participant observation (i.e., ethnographic field methods) now grouped in the social science methodological arsenal with open-ended interviewing, focus group study, and so on. Qualitative *and* quantitative methods are used in participatory action research (PAR), which gathers "hard" and "soft" data in its mission to implement social change. Following what Alfred McClung Lee calls a "radical interactionist" strategy, the articles herein demonstrate that these sources of data serve the purposes of social action in complementary ways.

Lee counsels sociologists to open their perceptual portals to mind-stretching humanizing experiences by carrying out "extensive participant observation, perceptive listening, and experimental involvement in social action," which "can take place concomitantly as you break down your own barriers against hearing and understanding . . . in *their* . . . terms what those interviewed have to tell you." He notes that "after such humanizing experiences, the stereotyped ideas with which sociologists 'handle' a different sort of person start to crumble" (1986, 60, 61). The deceptively simple tactics of "looking and seeing" have tremendous epistemological ramifications.

It is noteworthy that William Foote Whyte, the author of the sociological classic *Street Corner Society*, a landmark ethnographic sociological study published in 1943, writes that PAR is "a powerful methodology for advancing scientific knowledge" (1989). He notes, "Where the social researcher gets involved in a continuing process of organizational change, the professional expert role is much less useful for generating knowledge or for determining the course of change" (368).

Reflecting on his own earlier work in PAR on the Xerox business setting, he notes that "key informants" who "may become collaborators in the research process . . . may reach the point of joint authorship." That study reflected a different context than those herein. Workers and management at Xerox were selected to work together and carry out a study "to determine whether Xerox could cut its manufacturing costs sufficiently" to meet an outside bid "and thus save . . . jobs" (371). He concludes that "if professional researchers pursue the PAR strategy, reaching out for technical knowledge and analytical skills among practitioners in fields of action different from our own disciplinary bases, we find mutually profitable ways of combining intellectual forces" (380).

The close association of research methods with social ethics and social action is embodied in Alfred McClung Lee's *Sociology for Whom?* (1986). A cofounder of the Society for the Study of Social Problems (SSSP) in 1950–1951, he quotes an eminent member of the American Sociological Society who objected to the SSSP's "anti-systematic, anti-theoretical and anti-quantitative views," suggesting that the "humanist" qualitative research modality is more likely to recognize elites' manipulation of social conditions. Thus humanist activist researchers risk paying the price of endangering their academic and professional respectability (Lee 1986, 70, 94–96).

As Lee suggests, positivist sociologists are prone to rationalize social inequality and proclaim that the so-called impersonal ethical neutrality of their findings is "natural." They therefore "erect a scientistic fabric of symbols which presumably reflects 'reality.'" Activist researchers clearly disagree with this assertion and recognize that ethical neutrality "is neither possible psychologically nor desirable socially and scientifically" (96–97). In other words, such neutrality betokens sterility. We note that PAR researchers frequently utilize "mixed methods" approaches in their organizations' campaigns and campaign strategies, underlying our contention that the uses to which research methods are put spill over into the fundamental truth-telling meanings and significance of social action.

Although some may object to calling PAR a distinct *method* of social science research, the contents of this book testify that the partnership of academics and local community activists fosters a hybridization of methods and researcher and researcher-activist roles involving the seeking and determining of social truth that is not apparent to the "naked eye." It is worth noting that, owing to its relative newness as a method, PAR's hybridity or its messiness and "mongrel" nature—its "dirtiness"—might be rejected, discounted, or ignored according to established disciplinary standards. To repeat, an academic practitioner of PAR thus runs the risk of sacrificing her/his professional respectability and reputation (see, e.g., Croteau 2005, 32–34). Nonetheless, in defying "respectable" social and disciplinary boundary lines and precepts and the normative criteria of purity and danger, the "messiness" of PAR research practitioners' methodological and social border crossings of class, race, ethnicity, gender, and sexuality is likely to reveal more social truth than the established intellectual orthodoxies and verities of power, wealth, and privilege suggest.

Social truth is ascertained, incorporated, and exercised through what is ubiquitously called *praxis* by PAR practitioners. It is a term traceable to Marx's thought and recently derives from Paulo Freire's usage in *Pedagogy of the Oppressed* ("There is no true word that is not at the same time a praxis").[1] Prominently figuring in Freire's and Antonio Gramsci's writings, it simply refers to the union of theory and practice, thought and action, and as exemplified herein, investigation and action, processes that PAR so pungently exemplifies (Freire 1970, 75; Gramsci 1971, 334–335, 364–365). In the realm of participatory action research, this translates into the partnerships of college professors and local community members working together, developing interpersonal familiarity with each other and coinvestigating the social issues generating knowledge utilized to initiate social change.

As a result of the way PAR crosses the social lines and blends the relationships of the observer and the observed and academic social scientists and laypeople, the corresponding line between what anthropologists distinguish as "etic," or outsider observer orientations, versus "emic," or local populations' or insiders' perspectives, becomes blurred. Thus as depicted here, for example, the San Francisco Coalition on Homelessness cleverly uses and manipulates taken-for-granted public stereotypes of the homeless to combat their criminalization. Its success in doing so is a product of its members' crossing of the interpersonal and social boundaries of race, gender, sexual orientation, ethnicity, education, social class, and occupation. The organization's representations of the homeless and their incorporation in public presentations are clear markers of the uniqueness of the method.

Similarly, the frequent use of quantitative data by activists to drive PAR findings home in legislative and public fora, coupled with their adoption and use of local idioms to rhetorically frame their messages, publicity, and accounts of their constituencies, drive the success of their missions. Thus for the sake of credibility, a statistical "face" may be presented at public and legislative presentations in reports and fora, and the profundities revealed in their qualitative data gathering via focus groups, open-ended interviews, and participant observation often are channeled into the explanatory sections of reports or reserved for their internal organizational dialogues and strategy sessions.

While their presented materials appear to be heavily loaded to favor academic world views, the actual communal, qualitative, and quantitative social scientific and interpersonal experiential hybridization experienced on both sides of PAR partnerships betoken the simple fact that academics and community folks in varying degrees become socioculturally "bilingual" and communicatively hybridized or cross-fertilized by experience and *praxis*! As we see here, activists frequently adopt and selectively employ the communicative techniques and forms of reasoning of their academic counterparts, while the latter informally assume the attitudes, loyalties, and even local populations' values and idioms and occasionally "go native" by developing ties and relationships in their researched communities or marrying and living together with local residents.

To the dismay of purists on either end of the academic-community spectrum, the contents of this volume plainly testify to the fact of such academic-communal sociocultural hybridization. Here we might ask if academic folks taking on the views and the causes of their local partners is a two-way process. Moreover, what does this tell us about the so-called methodological hybridity we speak of? We look forward to more study and writing on these "informal" dimensions of PAR to flesh out the answer to this question.

Bud Hall, the former secretary-general of the International Participatory Research Network who teaches PAR at the Ontario Institute for Studies in Education, tells us PAR "is a way for researchers and oppressed people to join in solidarity to take collective action . . . for radical social change" (1993, xiv). Such action by and on behalf of subaltern groups frequently entails making claims to public officials and legislators who demand plausible quantified (i.e., statistical) evidence such as survey data, which might be coupled with other factual evidence and testimony from focus groups and open-ended interviews. Thus both quantitative and qualitative data fit the interests, organizations, and publics seeking and using information to understand and make social change. As the authors of an article focusing on PAR in schools suggest, "PAR projects can utilize qualitative, quantitative, and/or less traditional data collection and analysis methods" (Irizarry and Brown 2014, 64).

PAR praxis exemplifies how participatory action research avails itself of quantitative and qualitative methods of truth seeking. As suggested, the matter of *authenticity* is closely related to the issue of plausibility. Once again, due to the fact that subaltern[2] individuals and groups frequently work in close partnership with academicians, where they participate in conceiving the research and formulate questions and carry out the research work, the lines of social distance become blurred and break down. Thus as Hall tells us, "Participatory research attempts to break down the distinction between the researcher and the researched, the subjects and objects of knowledge production of the people-for-themselves in the process of gaining and creating knowledge" (Hall 1993, xiv).

Clearly, the epistemic, or truth-telling, value of community-based participatory action research, exemplified by the contents of this book, cleaves to the criteria of context and relevance. As Alfred McClung Lee puts it, action-oriented research "stress[es] the sense of being germane to important human concerns . . . with what lies behind veils obscuring the behavior of [so-called] problematic groups" (Lee 1970, 10, 14).

Thus the epistemological question is no longer simply an abstract one, particularly in its bearing on those people who are the subjects of the research and who for the most part *do* it as well. Paulo Freire, the much-cited eminent advocate of critical pedagogy, in a foreword to an anthology of participatory research in the United States and Canada, proclaims that "the silenced are not just incidental to the curiosity of the researcher but are the masters of inquiry into the underlying causes of the events in their world" (Freire 1993, x). Freire's proclamation is holy writ in the realm of PAR where local researchers *ideally* command and participate in every stage of the research process: identifying problems; posing the research question(s); designing the study and research instruments; "collecting, analyzing, and presenting data"; and "carrying out action" (Irizarry and Brown 2014, 65).

As the work herein demonstrates, academic and community partners participate in conceiving the research question(s) and designing and interpreting the data in consultation with the latter (Taylor and Rupp 2005). Several examples from this volume illustrate the hybrid nature of PAR "truth telling." As the Northwest Forest Worker Center (NFWC) selection states, "In addition to employing members of the forest worker community as staff, NFWC has a long-standing worker advisory committee . . . to identify priority issues to cover in the interviews . . . , provide guidance in developing interview questions, assist with the analysis of the interview data as well as with the development of the educational materials, and provide direction to NFWC based on project results" (see chapter 8).

We find a similar sharing of skill and information in the Workers Defense Project (WDP), and in the case of the Restaurant Opportunities Center (ROC), social action, research, and writing are totally worker-driven activities and have been demonstrably successful from a tactical standpoint in achieving hard-won victories regarding wages and working conditions for "front-of-the-house" and "back-of-the-house" restaurant workers. ROC's success in integrating research on all status and job categories of restaurant workers promises the coming of a new stage in national worker activism. As they put it, "Since its inception, ROC United adopted an ambitious research agenda as a tool for worker organizing and as an effective means of pushing an assertive policy agenda." Thus ROC "weaves in a forceful participatory research strategy that captures and draws on the collective knowledge of restaurant workers around the country." Moreover, "restaurant workers need to take the lead in research on their industry to get the best picture of what's really happening in their communities and workplaces, . . . so that knowledge can be used to create policies that address restaurant worker's needs."

The research by the recently Sociological Initiatives Foundation (SIF)–funded Brazilian Worker Center also comes close to the ideal of a parity of skill and worker leadership experience in its research and development of organizational strategy and tactics. The organization's director, Natalicia Tracey, who migrated from Brazil, became an exploited nanny, did domestic work, and subsequently achieved a PhD in sociology. In partnership with University of Massachusetts Boston anthropologist Tim Sieber, survey research was fed into successful legislative negotiation and the enactment of a state-level Domestic Worker Bill of Rights in 2014. Thus "the Massachusetts campaign was the context for our worker-based participatory research, funded by the Sociological Initiatives Foundation during 2013." Moreover, they "knew results from empirical studies of problematic working conditions can give power and heft to advocacy, public messaging, and testimony used to advance grassroots campaigns for change."

Similarly, the Nobody Leaves Mid-Hudson (NLMH) selection contends that "in this community-academic partnership, the community organization was in the lead. . . . In forging a relationship with two academic partners, NLMH sought to increase its capacity, systemize and extend its knowledge, further specify areas for potential policy work, and distribute its systematized knowledge about an under-named issue: *household energy insecurity*." NLMH states that the academic component directly fed into the group's campaign organizing model oriented toward "building relationships within an ongoing organization, not just turning people out to protest or to make demands of public officials."

By the same token, the National Day Laborers' Organizing Network states, "The origins of NDLON's research program date back to the early 1990s and the beginnings of immigrant day laborer organizing in the United States." Founded in 2001, NDLON "began with efforts to systematically understand the conditions facing day laborers and their families, so that day laborers themselves could analyze the sociopolitical and economic conditions that give rise to their marginalization as immigrants and as contingent workers in the United States."

Dismissals of egalitarian PAR intellectual partnering are often facile for they distort the "dirty hands" elements of the intellectual side of the work, as shown in a gritty example from the New York dairy industry study, wherein researchers had "to engage in a painstakingly laborious process of jotting down responses to survey questions by hand in the field and then ... [enter] that data into an online survey platform."

The foregoing illustrates the fact that PAR is neither socially nor methodologically monolithic. PAR's research roles, practices, and epistemological rectitude are as varied as cases and circumstances demand. These cases clearly testify to the integral ties of social research, social action, and perception. As the selection on the native sociocultural revival of the Nimiipuu (i.e., the so-called Nez Perce) and the environment asserts, the purpose of the work is "to decenter the university researcher's gaze and open space for Nimiipuu." Thus as Michelle Fine puts it, "PAR [is] ... a radical *epistemological challenge* to the traditions of social science, most critically on the topic of where knowledge resides." PAR thus represents a "democratic commitment to break the monopoly on who holds knowledge and for whom research should be undertaken" (2008, 215). Clearly, PAR's epistemological truth varies no more or less than its instances, role requirements, and circumstances demand, thus making epistemology in its constructive sense a socially negotiated and negotiable matter.

Our first selection views the class cultural attitudes of progressive activists of working-class and more privileged backgrounds who participated in the Class Action group's Activist Class Cultures workshop modules, which in a novel way put into praxis Freire's popular education method. What better way to lead off a volume arraying a collection of studies whose leitmotif *is* praxis?

Notes

1 Marx's idea is pointedly expressed in *The German Ideology*, where he explains, "The ideas of the ruling class are in every epoch the ruling ideas" (1947, 39), and most evidently in the appended "Theses on Feuerbach," in numbers 2 and 11—namely, "The dispute over the reality or non-reality of thinking that is isolated from practice is a purely *scholastic* question," and "The philosophers have only *interpreted* the world differently, the point is, to *change* it" (197, 199). True to this intellectual genealogy, the first selection in our book is Class Action sponsored the Class Cultures Project, whose project of raising class consciousness might be considered an important first step "in the world."

2 The term *subaltern*, now widely used in social science circles, derives from Antonio Gramsci's usage referring to the necessity of studying oppressed classes and groups falling under that heading (1971, 52).

References

Collette, Will. 2004. "Research for Organizing." In *Roots to Power: A Manual for Grassroots Organizing*, 2nd ed., edited by Lee Staples, 222–233. Westport, Conn.: Praeger.
Cooley, Charles Horton. 1926. "The Roots of Social Knowledge." *American Journal of Sociology* 32 (1): 59–79.
Croteau, David. 2005. "Which Side Are You On? The Tension between Movement Scholarship and Activism." In *Rhyming Hope and History: Activists, Academics, and Social Movement Scholarship*, edited by David Croteau, William Haynes, and Charlotte Ryan, 20–40. Minneapolis: University of Minnesota Press.
Fine, Michelle. 2008. "An Epilogue, of Sorts." In *Revolutionizing Education: Youth Participatory Action Research in Motion*, edited by Julio Cammarota and Michelle Fine, 213–234. New York: Routledge.
Freire, Paulo. 1970. *Pedagogy of the Oppressed*. New York: Herder and Herder.
———. 1993. "Foreword." In *Voices of Change: Participatory Research in the United States and Canada*, edited by Peter Park et al., ix–x. Westport, Conn.: Bergin and Garvey.
Gramsci, Antonio. 1971. *Selections from the Prison Notebooks*. New York: International Publishers.
Hall, Budd. 1993. "Introduction." In *Voices of Change: Participatory Research in the United States and Canada*, edited by Peter Park et al., xiii–xxii. Westport, Conn.: Bergin and Garvey.
Irizarry, Jason G., and Tara M. Brown. 2014. "Humanizing Research in Dehumanizing Spaces: The Challenges and Opportunities of Conducting Participatory Action Research with Youth in Schools." In *Humanizing Research: Decolonizing Qualitative Inquiry with Youth and Communities*, edited by Django Paris and Maisha T. Winn, 63–80. Los Angeles: Sage.
Jacobs, Glenn. 2006. *Charles Horton Cooley: Imagining Social Reality*. Amherst: University of Massachusetts Press.
Lee, Alfred McClung. 1970. "On Context and Relevance." In *The Participant Observer*, edited by Glenn Jacobs, 3–16. New York: George Braziller.
———. 1986. *Sociology for Whom?* 2nd ed. Syracuse, N.Y.: Syracuse University Press.
Marx, Karl, and Frederick Engels. 1947. *The German Ideology*. New York: International Publishers.
Sandwick, Talia, et al. 2018. "Promise and Provocation: Humble Reflections on Critical Participatory Action Research for Social Policy." *Urban Education* 53 (4): 473–502.
Taylor, Vera, and Leila J. Rupp. 2005. "Crossing Boundaries in Participatory Action Research: Performing Protest with Drag Queens." In *Rhyming Hope and History: Activists, Academics, and Social Movement Scholarship*, edited by David Croteau et al., 239–264. Minneapolis: University of Minnesota Press.

Part I

Social Justice Organizing

• • • • • • • • • • • • • • • • • • • •

This part describes challenges in organizing the powerless, the importance of building interclass alliances, and the extent to which knowledge is power. The chapters review reasons for success and failure and discuss overcoming bias, building mutual respect, and mobilizing and engaging members. The critical dynamic combines grassroots wisdom with expert power and grassroots power with expert wisdom.

3

The Activist Class
Cultures Project

• • • • • • • • • • • • • • • • • • • •

Helping Activists Become
More Class Inclusive

BETSY LEONDAR-WRIGHT

Progressive activism in the United States today is class diverse, but inside social movement organizations with different class compositions, groups are run differently, and activists interact differently. To learn about these differences, the national nonprofit Class Action (CA) created the Activist Class Cultures Project with help from the Sociological Initiatives Foundation. By studying twenty-five varied U.S. social justice groups, the project identified key class differences in how activists dealt with common situations. Approaches to recruitment, leadership, and especially language correlated with class. After turning the findings into a book, *Missing Class* (Leondar-Wright 2014), Class Action organized a national tour that put into practice the organization's inclusive values. Project goals included raising awareness of class-based cultural traits, offering advice on more class-inclusive activism, and convincing skeptics that a focus on class cultures is congruent with progressive values. The "culture of poverty" theories that skeptics find classist have been upended by the radical social critique of Pierre Bourdieu (1977, 1984), whose criticism of the French intelligentsia turns out to be surprisingly relevant to social movement groups today. The Activist Class Cultures Project helped disseminate this theoretical shift from pathologizing working-class cultures to making respectful comparisons based on empirical evidence as well as helping activists make their practices more class inclusive.

Progressive activists in the United States today come from every part of the class spectrum. Unions have recruited low-wage fast food workers into the Fight for $15, a movement that advocated for a higher per-hour minimum wage. Wealthy inheritors have advocated for increased taxes on upper-income brackets. Straddlers—first-generation college graduates from working-class backgrounds—predominate in Black Lives Matter chapters and in the DREAMers movement. Teachers in several states have gone out on strike for better education funding. Professionals predominate in efforts against climate change. High school students, mostly middle-class, have sparked a mass mobilization about gun violence. Undocumented immigrants on the margins of the economy have taken leadership in immigrant rights struggles.

These varied struggles are alike in their progressive visions of a better society, but within them are significant class differences in how organizations tend to run and how people tend to interact. Investigating the microlevel of dynamics inside social justice groups can lead to increased intragroup understanding as well as new solutions to common problems. Research on activism reveals class culture differences as obstacles to movement building (Cohen 1999; Croteau 1995; Doerr 2018; Rose 2000; Stout 1996). What are significant cultural differences based on class among activists in the United States today? The Activist Class Cultures Project tackled that hard-to-answer question.

Identifying Class Culture Contrasts in Social Justice Organizations

Class Action, since its founding as a national nonprofit in 2004, has spread class awareness in ways unfamiliar to most Americans. We foster cross-class dialogue about classism as a diversity issue parallel to and intersecting with racism, sexism, and other "isms"; about people's lived experience of class in schools, organizations, neighborhoods, and families, not only in workplaces; and about class culture differences.

Class Action works primarily with organizations whose missions imply serving everyone without class or race bias but whose actual practice falls short of those ideals. Besides schools, nonprofits, and the philanthropic sector, our other key constituency is social justice organizations because building progressive social movements is essential to reaching our vision of a world without classism. The research question for this project arose in our first few years of doing workshops for activist groups: how are class culture differences showing up in social justice efforts?

We knew our workshops and materials would be deepened if we could answer that question with empirical data. We did not want to rely on informal impressions from our own work with activists. It was clear that only a rigorous social science study could identify class culture contrasts that held up across regions, races, generations, and movement traditions. Our research question propelled me, a Class Action board member, into a sociology PhD program at Boston College and to a 2006 funding proposal to the Sociological Initiatives Foundation to cover the research expenses.

The fieldwork, done in 2007 and 2008, involved observing meetings of U.S. social justice organizations, aiming for class and race diversity within and between groups, and surveying and interviewing members.

Sociological Initiatives Foundation (SIF) funding enabled us to hire a Spanish-speaking Latino researcher to observe the Latinx groups and a Florida-based graduate student to observe groups in the southeast. We collected full data for twenty-five activist groups in five states and in five movement traditions (labor, community organizing, progressive protest affiliated with nonprofits, anarchist, and militant anti-imperialist). We attended their meetings and events (audiotaping when granted permission), collected demographic surveys from 362 members, and interviewed two to four members diverse in class and race per organization. The sixty-one interviewees were paid for their time out of the SIF funds.

The 362 survey respondents were categorized by class background and current class, based on parents' and own education level, occupation, and type of housing (such as owning, renting, public housing, or second homes). By taking two generations into account, the study could specify activists' class trajectories of upward or downward mobility or of remaining in the same class.

Thanks to SIF funding, meetings and interviews were transcribed verbatim, which enabled detailed analysis of speech differences based on class background and current class. For example, because the transcripts recorded laughter, we discovered that majority-working-class groups tended to laugh at different kinds of humor, with more teasing and fewer puns, than in majority-professional-middle-class groups. The analysis used mixed methods, with qualitative coding of more than a thousand pages of transcripts as well as statistical analysis on the association of class with cultural traits.

Class culture differences between and within activist groups turned out to be pervasive. Hundreds of variables correlated with class! Besides humor, activists of different classes tended to use different vocabulary; approach recruitment, group process, conflict, and leadership differently; think differently about diversity and racism; and respond differently to overtalkers and other problematic member behavior. The findings of the study were published by Cornell University Press as *Missing Class: Strengthening Social Movement Groups by Seeing Class Cultures* (Leondar-Wright 2014).

What Are Activist Class Culture Differences?

It can be hard to talk with Americans about class because of two pervasive myths. The first is that we are a classless society. We have no agreed-upon vocabulary for class identities; *middle class* is an overused and thus almost meaningless term. When asked about class diversity in their neighborhood or organization, many people answer about race, a difference they are more familiar with. But in fact, our lives are profoundly shaped by our parents' and our own education levels, occupations, finances, and neighborhoods. Along with those differences in lived experience come class cultural differences, which cut across ethnic differences far more than most people realize. "Culture" incorporates habits of behavior, speech, and thought. Of course, not all people within a certain class act, talk, or think alike, and overgeneralized stereotypes are harmful, but it can be illuminating to generalize based on factual tendencies.

The second myth is that more class-privileged people are superior to working-class and poor people. Politicians, media, and people on the street often explain negative financial outcomes in classist ways, blaming the supposed character flaws and dysfunctional behavior of those who struggle without recognizing the context of a changing economy or the policies that promote extreme inequality. Particularly among education scholars and policy makers, the achievement gap is often explained by the supposedly dysfunctional families and oppositional cultures in which poor students are presumed to have been raised (Payne 2005; Diamond and Lewis's [2017] critique of Ogbu 2003). Our country prides itself on rejecting aristocracy, but in fact we have elite classes that pass their advantages on generation after generation.

Class-based cultural traditions confer strengths and impose limitations on activists, as on everyone. Almost none of us are socialized in childhood to be an empowered and effective confronter of injustice; we all must move away from our socialization to become strategic activists. We all can learn from the cultures of other classes and ethnicities. Some may need more prodding to learn cross-class lessons than others. Our classist society deludes us to believe that professional middle-class ways are normal and functional, with no major downsides and that working-class and poor communities are pits of dysfunction, with no positive practices to bring to the coalition table. Nothing could be further from the truth.

In this myth-breaking spirit, Class Action undertook a class-cultural analysis of progressive activist groups. Our priority was class culture differences related to common activist dilemmas. Whatever their class composition, voluntary groups face similar challenges, such as how to get more people involved, how to activate the inactive, and how to handle conflicts. The focus on class differences in solving these common problems has the potential to offer practical tips for groups of any class composition.

More privileged activists would do well to tap some working-class cultural norms that could enable them to better reach their missions. The clearest example is how differently working-class and college-educated activists speak. Working-class styles, regardless of race or nationality, are more colorful and concrete and generally more effective at persuading the unconvinced about a cause than is the more abstract and impersonal communication style learned in college and in upper-middle-class social settings.

A striking example from the interviews of this class cultural difference is seen in how two members of the same group, both middle-aged African Americans, answered the question "What are the goals of your group?" An upper-middle-class man answered with a compact statement of broad political principles and vision: "One, we want to end the war, two is to become a multi-racial, multi-class, multi-ethnic peace movement for social and economic justice." A working-class woman answered with a vivid vignette that fit characters and dramatic conflict into just thirty-five words: "We don't want to see the war in Iraq, we want to see that come to an end. We don't want to see the recruiters harassing the kids in the high school, which they do." Both answers have strengths, but her answer might work better to persuade new recruits to join the group.

The following are two other examples where working-class ways seemed to have some advantages in solving activist dilemmas: recruitment and understandings of leadership.

Recruitment and Food

Food was shared at every single meeting observed in the study that had a working-class majority or that was run by people from working-class backgrounds. Sometimes the organization provided pizza, sometimes members put together a potluck, and sometimes bags of chips or candy were passed around. By contrast, many groups with progressive middle-class (PMC) majorities and facilitators did not have shared food at meetings.

When interviewees were asked "How could you get more people involved in the group?" the most common answer from working-class and poor activists was food: serve better food or advertise the food. Some also suggested offering entertainment. In other words, entice people in the door and then get them more involved once they are there.

When college-educated activists with PMC parents were asked the same question, *not even one* mentioned food. Instead, their most common answers focused on the ideas behind the group's work, whether to add appealing new issues or shift the ideological tone. Yet several majority PMC activist groups were observed sitting around at small meetings at 6:30 p.m., with not a calorie in the room, asking, "Where is everybody?" Knowing that meetings in the community organizing and labor traditions typically include food might have suggested new solutions to their problem.

Perspectives of Leadership

Understandings of leadership roles varied by activists' class and by movement tradition: attitudes favorable to strong leadership strongly correlated with working-class people and with labor and community organizing traditions; antileadership attitudes correlated with more privileged-background people and with the anarchist and nonprofit-affiliated protest traditions.

When activists were asked in interviews "Who are the leaders of your group?" vehemently antileadership responses were heard only from college-educated people, most often from young, white activists. For example, Leon, a protester at a 2008 political convention, answered, "I hate the word 'leaders.' I see it come up over and over, informal hierarchies." Almost no second-generation college-educated interviewees answered that question with any leaders' names; most problematized the question.

In contrast, upbeat descriptions of strong leaders were most often heard from working-class activists in labor-sponsored coalitions and community-organizing groups. Many praised both leaders' authority and their empowerment of members, as if those were not opposites but went together. For example, a black working-class woman said of a well-known African American leader that he "was a very good teacher" and "kept [them] hopping." A white working-class woman said of her community group's white founder, "He's very organized. He knows how to recruit people to get them where he needs them."

Effective leaders of working-class-majority groups in the study had some shared practices for activating inactive members. Some spent time one-on-one with new recruits, forming personal relationships. Their meeting process often included asking questions of individual members. One common practice, taught to community organizers by the Midwest Academy, was to ask disempowered members to play specific roles, starting with tiny, low-risk tasks such as bringing cookies to a meeting and gradually escalating to speaking in public and taking on organizational responsibilities. For example, a working-class black woman in Low-Income Women Rising said, "When I came into welfare rights, I wasn't a leader in anything. . . . They make you—they don't 'make' you, they empower you to stand up, speak out, and fight back. My first task was holding a sign. I never was holding a sign. . . . And then from there . . . my first time [speaking in public] was in reading a press statement from the people,

I was so nervous, my voice was chattering. . . . It's been a good experience for me."

By contrast, rigid antihierarchy attitudes and the pretense of leaderlessness were prevalent among some class-privileged groups. Suspicious attitudes toward leaders are healthy when there is evidence of corruption or top-down abuses of power. But when it is chronic, the impulse to shoot down anyone taking leadership can get in the way of groups reaching their missions. In a Green Party chapter whose members averaged more than four years of higher education, Lichterman (1996) found that there were as many projects as there were active members, as each member had started his or her own project. One of them told him, "All members are leaders."

For some college-educated activists in anarchist and other protest groups who come from class-privileged backgrounds, the word *leader* means "dominator." Many put their egalitarian ideal of "sharing airspace" into practice by employing stylized group processes in which each person is required to speak the same amount, such as go-arounds or small-group report-backs.

College-educated interviewees sometimes responded to the question "How could you get more people involved in the group?" by advocating self-monitoring by dominant members to allow others more room to speak. Sometimes this strategy works to draw out quieter members, but sometimes it fails. An example of ineffective self-restraint was seen in one unusually silent meeting of a globalization group. Concerned that most members were inactive, two male college-educated core members left long pauses, which one of them later described as "stepping back and not taking up so much space." They asked no questions of the group and made no requests of anyone to take on tasks. To perform their egalitarian ideal, they eschewed acting like dominant leaders. But in that meeting, their strategy backfired, as the less active members also sat there silently and didn't volunteer for action steps.

Antileadership attitudes can reinforce informal hierarchies (Freeman 1972; Cornell 2011) and can result in intensifying the individualism of PMC culture. PMC activists most commonly become politically aware in college, feel called to a cause as an individual, and then go looking for a group to join. Their activism is "personalist" (Lichterman 1996): their commitment to the cause came first, before group membership. Working-class activists, on the other hand, most commonly enter activism through prior affiliations, such as shared neighborhood, workplace, social circles, or family ties. Membership is often viewed as a collective bond with specific members, including leaders. To build durable social justice groups, the healthiest approach is a balance of loyalty to particular people (unless it means betraying the cause) and loyalty to the cause (unless it means harming other activists). Understanding these two different class cultures can help activists find that balance.

Recruitment and food, language, humor, leadership: understanding these activist class culture differences seemed potentially useful to movement builders, so we at Class Action decided to take them on the road.

Practicing What We Preach

We hoped to use the publication of *Missing Class* to bring the Activist Class Cultures Project to progressive groups around the United States. We wanted to do something more class inclusive than a traditional book tour, which invokes a certain classed setting—a book-reading audience of intellectuals, sitting in a bookstore, passively listening to an expert author. How could we inject our inclusive values and mission into the tour?

The popular education method that CA uses in our workshops was essential. This philosophy grew out of Paulo Freire's work with landless Brazilian peasants (Freire 1970); he drew out their own life experiences and fostered community dialogue to generate energy and ideas for collective resistance. CA workshops start with participants' direct experience, either through drawing memories from their own lives or through doing a group interactive activity. Generalizations about theory or practice come only after the group has reflected on lived experience (Lakey 2010). The last stage is always to apply the learning to action steps to do after the workshop. This practice is inherently more class inclusive and race inclusive than other educational methods, as all voices are heard, and working-class and poor people's lived experiences are given as much attention as more privileged people's. With help from workshop-design specialist Erika Thorne of Training for Change, we created interactive popular education modules for five of the major findings on activist class cultures.

Second, we included a cofacilitator who was working class or raised poor and/or a facilitator of color whenever possible. Our standard practice is a diverse two-person team of trainers so that most participants will find commonalities with one trainer or the other. I, the book's author, am a white woman from an upper-middle-class background and with an elite education, so sending me alone on the road wasn't ideal. We held online video-linked "training of trainers" sessions and prepared eleven more Class Action trainers around the United States to lead the Activist Class Cultures workshop modules. I cofacilitated most of the full-length workshops with them.

Third, we made the workshops financially accessible to all kinds of groups and activists. We raised enough money through a special appeal to our donors to be able to offer free workshops to low-budget grassroots groups and informal gatherings of individual activists.

Class Action's executive director at the time, Anne Phillips, was a mastermind at organizing complex projects with far-flung partner groups on a shoestring budget. She publicized the Activist Class Cultures workshops to social justice groups of all classes, ethnicities, and issues and put together a tour of workshops, presentations, and media coverage for six months in 2014.

The tour included more than thirty events in eleven states in the Northeast, Southeast, Northern Midwest, and West Coast. The typical workshop length was three or four hours, but events ranged from ninety minutes to a three-day weekend. Venues included religious congregations, grassroots community organizing offices, union offices, conference centers, foundation offices, colleges, and a museum. Even in traditionally passive-audience settings such as bookstores and speaker series, the events involved interactive exercises in Class Action's trademark style. Event sizes ranged from 5 to 450 people, with most workshops having between 12 and 35 participants. One highlight was a weekend-long workshop for southern activists at the Highlander Folk Center in Tennessee.

Participant evaluations were overwhelmingly positive. The most popular workshop module, described in the next section, was about using class speech differences in persuasive messaging.

The final way that the tour exemplified Class Action's class-inclusive, "listen first" approach was in the awards we gave. We did not want to arrive in a strange city as outside experts; we knew that local wisdom about cross-class alliance building would be found everywhere and could be disseminated during the tour if only we could find ways to tap local activists' knowledge in advance of our arrival. Our solution was the Cross-Class Bridge Builder Awards, which we awarded in nine cities.

Before coming to a town, we emailed all our contacts there and asked the sponsoring organization(s) to do the same. The email requested nominations of local organizations that met three criteria: "actively pursuing participation by people of diverse classes and races; raising the voices and supporting the leadership of working class and poor people; and demonstrating an organizational culture that draws on the strengths of all class cultures." Once the nominations came in, we circulated a ballot through all the nominated and cosponsoring organizations asking local people to vote for the best cross-class bridge builder in their area and explain why. It was a pleasure to inform the winners that their communities had honored them in this way and to share with them the exuberant praise of their supporters.

We made charming awards with a shiny little red bridge, intended for fish tanks, on a black base with a plaque honoring the winning organizations. At one event per city, I gave the award and then turned the floor over to representatives of the winning organization. Sometimes only a staff member spoke, but sometimes it was a grassroots member who had rarely spoken in public, including a farmworker, high school students, a recovering addict, and a homeless activist. Inviting the memberships of all the nominees increased the diversity of the attendees. The winners were so varied that announcing them to our national networks made the point that there is no formula for cross-class alliance building; it can be practiced by all kinds of organizations.[1]

To reach more activists than came to the events, broadcast media and the internet were critical to the Activist Class Cultures Project. The highlight of the media campaign was more than fifty radio interviews around the United States, many on stations that reach progressive activists (Pacifica, NPR, college and community radio stations). The book's website, www.MissingClass .org, was augmented in 2015 when Class Action created an online toolkit, www.activistclasscultures.org. The talented web artist Tanya Albrigtsen-Frable brought stories in the book to life with line drawings, including animations that illustrate audio narrations. The site features a seven-session study group curriculum with readings and interactive features, some related to personal lived class experience, others to organizational class diversity. For common activist dilemmas—inactive members, too much conflict or conflict avoidance, and differences in how to deal with diversity issues—the site lays out how activists of different classes tend to approach them.

We asked a dozen diverse social justice organizations to promote the new online toolkit, and as a result, more than fourteen thousand people visited the site in its first three months. Class Action's internal evaluation of the project was very positive. It took much longer than the original timeline in the SIF grant proposal (eight years instead of two). But it was incredibly productive, widening our network, sparking a conversation about class culture differences and cross-class alliance-building, and shifting the practice of some progressive organizations.

A Highlight from the Workshops: Classed Speech Codes

The clearest impact from the workshops came from an often-requested module called "Persuasive Messaging." Almost all social justice organizations and activists are motivated to persuade the public and recruit more people, and this workshop promises to strengthen their outreach by drawing on the strengths of two class speech codes. This module continues to be frequently included in Class Action workshops.

First, participants learn the study's findings on how working-class activists and college-educated professional activists tend to speak differently by doing an exercise comparing quotes. They learn that working-class activists tend to use more first- and second-person pronouns and more concrete, specific words, while college-educated activists use more third-person pronouns and more abstract terms. Working-class activists tend to speak more colorfully and personally. Some in the study coined new metaphors; "I'm a pebble in their shoe," said a working-class court watcher. Some used sayings from their ethnic or local culture; a Caribbean immigrant activist said, "Back home, they say, 'You want good, your nose has to run'; you have to put that effort in it." A working-class white leader used a metaphor to explain why she felt compelled to organize against extreme poverty: "[It] is like seeing kids on a railroad track, and when you push those kids off that railroad track, is that a choice, or did you have to do that? I have to do that."

Participants then learn terms that were used far more often by college-educated members than by less educated members of the twenty-five groups in our study, words that might create communication barriers across class lines, such as "context," "strategy," and "perspective." They learn words used at equal rates by activists of all classes: "issue," "goal," "decision," and "task." Ironically, the abstract terms used much less often by working-class activists include the words "class" (in the sense of social class), "working class," and the longtime rallying cry of the labor movement, "solidarity" (Leondar-Wright 2013).

In the final exercise of the workshop, participants apply the strengths of both class speech codes to the issues they are passionate about. Each small group takes on one public issue to craft a message. Common choices in 2014 were climate change, police brutality, affordable housing, and sexual assault. The hypothetical scenario is that they have an opportunity to speak for ninety seconds on a popular radio show and need to write the most persuasive message they can. Since abstract terms are persuasive only when used sparingly and in context, their first task is to brainstorm a list of general phrases that convey the importance of the issue succinctly and compellingly. Then they cross out any that are dry, confusing, controversial or technical, and agree on one that remained to be their key term. In the example on the handout, "anthropogenic global warming" and "cap and trade" were crossed out, and "climate change" was chosen.

The next task was to create a short spoken message about the issue, incorporating the strengths of working-class speech styles. They were encouraged to make it personal with a first-person voice or vivid descriptions of human impact, to explain the key term using everyday words, to bring the issue to life with a story or analogy, and to offer hope by describing concrete plans to solve the problem. Then small groups gave their ninety-second speeches and received applause and positive feedback on how well they used both classed speech codes.

One group of grassroots activists used their whole ninety seconds to tell one human story that conveyed the issue but didn't name it with a general term or describe a solution. Another small group of older white Quakers had half a dozen abstract and ideological terms in their statement and almost no colorful language. But most groups of all classes and races gave compelling speeches that seemed to be more powerful thanks to the guidance of the workshop's explanation of the two class speech codes.

More than with any other workshop module, this one showed immediate evidence of impact. In evaluation forms and follow-up conversations, and even during the workshop, participants reported that they had new ideas for their organization's outward-facing communications. One nonprofit staffer told us that after the workshop, she persuaded her board to rewrite the mission statement to have fewer abstract terms. Two members of one grassroots community-organizing group said they planned to report back that funders might respond better if they framed their heartwarming stories as examples of a general trend. Two organizations reported that they changed their websites, in one case pushing photos and human stories higher toward the top.

There was also pushback from a few college-educated activists about limiting the use of abstract words. One thing we have learned from doing this module so often is how attached some activists are to their ideological terms. *White supremacy, sustainability, neoliberal capitalism, democratic socialism, institutionalized racism, patriarchy*, and *nonviolence* all have their passionate defenders. Our goal is not to persuade activists to avoid these terms, all of which encapsulate macrolevel analyses well, but to use them sparingly and to surround them with more vivid words. We want advocates of these terms to remember that many listeners won't be familiar with them (in particular, those with little formal education or limited English), so the terms require explanation; that adding the working-class style of colorful and personal speech can strengthen the terms' impact; and finally, that many listeners, including many working-class and poor people, are put off by overly ideological speech. So it often makes sense to draw people in first with stories, shocking facts, analogies and metaphors, or questions and conversational back-and-forth before introducing an abstract key term.

For anyone with a goal of building a cross-class, multiracial movement, incorporating the strengths of the working-class speech code can be a political act against classism. For audiences of any class, persuasion involves connecting with listeners' emotions as well as their minds, with their personal experiences as well as their big-picture worldviews, and thus a mix of the two class speech codes will be the most persuasive. These advantages of becoming a class-bilingual code switcher are one example of how awareness of class culture differences can strengthen social justice work.

Shifting Progressive Views on Class Cultures

Beyond giving activists tips on becoming more class inclusive in their language and organizational practices, the Activist Class Cultures Project also promoted Class Action's broader mission of shifting Americans' attitudes toward class overall. When we reached out to social justice organizations to offer workshops, not everyone responded positively to the topic of class cultures. Many progressives reject class culture analysis as inherently conservative. They are understandably leery of the old "culture of poverty" tradition (Lewis 1959; Moynihan 1965), which frequently fell into the canard of blaming the victim (Ryan 1976; McNamee and Miller 2004; Greenbaum 2015). Rejecting this approach leads some progressives to promote structural critiques as the one and only progressive approach to inequality. Class Action often encounters this view in resistance to our combined culture-and-structure approach. As we promoted the Activist Class Cultures Project, we knew we were entering a long-standing argument within the U.S. left today. For example, within the Working-Class Studies Association, principled discussions often spontaneously break out about structural versus cultural approaches to understanding how class works.

This discussion was influenced by the work of French sociologist Pierre Bourdieu (1984). He grew up working class at a time when France removed all financial barriers to higher education and made access to the formerly aristocrat-heavy elite universities open to all. But when he himself reached the highest levels of that system, he found almost no other students from working-class backgrounds like his. He made it his life's work to document the subtle social and cultural barriers that exclude nonelites even when financial barriers disappear. He coined the terms "social capital" and "cultural capital" for the intangible advantages held by the already advantaged. He called them "capital" because they can be converted into enhanced opportunities and financial gains.

Just as conscious, deliberate racism is not required for racial inequities to persist (Bonilla-Silva 2010), no overt classism is needed for social reproduction (which is the tendency for most children of elites to fill elite social positions and for most lower-middle-class, working-class, and poor children to end up in approximately the same classes as adults). Distinctions of taste are the main mechanism he identified. Gatekeepers such as hiring committees, admissions offices, editors, and publishers tend to select applicants who laugh at similar jokes, wear similar clothes, talk similarly, and enjoy similar food, music, and leisure activities.

Some activists from PMC backgrounds overlook how their rejection of mainstream America comes across as classist superiority toward mainstream working-class people and their tastes and values. Especially common among PMC activists is disdain for *white* working-class and lower-middle-class people who are Christians, rural southerners, big-box-store shoppers, or employees of for-profit corporations. Concentrating on how their progressive values conflict with the business sector of the UMC, they can ignore the privileged cultural and social capital that wins them more favor from funders, legislators, and the media compared with working-class and poverty-class activists. Classism in social justice circles hinges on this misrecognition of cultural capital. *Missing Class* was the first book to apply this concept to the field of social movement organizations.

Through the Activist Class Cultures Project, we hoped to shift the structurally focused gaze of the left toward more concrete lived experiences of class and to argue that the intangible forces of class reproduction are just as worthy of analysis as the policies and economic systems that widen inequality. A strict political-economy approach to class does not take organizations very far in a process of transformation. Foregrounding class cultures has led some to study the social and cultural obstacles facing first-generation college students (Hurst 2010, 2012; Lee 2016), others to develop classroom protocols for bringing out the best in working-class children (Heath 1983; Calarco 2018), and led Class Action to look inside activist groups to learn how they operate differently due to class culture differences.

Toward our vision of a world without classism, Class Action helps people recognize and escape the limitations of their class socialization. All our futures depend on powerful cross-class and multiracial/ethnic mobilization to counter the threats facing us. Understanding activists' class cultures is one ingredient necessary for successful movement building.

Note

1　The winning organizations were Neighborhoods Organizing for Change in Minneapolis; the East Bay Meditation Center in Oakland; Jews for Racial and Economic Justice in New York City; Sub/Urban Justice and the City School in Boston; Haydenville Congregational Church in Western Massachusetts; Put People First in Philadelphia; Student Action with Farmworkers in Durham, North Carolina; Real Change Homeless Empowerment Project in Seattle; and Madison Urban Ministry in Wisconsin.

References

Bonilla-Silva, Eduardo. 2010. *Racism without Racists: Color-Blind Racism & Racial Inequality in Contemporary America.* 3rd ed. New York: Rowman & Littlefield.

Bourdieu, Pierre. 1984. *Distinction: A Social Critique of the Judgement of Taste.* Cambridge, Mass.: Harvard University Press.

Bourdieu, Pierre, and Jean-Claude Passeron. 1977. *Reproduction in Education, Society and Culture.* London: Sage.

Brooks, David. 2001. *Bobos in Paradise: The New Upper Class and How They Got There.* New York: Simon & Schuster.

Calarco, Jessica. 2018. *Negotiating Opportunities: How the Middle Class Secures Advantages in School.* New York: Oxford University Press.

Cohen, Cathy. 1999. *The Boundaries of Blackness.* Chicago: University of Chicago Press.

Cornell, Andrew. 2011. *Oppose and Propose! Lessons from Movement for a New Society*. Oakland: AK Press.

Croteau, David. 1995. *Politics and the Class Divide: Working People and the Middle-Class Left*. Philadelphia: Temple University Press.

Diamond, John, and Amanda Lewis. 2017. *Despite the Best Intentions: How Racial Inequality Thrives in Good Schools*. New York: Oxford University Press.

Diamond, John, Amanda Lewis, and Lamont Gordon. 2007. "Race and School Achievement in a Desegregated Suburb: Reconsidering the Oppositional Culture Explanation." *International Journal of Qualitative Studies in Education* 20 (6): 655–679.

Doerr, Nicole. 2018. *Political Translation: How Social Movement Democracies Survive*. Cambridge, U.K.: Cambridge University Press.

Dyson, Michael Eric. 2005. *Is Bill Cosby Right, or Has the Black Middle-Class Lost Its Mind?* New York: Basic Civitas Books.

Freeman, Jo. 1972. "The Tyranny of Structurelessness." *Second Wave* 2 (1). http://www.jofreeman.com.

Freire, Paulo. 1970. *Pedagogy of the Oppressed*. New York: Continuum.

Greenbaum, Susan D. 2015. *Blaming the Poor: The Long Shadow of the Moynihan Report on Cruel Images about Poverty*. New Brunswick, N.J.: Rutgers University Press.

Heath, Shirley Brice. 1983. *Ways with Words: Language, Life, and Work in Communities and Classrooms*. Cambridge, U.K.: Cambridge University Press.

Holt, Douglas. 1997. "Distinction in America? Recovering Bourdieu's Theory of Tastes from Its Critics." *Poetics* 25 (2–3): 93–120.

———. 1998. "Does Cultural Capital Structure American Consumption?" *Journal of Consumer Research* 25 (1): 1–25.

Hurst, Allison. 2010. *The Burden of Academic Success*. Lanham, Md.: Lexington Books.

———. 2012. *College and the Working Class*. New York: Sense Publishers.

Jensen, Barbara. 2012. *Reading Classes: On Culture and Classism in America*. Ithaca, N.Y.: Cornell University Press.

Lakey, George. 2010. *Facilitating Group Learning*. San Francisco: Jossey-Bass.

Lamont, Michèle. 1992. *Money, Morals, and Manners: The Culture of the French and the American Upper-Middle Class*. Chicago: University of Chicago Press.

———. 2000. *The Dignity of Working Men: Morality and the Boundaries of Race, Class and Immigration*. Cambridge, Mass.: Harvard University Press.

Lamont, Michèle, and Annette Lareau. 1988. "Cultural Capital: Allusions, Gaps and Glissandos in Recent Theoretical Developments." *Sociological Theory* 6 (2): 153–168.

Lareau, Annette. 2003. *Unequal Childhoods*. Berkeley: University of California Press.

Lee, Elizabeth. 2016. *Class and Campus Life*. Ithaca, N.Y.: Cornell University Press.

Leondar-Wright, Betsy. 2013. "Pretense, Put-Downs and Missing Identities in Activists' Class Talk." *Humanity & Society* 37 (3): 225–247.

———. 2014. *Missing Class: Strengthening Social Movement Organizations by Seeing Class Cultures*. Ithaca, N.Y.: Cornell University Press.

Lewis, Oscar. 1959. *Five Families: Mexican Case Studies in the Culture of Poverty*. New York: Basic Books.

Lichterman, Paul. 1996. *The Search for Political Community: American Activists Reinventing Commitment*. Cambridge, U.K.: Cambridge University Press.

McNamee, Steven J., and Robert K. Miller. 2004. *The Meritocracy Myth*. New York: Rowman & Littlefield.

Moynihan, D. Patrick. 1965. *The Negro Family: The Case for National Action*. Washington, D.C.: Office of Policy Planning and Research, United States Department of Labor.

Ogbu, John. 2003. *Black American Students in an Affluent Suburb: A Study of Academic Disengagement.* New York: Routledge.

Payne, Ruby. 2005. *A Framework for Understanding Poverty.* Highlands, Tex.: aha! Process.

Peterson, Richard, and Roger M. Kern. 1996. "Changing Highbrow Taste: From Snob to Omnivore." *American Sociological Review* 61 (5): 900–907.

Rose, Fred. 2000. *Coalitions across the Class Divide: Lessons from the Labor, Peace, and Environmental Movements.* Ithaca, N.Y.: Cornell University Press.

Ryan, William. 1976. *Blaming the Victim.* New York: Vintage.

Stout, Linda. 1996. *Bridging the Class Divide and Other Lessons for Grassroots Organizing.* Boston: Beacon.

4

Fighting Antihomeless Laws and the Criminalization of Poverty through Participatory Action Research

• • • • • • • • • • • • • • • • • • • •

LISA MARIE ALATORRE, BILAL ALI,
JENNIFER FRIEDENBACH, CHRIS
HERRING, T. J. JOHNSTON, AND
DILARA YARBROUGH

Formed in 1987, the San Francisco Coalition on Homelessness (COH) has been organizing against the criminalization of poverty for more than twenty years. In collaboration with sociologists, we conducted a participatory action research (PAR) study about the effects of the criminalization of homelessness in San Francisco. This chapter discusses how our participatory research process enhanced the quality of data and worked as a vehicle for organizing; how our project impacted the organization, city, and narrative on the criminalization of homelessness; and how we confronted assumptions about expertise as we worked to establish homeless people as leaders and experts in the local policy arena. Our successes, struggles, and process can be useful to other researchers and organizers designing and implementing projects that establish the expertise and leadership of directly affected communities.

Antihomeless laws that criminalize sleeping, sitting, and panhandling in public spaces have increased across the nation, most rapidly in the last ten years. For more than two decades, members of the COH have done weekly outreach to unhoused San Franciscans, reported on the impacts of criminalization, and advocated for policy change. Yet policy makers and the public were often skeptical of these anecdotes about what was essentially an invisiblized process of punishment, with no city agency tracking arrests, citations, or move-along orders aimed at the unhoused, let alone investigating their impacts. Our participatory action research project documented and analyzed the impacts of the rising tide of antihomeless laws on those experiencing homelessness in San Francisco, with more antihomeless laws on its books than any other California city. The COH in partnership with sociologists affiliated with the University of California, Berkeley Law School's Center for Human Rights carried out a citywide survey of 351 unhoused individuals in all neighborhoods in San Francisco's central city as well as forty-three in-depth interviews. We also collected and analyzed data obtained through public record requests from various city departments on policy protocols, citations, and sanitation sweeps.

The survey and interview instruments were directed by COH's Human Rights Work Group, surveys were conducted by COH volunteers, and the in-depth video interviews were completed by a team of five currently or formerly unhoused peer researchers. The sociologists translated the working group's questions and goals into a rigorous research design and provided training and direct guidance through the data-collection phase. Sociologists completed the technical aspects of statistical analysis and report writing, but the interpretation, presentation of findings, and recommendations were formed through a consensus-based process in the COH's working group of which both sociologists were members. We shared our findings in an in-depth report and a fifteen-minute video documentary featuring a selection of interviews completed by the peer research team (see http://www.cohsf.org/punishing-the-poorest/). The report provides an in-depth analysis of each step in the criminalization of homelessness—interactions with law enforcement, the issuance and processing of citations, incarceration and release—demonstrating how criminalizing homelessness not only fails to reduce it in public space but actually perpetuates homelessness, inequality, and poverty. The video provides powerful testimony to the analysis. Just as our organizing priorities informed our research questions, these findings have informed our policy advocacy.

This chapter, collaboratively written by human rights organizer Lisa Marie, peer researchers Bilal Ali and T. J. Johnston, COH director Jennifer Friedenbach, and sociologists Chris Herring and Dilara Yarbrough, addresses our experience. We discuss using data collection as a tool for political organizing, establishing homeless people and the COH as experts, and using our research findings to create policy change. Despite many challenges, community-based participatory research can provide superior data, more precise analysis, and broader impact than traditional academic studies lacking grassroots partnerships. We hope that our successes and struggles will be useful for other researchers and political organizers who hope to design and implement projects led by directly affected communities.

Improving Data and Analysis through Collaboration

Community-based research is often perceived as biased and therefore less methodologically sound than research carried out by professional academics. But in fact, the leadership of directly affected communities can make research more robust. In this study, a combination of personal knowledge of housing deprivation and training in social science research methods improved the quality of data collection and analysis. It was very important that our data be collected in an unbiased way and that our findings be taken seriously, so the sociologists followed the same training and design protocols as they would in their academic studies. Sociologists not affiliated with the COH reviewed our questionnaires, and then Dilara and Chris provided a ninety-minute training for thirty volunteer proctors, including local service providers and unhoused members of the COH. Proctors practiced using a script to introduce the research project in a way that would not bias responses. We used the COH's organizational knowledge to assign locations to each survey proctor to capture the most representative sample possible of people who had experienced homelessness in the last year. After the survey phase, currently and recently unhoused peer researchers conducted oral history interviews about interactions with law enforcement with forty-three more currently unhoused participants. Dilara and Chris provided eight hours of formal methodological training, covering recruitment and informed consent, prescreening, interviewing and effective follow-up questions, supportive listening, and writing postinterview summaries. Weekly research team meetings provided a forum for discussion of the process and mutual support.

Although this academic training and design created a more rigorous study than COH's past reports, COH's institutional knowledge, legitimacy among the unhoused, and its members' intimate knowledge of homelessness improved the quality of data collection. Survey proctors were deeply familiar with unhoused communities, making them better able to recruit and connect with survey participants. Their practical knowledge from the streets and shelters allowed them to access otherwise hidden groups. Their personal experiences and affiliation with the COH, a trusted poor people–led organization, gave proctors substantially more credibility among unhoused respondents, who were rightfully suspicious of "poverty pimping." Many unhoused San Franciscans suffer from "research fatigue," persistently being questioned for program evaluations, or governmental and scholastic studies that often employ paid contracted proctors. Yet because the COH conducts outreach almost every day—checking in on encampments, listening to what the unhoused think about city policies, and offering peer-based legal advice about citations—many respondents not only were willing to participate but did so more openly and honestly.

The practical and experiential knowledge of homelessness among peer researchers was even more beneficial in conducting the in-depth interviews. The peer researchers included three women, two men, two transgender people, and three cisgender people. One of the peer researchers was white, one Latina, one multiracial, and three black. We ranged in age from early twenties to early sixties. Peer researchers stayed in shelters, on the streets, in transitional housing, and in a community land trust at the time of the study. Shared experience with those we interviewed and intimate knowledge of criminalization allowed peer researchers to connect with participants quickly and ask thoughtful follow-up questions in ways that would require far more training for academics or other professionals. This was especially important as participants were being asked sensitive questions about criminal records, illegal activities, and often traumatic experiences.

Initially, we assumed that peer researchers would recruit from their own social networks and that each researcher could connect with unhoused peers who had similar experiences based on race, gender, or age. Although our research team successfully forged connections with other unhoused people that often felt empowering, we found that certain commonalities could make interviews traumatic. One peer researcher found her interviewee's experiences of victimization similar to her own past experiences, triggering unwanted memories and feelings of panic. At first, she tried to push through doing interviews, but when she finally shared her feelings with another member of the research team, we agreed that it would be best to stop any interviews that felt too difficult or triggering.

To take care of ourselves while completing the interview portion of our project, some of us had to seek out and interview people outside of our networks, with different identities and experiences. Sometimes, we had to stop the interview to take a break and ground ourselves in the now. We talked about how to end an interview early using words that would feel caring and respectful to the interview participant.

After completing the surveys and interviews, we discussed our findings and their implications in our weekly Human Rights Work Group meetings. These meetings included anywhere between ten to thirty people, many of whom were unhoused, as well as COH staff and volunteers. To analyze the survey data, Chris and Dilara presented tables and graphs and facilitated discussions to interpret patterns and trends. For our discussion of the interviews, T. J. and Bilal worked with Lisa Marie to present excerpts to the workgroup. Together the sociologists and organizers collaboratively analyzed this data, with the sociologists being careful that the group's interpretations stood up to alternative hypotheses and met scientific criteria of validation while the workgroup provided a diversity of interpretations grounded in experience. This collaborative approach provided a richer and more accurate analysis than could have been completed by scholars or organizers alone.

Advancing Community Organizing through Data Collection

The survey and interview process simultaneously advanced the COH's mission of outreach, education, and political organizing. After completing the survey and interview, many people asked about the COH's latest campaigns and learned how to get involved in supporting local initiatives to curb criminalization and the statewide "Right to Rest Act," which would make it illegal to cite or arrest people for resting in public spaces when shelter is unavailable. There were promises being heard in the California State Senate that spring that it would be considered. Several participants who had been given citations learned about the COH's "citation defense" program and received advice about how to get their tickets dismissed. We also distributed pamphlets about people's rights when interacting with police. Through the survey and interview processes, hundreds of people experiencing homelessness in San Francisco learned about the work of the COH. As we invited participants to join in the fight against criminalization, the research process itself facilitated community organizing and amplified the COH's ongoing outreach.

However, we were also reminded that romanticized ideas of "community" or "solidarity" don't always reflect lived experiences of identity. Some members of the research team struggled because they felt targeted and marginalized within the larger unhoused community. One member of our team, a black transgender woman, initially experienced verbal harassment from unhoused people she was trying to recruit to be part of the study and ended up dealing with this problem by making herself a very official-looking "COH Researcher" name tag to emphasize her special role and gain more respect.

In contrast, another member, a black cisgender man, adopted an informal style. He told his interview participants that he was camping on the street and explained how this was because of the injustice of the capitalist system. For this researcher, shared identities provided a basis for shared political action. While participants in the study had varying degrees of interest in discussing how broader political and economic systems produce homelessness, we found that the research process provided an opportunity for dialogue about common experiences of injustice. This is particularly important in unhoused communities, where race- and gender-based divisions and myths about individual responsibility and deservingness can preclude broad-based political organizing. Collaborative data analysis provided additional opportunities to frame shared experiences of criminalization in terms of state violence rather than individual failure.

Presenting All of Us as Experts

In an era of extreme poverty and given a culture that tends to blame people for their own suffering, it is more urgent than ever for social scientists to develop ways to ethically and effectively engage marginalized people in research. A primary goal of the project was to make the intellectual labor of unhoused people visible and to make policy makers view unhoused people as experts on homelessness. In a context where many people making policy decisions about unhoused people's lives are white, middle class, able-bodied, and cisgender, calling attention to unhoused people's expertise also helps ensure that our campaigns challenge white supremacy, heteropatriarchy, and ableism. One political tactic for achieving this goal is having unhoused members of our research team be highly visible as we present our findings and for academic researchers to be less so. Whether meeting with city supervisors, the district attorney, police chief, community groups, or university classes, peer researchers actively opposed the social stigma attached to the unhoused by presenting the research they conducted.

Except for a few strategic instances in which we needed to get key stakeholders' support more expediently than deeper conversations would allow, we talked about audience members' hidden assumptions. We asked them to see us all as experts—not just the white people, housed people, cis people, or academics. We named the danger of reifying racist sexist and classist notions of expertise. And we reflected on our mistakes to make sure we do better next time. This section contrasts the way we presented ourselves to different audiences to draw lessons about the construction of expertise based on academic credentials versus lived experience.

In almost all our fifty-plus presentations, peer researchers presented sections of the report, and we prioritized our goal of presenting unhoused people as experts, even if that brought skepticism from biased audiences. Sometimes, however, we strategically marshaled our privilege and academic affiliations to prioritize getting our message across to audiences that we thought would dismiss unhoused presenters. Strategic use of unearned privilege is a double-edged sword. We constantly weighed the tension between our goals of establishing unhoused people as experts on homelessness and establishing the credibility of our research among those more likely to believe academics than unhoused people. We challenged assumptions about methodological rigor and expertise explicitly, encouraging audiences to question their biases about who can be an expert. On a few occasions, we made regrettable decisions about how to present ourselves and our project.

As the lone white male academic on our team, Chris attended countless meetings with police and bureaucrats who were willing to engage with his authoritative assertions of our research findings. Chris's confident and informed speech, coupled with his embodied identities and affiliation with an elite academic institution, helped him become a broker of information in the local homeless policy sphere, a role that was unavailable to most other team members. His connections with a variety of local bureaucratic actors—facilitated by his role as a professional researcher—gave him power to which unhoused activists did not have access. "Chris has that white guy charm," we'd joke, simultaneously exasperated by the more respectful way police officers, city supervisors, and other officials responded to white middle-class masculinity and grateful that our team of women, poor people, queer and trans folks, and people of color could strategically marshal Chris's embodied identities.

Academic-community collaborations are not uniform, nor are there clear definitions of "academic" or "community." These essentialist notions elide the complex subject positions that all of us hold based on our race and gender identities, class background, and experience in a variety of institutions. For example, Dilara and Chris had to learn to accommodate one another's gendered self-presentation styles. At the beginning of the project, both were graduate students in sociology. However, many outsiders assumed that Chris was the only professional researcher on the team. Reflecting on their different approaches as academics and members of the COH, we noticed that Chris spoke about the research in an authoritative style that underscored his personal contributions. In contrast, Dilara spoke about the research using "we" statements that downplayed her central role in study design, analysis, and writing. Over the course of our collaboration, the academic researchers learned to accommodate each other's styles, with Chris consciously trying to ensure that the way he presented himself did not erase the contributions of other team members and Dilara working to become more visible as a professional researcher.

The academic researchers were invited in 2018 to present our findings to the visiting United Nations special rapporteur on extreme poverty. Dilara was eager to use her new credential as a university professor to bolster the work of the coalition and lend academic credibility to our project. She felt honored to have been invited to present to the U.N. rapporteur and excited to be at an activist event doing something that felt meaningful after a long semester of soul-crushing academic committee work. She had dressed for the occasion in her most professional-looking blazer and, to be extra prepared, had typed out notes for this presentation we'd all done dozens of times.

Before the presentation, Dilara noted that she was presenting on behalf of the research team led by unhoused researchers and that peer researchers T. J. and Bilal were in the room. In other contexts where we were presenting as a team, this standard introduction felt like enough to establish unhoused people's status as experts. Dilara launched into the "Punishing the Poorest" slide show.

At the end of the presentations, there was an "open mic" for anyone who wanted to speak. The founder of Poor News Network, whose concept of "we-search" by and for poor people was an inspiration for our project, looked directly at Dilara and Jennifer and told us that she was tired of hearing about research because we already know everything we need to know to take action. Another prominent housing and disability justice activist wondered why everyone invited to speak was a service industry, legal, or academic professional. Why had this event centered elite voices and marginalized the voices of directly affected people?

Debriefing the following week, Dilara told Bilal about the horror she felt seeing unhoused people waiting in line to speak after her panel presentation, and Bilal agreed that many of the unhoused activists in the room felt deeply hurt seeing yet another "community event" privileging a group of "suits" (including Dilara in her blazer alongside the service providers and lawyers) chosen to speak on their behalf. How could we prevent similar situations from happening in the future? In her excitement to be part of the event, Dilara didn't check to make sure that the event was representing the voices of directly affected communities. She realized that if she had, she could have suggested that a different team member, one who was currently unhoused rather than a stably housed professor, take her place on the panel. It is academic researchers' responsibility to make sure that the presentations we are part of do not (however unintentionally) perpetuate harmful hierarchies and exclusions. When we see that we're part of an "expert" panel of academics, lawyers, and service providers analyzing issues that no one on the panel has personally experienced, we can step back and realize that we need to make this change.

Although it is important to avoid exclusions like the ones previously described, strategic deployment of unearned privilege can at times be useful. In a few instances, Dilara and Chris strategically performed their academic expertise and their white, middle-class embodied identities to advance the coalition's policy change goals. A few hours after the presentation to the U.N. rapporteur, we presented to the San Francisco Police Commission. As we decided who would cover the different sections of our findings, Jennifer told Dilara, "The more you cover, the better. You'll have more credibility than I do because you're a professor." Dilara laughed, thinking that much of what she knew about local politics and policies she learned from Jennifer, whose knowledge came from more than twenty years of experience in local policy advocacy and at the COH. For the police commission, Dilara strategically performed her role as the expert professor, conscious of the temporary subordination of the long-term goal of establishing unhoused people as experts on "homelessness" to the more immediate goal of getting the police commission to enact policy change. The key difference between Dilara's performance of professor for the U.N. rapporteur in the morning and the police commission in the evening was that one was at a community event in which the context meant it had unintentionally exclusionary outcomes and the other was an intentional choice by the team to strategically use Dilara's PhD to convince people who would invest authority in this credential. We couldn't immediately change the police commission's stereotypes about homeless people, but we could give them the facts in a way they would find credible, using Dilara's and Chris's academic voices and credentials.

The benefits of activist scholarship are not only to community organizations seeking deeper understanding of the causes of the oppression they're fighting against. People considering professional research careers also benefit from doing applied work in the service of social justice. When we first started discussing the citywide survey that resulted in our "Punishing the Poorest" report, Dilara was disillusioned with mainstream sociology's focus on depoliticized analyses with no policy impact. When we came up with the idea for a citywide survey of unhoused people's experiences of criminalization and displacement, she had been volunteering at the COH for two years and had collaborated with Lisa Marie, T. J., and the Human Rights Work Group to design and coordinate a smaller-scale study of policing and displacement. Before she started doing research with the COH, Dilara was considering leaving her PhD program to focus on more applied antipoverty work. Inspired by the political analysis of the COH's Human Rights Work Group, Dilara once again became excited about the potential of research to produce knowledge that could help transform conditions of oppression. Chris, who had also worked in advocacy and policy fields before entering graduate school, felt similarly alienated and isolated carrying out a lone ethnographic study for his dissertation. Unlike conventional academic work, doing research designed to instigate social change felt useful, meaningful, and worthwhile. Being able to use their academic skills to bolster the COH's campaigns renewed Chris and Dilara's commitment to research as an integral part of activism and organizing.

The Politics and Contradictions of Human Rights Research and Funding

Funding for work to end poverty is complicated because funders prefer to back service-oriented work, especially short-term or "immediate needs" rather than investing in long-term solutions and policy-oriented work aimed at infrastructural changes. At the COH, we are committed to work based on the needs and asks of our communities—not the vision of a funder. Most funders take a top-down and ameliorative approach, while we focus on a bottom-up approach to challenge the conditions that produce poverty. Attempting to build the political power of our unhoused members makes our goals incompatible with the priorities of many funders. Our groundbreaking work of political organizing and policy change often fails to produce the "evidence-based" examples and quantifiable outcomes that most funders require.

As an underfunded, grassroots organization, we are used to doing a lot with a little. In the past, we successfully launched unfunded PAR projects, but the Sociological Initiatives Foundation (SIF) grant made our project stronger, more impactful, and farther reaching. The SIF grant specifically allowed compensation for peer researchers, an academic researcher to coordinate peer researchers, and research participants; it covered printing costs for report development and refreshments for launch events and trainings. As a poor people–led organization, we frequently experience the denial of academic-type funding toward our community-organizing efforts. Instead, we see those resources fund work that will likely never impact the lives of those being studied. All too often, we are asked to speak at academic gatherings to study poverty, events that are often flush with free food and wine, and events where researchers who have never been without housing are provided with monetary support for which our currently unhoused researchers are not even eligible.

A clear example of this happened when Chris and Dilara were awarded a research fellowship from the University of California, Berkeley Law's Human Rights Center. This was an award for which only current University of California law students or doctoral researchers were eligible. Chris and Dilara's fellowship presentation at Berkeley Law's Human Rights Center was the first time they had presented the project without the peer research team. We remarked on this fact in our presentation, pointing out T. J. sitting in the audience rather than onstage with the fellows. We noticed that day the abundant spread of catered appetizers, lunch, coffee, tea, cookies, and wine meant for academic fellows at the University of California, a sharp contrast from our COH Human Rights Work Group meetings where unhoused organizers' stomachs growled because we had no organizational budget for food to serve during our lunchtime meetings.

By supporting academic researchers who dedicate their time to human rights work, fellowships like this one indirectly subsidize the allocation of academic time and energy to human rights organizations. Without additional financial support, Chris and Dilara would have struggled to balance their own needs for income with their commitment to the COH as long-term unpaid volunteers. The fellowship also provided us with a prestigious affiliation that increased our research team's credibility when presenting our project to city officials. Ironically, however, the funder's requirements for academic affiliation exclude the communities whose human rights are the topic of our research.

After the fellowship, Chris and Dilara were invited to apply for a summer writing residency. When we asked if T. J. could apply, the fellowship coordinator said that he was not eligible. In other words, a human rights organization was inviting housed members of our research team to access free housing and meals in a beautiful retreat center, while T. J., an unhoused peer researcher and full-time journalist who does his writing each day in the loud and hectic environments of the COH office and temporary homeless shelters, was not eligible to apply.

With the SIF funding, the COH could finally pay currently and recently unhoused people for their research and activism. We were limited by the punitive requirements imposed by workfare bureaucracies, careful that the monthly stipends did not exceed allowable income in ways that would cause members of our research team to lose government benefits. Nonetheless, the SIF grant was a welcome change from our frequently demoralizing experiences with funders and affirmed the project's broader goals of establishing the expertise and leadership of directly affected communities and producing rigorous research to fight the criminalization of homelessness.

Using Research to Change Policy

Our research findings challenged many popular beliefs about the criminalization of homelessness. First, there was the general myth that San Francisco is a liberal city that doesn't criminalize homelessness but only enforces antihomeless laws on those whose behavior threatens public safety. However, our survey found that the majority of San Francisco's unhoused were impacted: 70 percent had been forced to move and 69 percent were cited in the past year, with nearly a quarter receiving five or more citations. Surveys and interviews revealed how citations and move-along orders resulted in a cycle of bench warrants, revoked driver's licenses, denials of housing, and increased people's exposure to violence and illness that prolonged homelessness. The report also challenged official statements and popular beliefs that the enforcement of antihomeless laws pushed people into services through "tough love." Of the

204 respondents who had been displaced by the San Francisco Police Department (SFPD), only twenty-four reported being offered services, which mainly included Band-Aid referrals that reinforced punitive practices—for example, handing out a sandwich or a pamphlet accompanied by warnings that if the person did not leave the area, he or she would be cited or arrested. The COH knew these to be myths prior to the research, but now we had data to articulate the immense social suffering caused by antihomeless laws.

Since the release of our policy report in 2015, we have presented this research to thirteen city agencies and commissions, each of the city supervisors, six state senators, and investigators from the U.S. Department of Justice reviewing San Francisco's police department and in more than a dozen community forums. In the days following its release, six newspapers dedicated entire articles to our report findings, and we are frequently cited in local media coverage about homelessness. Transforming the media narrative is crucial for public advocacy. Public opinion drives antihomeless policy and enforcement, so public education is just as critical as the immediate policy gains. The COH continued to use the report and its findings with media in the local, national, and even international coverage of the mass eviction of a tent city leading up to the 2016 Super Bowl. The study and video have been featured in more than a dozen educational and community presentations at local universities and homeless service centers. Wide local media coverage of the report helped reframe the discourse around the city's approach to clearing unhoused encampments from a "quality of life" issue for the housed to a human rights issue for the unhoused.

The widespread media coverage and ability to gain an audience with agency directors, city supervisors, the district attorney, a public defender, the police chief, the police commission, and the Local Homeless Coordinating Board did not rely mainly on the power of the findings or our academic credentials but was made possible by the community and political ties of the COH.

Just as the COH's political ties gave our research a greater impact, our affiliation with academic institutions made policy makers take our work more seriously. In much of our anticriminalization work in San Francisco and California, we have been met with resistance. Many policy makers have even refused to accept that criminalization is a primary policy response to homelessness and visible poverty, let alone acknowledge that criminalization harms unhoused and marginally housed people. This project provided groundbreaking research demonstrating that criminalization is a pervasive and primary response to poverty and documenting how criminalization affects unhoused communities. The launch and dissemination of our final report and video had lasting impacts both in media coverage of criminalization of homelessness and on local policy.

One clear policy gain was convincing the city's district attorney (DA) to end the practice of issuing warrants for unpaid fines for quality-of-life violations and dismiss those already on the books. Peer researchers and organizers met with the DA's office multiple times about our findings and recommendations. Since then more than thirty thousand warrants for quality-of-life violations were dismissed. Unpaid fines related to quality-of-life violations no longer result in the issuance of warrants or the revocation of driver's licenses. This policy change means that thousands of unhoused and poor San Franciscans are not prosecuted for being visibly poor and the city is no longer able to collect money or time from these folks due to their housing status. To help preserve the quickly diminishing rights of people currently living in their vehicles, we also used our data to lobby successfully for the reduction of fines and fees when someone's home is impounded.

The report's findings provoked a city supervisor to request that the Legislative Analyst's Office study the cost of criminalizing homelessness. The revelation that San Francisco spends more than $21 million a year to police and prosecute unhoused residents spurred a hearing on the criminalization of homelessness at the board of supervisors. Our findings of widespread search and seizure of property resulted in a general order from the chief of police and new interest by civil rights attorneys in challenging the city sanitation crew's policy of sweeping encampments. And our presentations have garnered new support for California's Right to Rest Act, statewide legislation proposed as part of a coordinated campaign by members of the Western Regional Advocacy Project. Most of all, the study gave the COH a new legitimacy that has increased our political and policy capital across our work.

Our report also helped initiate and inform the first proposed legislation in the city of San Francisco to partially decriminalize homelessness. The legislation, drafted in part by our research team, was designed to halt the destruction of property, requiring the city to post warnings before camp evictions and offer shelter, housing, or an alternative safe location before issuing citations. The proposed legislation also requires the city to provide garbage removal and portable toilets to encampments, thus resolving public health emergencies used as a pretext to force eviction. We predict our research findings will help garner support for the future passage of this proposed legislation.

Most of our work has been positive in shifting opinions and rolling back criminalization, but we have also found it difficult to hold our political ground while supporting incremental shifts in harmful policies. Following our report release, we met repeatedly with various city agencies. This included many meetings with the SFPD and police commission about how to reduce the volume of housed people's 911 and 311 calls to complain about unhoused people's existence in public space. Sometimes our findings were co-opted to push for a watered-down political goal. For example, when we met with law enforcement officials and explained our recommendation that the city divest completely from criminalization efforts, law enforcement met this request with a promise of a shift from citations to a kinder, gentler "warning." Our team was divided about how to respond. Although warnings are less harmful than citations, they continue the damaging policies of displacement and ignore that police contact is inherently harmful: homelessness should not be a police issue.

The COH is always grappling with this tension between reform versus abolition. We try to prioritize long-term change and support reforms that don't give more power or allocate more funding to policing and incarceration. Even as we worked with city agencies to institute moderate reforms, we also joined with partner organizations for more radical change. Our research findings provided useful talking points in a successful grassroots campaign against the construction of a $320 million new jail in San Francisco.

Toward the end of 2016, this campaign was ultimately successful in defeating the proposal for the construction of a new jail and relied heavily on data and recommendations from our project as evidence. Our data clearly showed the cyclical relationship between lack of housing and incarceration. Many of our policy recommendations were used in the No New SF Jail campaign's demands, including ending money bails and prosecution of quality-of-life infractions. These are now part of larger campaigns to reform the San Francisco criminal (in)justice system.

Despite these important gains, criminalization of homelessness continues unabated in San Francisco and throughout the United States. In direct response to our proposed legislation to decriminalize homelessness, supported by four of the eleven city supervisors, the opposing faction devised an "anti-camping" ordinance as a ballot initiative, which passed by a voter majority. Although some cities, such as Indianapolis and Seattle, have recently passed ordinances intended to reduce criminalization, our experience in San Francisco shows this to be incredibly difficult. Even in "left-coast" San Francisco, we found that more immediate gains are possible with agency technocrats who can make internal reforms or by assisting local legal struggles protecting the rights of the poor.

The limits and barriers to local reform that we found in our research suggest that we must continue pushing for policy solutions at the state and national levels. Since 2013, a coalition organized through the Western Regional Advocacy Project (WRAP) has had bills presented at state legislatures in Oregon, Colorado, and California called the Right to Rest Act. While no bill has been successfully passed, the legislation is increasingly becoming a point of distinction in progressive credentials among left-leaning politicians and political groups in forcing them to support or oppose a right to rest and has squarely shifted the concept of "the criminalization of homelessness" from a social movements slogan into the lexicon of journalists, lawyers, politicians, and policy makers. Just as our work has supported this legislative campaign, we hope that future research will do the same.

5

Organizers and
Academics Together

•••••••••••••••••••••

The Household Energy
Security Crisis and Utility
Justice Organizing

JONATHAN BIX, WILLIAM HOYNES,

AND PEGGY KAHN

The partnership between Nobody Leaves Mid-Hudson (NLMH), a community organization in New York State's Hudson Valley, and two academic researchers, one at Vassar College and one at the University of Michigan-Flint, culminated in the writing and dissemination of a report, *Just Utilities: Organizing for Solutions to the Household Energy Crisis*, in 2016.[1] The report systematized traditional forms of data and incorporated organizers' and members' experiences, and it articulated Nobody Leaves' organizing model. Both the writing and dissemination were tied to NLMH's People's Power campaign arguing that household energy (heating and electricity) security was a basic need and social right, not a mere market commodity, but often out of reach of low-income households. Led by the staff organizers and member leaders, the campaign aimed to highlight household energy security as an element of housing and land justice, empower directly impacted community members through building an active membership organization, relieve household energy insecurity in individual member households, and achieve significant changes in utility company practices and public policy. The multifaceted utility justice campaign won multiple victories.

In this community-academic partnership, the community organization was in the lead. Nobody Leaves Mid-Hudson's knowledge of the local community and of organizing strategies put them several steps ahead of their prospective academic partners. Nobody Leaves had identified key community problems, developed relationships with community members, and defined strategies of mobilizing and possible policy-making interventions. NLMH was fully invested in the work of base-building community organizing. In forging a relationship with two academic partners, NLMH sought to increase its capacity, systematize and extend its knowledge, further specify areas for potential policy work, and distribute its systematized knowledge about an undernamed issue: *household energy insecurity*. Organizing and activism produced research knowledge, and the academic research and writing fed back into action and advocacy. Other professional experts and community organizations were also essential to the People's Power campaign and report writing.

Many participatory action research projects emphasize direct contact between academic researchers and community members, but the NLMH project was primarily a relationship between community organization staff embedded in the community and academic partners. The two academic partners recognized the organization's relationships, experience, and roots in the community. The academics, through and with the community organization staff, incorporated the knowledge of community members and organizers and amplified the voices of those with limited access to the research and writing process.

The academic resources of the partnership were mainly two individual faculty members who had prior relationships with the key staff organizers of Nobody Leaves Mid-Hudson. Professor Bill Hoynes was a senior member of the Vassar College Sociology Department, in which several of the NLMH founding staff had been taught and mentored as undergraduate students. Hoynes was a public media and social movement scholar with roots in the Poughkeepsie area and was skilled in locating, interpreting, and presenting public social data. Peggy Kahn, professor of political science at the University of Michigan-Flint, had studied low-income, especially mother-headed, households and how they accessed employment and public benefits and services to meet a range of basic needs. Kahn had long-standing ties to NLMH's founding staff. Both faculty members were at advanced stages of their academic careers without traditional academic pressures faced by junior faculty, and both supported the project without any compensation.

The *Just Utilities* report strengthened the organization's household energy utilities campaign, mainly between fall 2014 and late 2017. This was a critical period. Nobody Leaves was transitioning from a thinly resourced organization growing out of the local Occupy movement that lacked full-time staff and focused primarily on eviction and foreclosure to a staffed organization undertaking household energy work. Starting in 2017, with many of the initial goals of the People's Power campaign achieved, the organization began using its organizing model to build campaigns on immigrant rights and protection. The name, Nobody Leaves Mid-Hudson, was originally a reference to housing justice and household energy security, but it has taken on a new meaning in the current period of intensified immigration enforcement, including detention and deportation.

The History of Nobody Leaves Mid-Hudson

The beginnings of Nobody Leaves Mid-Hudson lay partly in the formative experiences of the founding organizers during their undergraduate years at Vassar College between 2010 and 2015. They benefited from a small, socially engaged sociology program. Founding organizers had multiple opportunities to explore—through their curriculum, independent study projects, community-engaged field experiences, and senior thesis research—critical social and political theory, community organizing models, and the Poughkeepsie community itself. The sociology department required a substantial senior thesis. One of Nobody Leave's founding members studied Boston-based City Life / Vida Urbana—through academic and activist literature, participant observation, and interviews of members and leaders—as a positive example of radical community organizing that built local power using an organizational model based on solidarity and community. City Life / Vida Urbana was located within and engaged in a specific community, but its organizing addressed broader structural dynamics and power and connected to social movements for housing and land justice. Another founding organizer wrote a senior thesis on the value of Gramscian theory for twenty-first-century social movements, emphasizing the need to renovate Gramsci for the neoliberal moment and build tools for both strategically informed theory and theoretically informed activist practice.

The sociology department's undergraduate curriculum allowed students to gain academic credit for community-based field experiences. The campus had multiple student organizations engaged with politics and links to social-change-oriented community organizations, and several students experienced the Occupy Wall Street marches and assemblies. As the founding organizers moved between academic and organizing spaces, they were supported and guided by experienced community organizers as well as Vassar College faculty members. These early experiences exposed the future organizers to the importance of theory in shaping organizing activity and methods of practical organizing as well as embedding them in networks of academics and organizers interested in social transformation.

In late 2011, a group of community members and students from Vassar College formed the Anti-eviction and Foreclosure Working Group of Occupy Poughkeepsie. In February 2012, several Vassar College students and others reshaped the group into a more structured base-building, radical organizing group, Nobody Leaves Mid-Hudson. Drawing on City Life / Vida Urbana as a model, it described its approach as building a community organization of directly impacted people, mainly people of color bearing the burden of capitalist, for-profit, and racialized policies and practices. Its goal was to build an ongoing, relationally dense community organization that understood the structural roots of social problems, won incremental victories with and for members, and contributed to a powerful movement for social and political transformation.

The organization began by resisting eviction and foreclosure in and near the city of Poughkeepsie. Throughout 2012, they learned about antiforeclosure organizing by visiting Springfield No One Leaves, attending a Right to the City Alliance organizing training that featured City Life / Vida Urbana and Springfield No One Leaves, and working with local lawyers. In September 2012, they anchored and participated in a Right to the City New York City regional demonstration targeting the practices of Fannie Mae and Freddie Mac, and the Right to the City Alliance achieved some important concessions. Through legal support and direct action, the group prevented foreclosures and evictions for more than a dozen Poughkeepsie residents. Partnering with local allies, NLMH spearheaded the passage of the state's first municipal foreclosure bond law in 2014—a Poughkeepsie ordinance requiring owners of properties in foreclosure (mostly banks) to post a $10,000 bond to the city for upkeep. Poughkeepsie was only the seventh city in the country to pass such legislation.

While the antieviction and antiforeclosure campaigns were proceeding, community members and leaders were also telling Nobody Leaves Mid-Hudson about other central housing security and safety issues in the city: unaffordable household energy bills and power shut-offs. Many local residents were renters being displaced by landlord foreclosure, but more were struggling to manage unaffordable household utility bills. In July 2013, NLMH attended the Right to the City's Homes for All campaign retreat in New York City. The Homes for All campaign advanced a comprehensive housing agenda beyond foreclosure that also spoke to issues affecting public housing residents, homeless families, and renters. Homes for All worked to protect, defend, and expand housing that was affordable, accessible, stable, healthy, sustainable, and community controlled.

The Right to the City research committee, composed of academic and policy researchers, produced in June 2014 a well-researched report to frame the issue of housing for urban renters and point to policy objectives. Following the work of the Homes for All campaign beyond foreclosure and nearing the end of what it could accomplish on the foreclosure issue, NLMH noted the Poughkeepsie data in the *Renter Nation* report showing that Poughkeepsie residents, 60 percent of whom were renters, paid nearly 60 percent of household income (rather than the 30 percent identified by the federal Department of Housing and Urban Development as affordable) for rent and utilities. By late 2014, NLMH staff began planning a campaign around energy costs and shut-offs, targeting the local investor-owned utility, Central Hudson (CH).

The People's Power Campaign

In June 2014 as NLMH hired its first staff, they began to move toward household energy insecurity as the key local housing justice issue. At the same time, NLMH's new staff, recognizing the need to put the organization on a sustainable footing, began to seek foundation grants and do grassroots fund-raising. The organization found many mentors among College faculty and in community organizations. Professor Bill Hoynes supported NLMH in its early efforts to secure grants, including the Sociological Initiatives Foundation's (SIF) grants for academic-community partnerships, and he helped develop the SIF grant proposal. Not tied to a specific research project or community issue, his commitment was based on deep relationships with students and former students among NLMH staff and a belief that Nobody Leaves Mid-Hudson was a community organization with the potential to build its capacity and make a valuable impact. Although NLMH attracted several modest grants from Vassar College and private foundations, the Sociological Initiatives Foundation grant critically helped stabilize the organization and launch the People's Power campaign.

The initial proposal to the Sociological Initiatives Foundation envisioned a group of Vassar College faculty and students working on a survey-based housing-needs assessment in the city of Poughkeepsie. However, the traditional academic community needs assessment was overtaken by more practical organizing needs. When NLMH mounted a utility rights clinic with the Public Utility Law Project (PULP) of New York State,[2] attendees emphasized the household energy security problem. When organizational leaders surveyed clients at the social services offices and canvased door-to-door—with limited key questions tied to practical organizing against utility companies—the problems of energy unaffordability and utility shut-offs were confirmed.

Hoynes helped frame the short surveys, and Kahn wrote a research brief about household energy insecurity and health. NLMH members drafted a campaign framework and a set of action-related research questions. At the end of February, Nobody Leaves organized a large-scale member meeting focused on utility issues and an ongoing "rate case": the Public Service Commission's proceeding concerning a proposed increase in the rates charged by Central Hudson to its residential users. NLMH now had a clear picture of a vital community need; the People's Power campaign was under way.

This shift from an academically rigorous, survey-based needs assessment to an organizationally defined set of community needs and action priorities illuminates key dynamics underlying academic-community partnerships. First, academic and community organizing timetables and schedules are not easily reconciled. Academic needs assessment projects require considerable faculty (and student) planning and implementation time. Academic faculty members engage in long advanced planning and slowly unfolding projects. They face various demands across teaching, research, and service to their institutions, which are often priorities for career advancement. Community organizing, by contrast, often responds quickly to opportunities, needs, and events. Second, Nobody Leaves Mid-Hudson was already organically connected to community members through previous work, and they were committed to a certain model of community organizing. Rather than conducting a depersonalized survey, organizers opted for recruitment to meetings, where the issues could be more fully framed and deliberated, a style that grew out of their previous experience and a base-building organizing model.

The organizing model, modified from City Life / Vida Urbana in Boston, stressed the importance of building relationships within an ongoing organization, not just turning people out to protest or to make demands of public officials. It involved a member-leadership model in which members acquired leadership skills and decided on action together with the staff. While the idea of documenting community needs remained a critical element of the campaign, it became a task to accompany and follow, rather than precede, the initial organizing. The resulting documentation of community needs, which culminated in the *Just Utilities* report, used public data, organizational experience, and member stories rather than traditional survey techniques, and the report took a form that made information about energy insecurity and potential policy interventions more accessible.

Several factors solidified the community-academic partnership as it focused on a research-based advocacy report. The partnership would augment NLMH's capacity at a time when they faced organizing around a new issue. This involved building new relationships among the mainly women of color at the center of the crisis, listening to members' concerns and needs, discerning patterns of problems, learning a new and fairly technical field, developing new

types of interventions, identifying targets for protest and advocacy, and finding positive policy and practice models. The SIF grant application included
a proposal to document the local problem and offer advocacy recommendations, and Right to the City was generating reports on aspects of the postreces-
sion housing crisis. Household energy insecurity in its many dimensions was
relatively neglected by both community organizers and academics, and pieces
of the work were scattered, so academic collaboration was especially helpful. The partnership became more robust and explicitly aimed to gather both
quantitative and qualitative data around the critical and understudied area of
household energy security in the Poughkeepsie area.

Early discussions within the organization and between staff and academics retrieved the Homes for All argument that housing security was a basic
need and should be regarded as a social right, not a market commodity, and
this applied also to household energy security. NLMH and its collaborators
adopted the five-pillar framework of Homes for All and modified it to four.
Each pillar represented a principle that should govern utility justice but was
violated by current practices.

1 Affordability. Utility rates should be affordable relative to household
  income and other basic expenses.
2 Accessibility, long-term stability, and protection from displacement.
  Households should be able to access the household energy they require
  and be protected from shut-offs.
3 Health, sustainability, and quality. Household energy use should contribute to the health and social well-being of families, communities,
  and the environment.
4 Community control. Low-income communities should participate in
  regulatory and policy processes, benefit from weatherization and efficiency, and own and control distributed energy resources.

Both the practice of NLMH and the expertise of the two academics, however, meant that there would be an emphasis on the first two pillars: affordability and accessibility. The two academics, neither an expert on utilities and
the energy sector, had to surrender certain accustomed standards of depth of
knowledge in writing about aspects of these last two pillars and other elements
of the energy and utilities sector.

Action Shapes Research and Research Strengthens Action

By the time the report writers entered the field, NLMH had considerable
understanding of members' direct experiences, community needs, utility practices, and other related organizing efforts. The day-to-day work of NLMH

privileged the direct experience of its members and usable knowledge acquired from practical work. Academic researchers, in turn, were able to locate more systematic and extensive data related to NLMH's ongoing work, analyze those data, and present the data in an accessible form. The geographic dispersion of the researchers and organizers was resolved through digital communication and with a week-long face-to-face working session. Both writers and the NLMH executive director were present for all the sessions, and the most active community organizer was present for some. The report was developed in four main sections. The first section, "Household Energy Insecurity and Organizing for Utilities Justice," explained the Homes for All principles adapted to household energy, described Nobody Leaves' organizing model, and briefly explained the structure of regulated public utilities. The central section of the report, "Household Energy Insecurity in Local Perspective," detailed with data and member stories problems of unaffordability and shutoffs, inefficiency and lack of access to renewables, and lack of public participation and community control. The final section of the report, "Policy Solutions for Low-Income Households and Communities," offered recommendations and existing examples of "best" or "better" practices—policies that addressed each of the violations of principle documented in the section on "Household Energy Insecurity in Local Perspective."

NLMH was place-engaged in the city of Poughkeepsie, a compact city of about five square miles surrounded by sprawling more prosperous suburbs. The majority population in the city is people of color, black and Latinx, and Poughkeepsie suffers from a shortage of secure jobs, high unemployment, extensive poverty, and a variety of high social needs. The rental rate in Poughkeepsie is 60 percent, rental costs are relatively high, and much of the housing stock is older. The regulated private utility, Central Hudson Gas & Electric, had recently merged with the investor-owned utility and energy group, Fortis Inc. While the organizers knew a good deal about the city and the utility, academic researchers were able to document the city's social and economic characteristics, including its experiences of de-industrialization and job loss and of "urban renewal" and flight to the suburbs and its current social and economic profile, using public data from the American Community Survey and with the assistance of Kafui Attoh, an urban geographer living in Poughkeepsie and teaching at the Murphy Institute. From various public sources, they were also able to retrieve some of the history of the merger of the local utility with Fortis Inc. and some of its labor policies. These data and information showed how the household energy crisis was created by the intersection of employment precarity and a shredded social safety net on the one hand and developments in the utility sector on the other. It assisted NLMH not only in making the local case but in showing how the local setting resembled that of others in which households struggled to secure affordable household energy.

The main section of the report on household energy insecurity in the local perspective drew on multiple sources. The organizers knew their members' experiences, had some survey data, and were already familiar with some of the public data through the work of energy economists Fisher, Sheehan and Colton (FSC)[3] and the PULP of New York State. The academic researchers were able to systematize and add to this information using NLMH's suggestions and the public documents associated with the proceedings of the New York State Public Service Commission. An important starting argument was the definition of affordability compared with the actual charges in Dutchess County in which Poughkeepsie was located. Homes for All had used 30 percent of income as a baseline for housing affordability. The home energy affordability baseline was less well known but became important for NLMH's and its allies' public advocacy. FSC had defined affordable energy bills as 6 percent or less of gross household income, documented the state affordability gap, and shown that the Dutchess County burden—bills as a percentage of household income—was 44 percent for households below 50 percent of the official poverty threshold and 24 percent for those between 50 and 100 percent of poverty. The use and graphing of these percentages, generalized to all states by a household income segment at the end of the report, was an important local, statewide, and national advocacy tool that the People's Power campaign used repeatedly. Organizers had already heard stories from members—one member had to turn off the heat, and his wife and daughter had left ("the utility bill has literally divided my family"), and he cut back his food consumption and cable subscription. Others had to withhold their rent payments. Using national data and sources, the report was able to systematically extend the discussion of what happens in households when utility rates are high and incomes low.

Not only the household energy burden but also the structure of charges was problematic. Here the report disseminated information about the structure of the utility bills, focusing on fixed and variable charges. The partnership, with the assistance particularly of PULP, identified the rising proportion of fixed service charges for low-usage, primarily low-income customers. The second segment of the monthly charge, based on volume, also was explained and identified as a problem. Using the prior knowledge of NLMH and its allies and standard research tools, the report writers were able to generate a list of seven policy directions that would tackle rates and affordability.

NLMH had documented the level of utility debt (arrears) among their members, while the two academic researchers found PULP data on Central Hudson customers in arrears. As NLMH had worked with members on individual cases, they also discovered the limits of the utility's discounted bills and arrears forgiveness programs, a supplementary mandated low-income bill discount program, and the federal Low Income Home Energy Assistance

Program (LIHEAP). Members had also been approached by lightly regulated Energy Services Corporations (ESCOs), which misrepresented their services and charges, and using NLMH experience and the rigorous and extensive work of PULP, the report was able to summarize Energy Service Corporation practices that compounded unaffordability. The report was able to document better practices across the country that reduced energy bill arrears and their severe consequences, including shut-offs.

Terminations resulting from unaffordability violate the critical pillar of stable access to utilities and housing itself. NLMH's survey of 184 residents at the Department of Social Services had shown that 40 percent had experienced at least one termination, and several NLMH members had faced shut-offs under dire circumstances of their own serious illnesses or children undergoing at-home medical treatment. These dramatic member stories became an important part of the report. PULP data systematized termination information and led the Public Service Commission to express concern that Central Hudson relied heavily upon service termination to collect arrears and was endangering residents. At the beginning of its campaign, NLMH had found that fewer than 1 percent of the two thousand people they had approached at their doors and at social services offices had even heard of New York State's "energy bill of rights," the Home Energy Fair Practices Act. One of NLMH's first programs in 2015 had been a utility rights clinic mounted largely by PULP at which attendees were flabbergasted to learn that they had rights that might prevent shut-offs. Academic researchers were able to identify the gaps in these legal rights by looking at national databases of state utility rights laws. In addition, the report was able, using national data and policy examples, to recommend a focused multipronged effort to increase knowledge and use of existing HEFPA rights in New York State and a project to try to increase HEFPA rights.

Nobody Leaves Mid-Hudson's People's Power campaign focused on affordability and access, but as a Steering Committee member of the Energy Democracy Alliance of New York State, they took seriously the issue of environmental sustainability, which was linked to both affordability and control through the issue of weatherization and renewables. The two academic researchers had less knowledge and experience in this field and relied heavily on information about member experiences of old poorly insulated rental stock with often disinterested or uncooperative landlords, public information about Poughkeepsie's rental stock, and public information about efficiency and weatherization programs in New York State. NLMH identified some resources for renters and raised questions about the cost burdens of transitions to more renewable energy in the utility mix. The report recommended increased access to existing low-income weatherization and efficiency, public earmarking of renewable investments for low-income communities, community and local ownership of renewables, and expansion of good weatherization and solar installation jobs, citing some policy models.

NLMH noted the limits of low-income community voices in determination of energy and utilities policies in the county and state, and they worked through both protest and participation in regular processes to amplify members' voices. The report argued that low-income households and communities required stronger representation and more participation of low-income users and communities in developing household energy policies. One policy recommendation was to increase community and low-income representation on public bodies, such as the Public Service Commission that regulated investor-owned utilities. Others were to increase venues open to public participation and to adequately and consistently fund public intervenors in rate setting and other regulatory processes. Finally, the report recommended a shift toward publicly owned utilities, a complex and longer-term goal.

Changing Policy and Shaping a New Vision

The campaign, of which the research and written report were a part, heightened the visibility of the household energy insecurity issue, won material victories for NLMH households, brought changes to the local utility's practices, and together with partner organizations, made serious policy inroads at the state level. There was progress on each of the four critical policy pillars.

Framing the Issue and Creating Awareness

NLMH created a surge of local, regional, and national public and social media coverage and developed a range of media practices and connections. The campaign framed its public discussion of household energy security as a basic need that should be a social right rather than contingent on the profit-making strategies of insufficiently regulated investor-owned utilities. It noted the negative impacts of existing practices on communities of color and appealed to the importance of protecting children and families. The campaign combined its critique of for-profit utilities with pragmatic practice- and policy-specific arguments with different emphases in different venues.

In April 2015, geographer Kafui Attoh wrote an extensive post on Nobody Leaves and the household energy utilities campaign on the Murphy Institute Blog (CUNY). As the campaign unfolded, the *Poughkeepsie Journal* covered early street protests, met with NLMH to discuss the rate case, ran an editorial against the rate hike, and published NLMH's op-ed piece opposing the rate hike along with Central Hudson's justification for it. Regional public radio, television, and newspapers covered the opposition to the rate hike and NLMH's advocacy work mobilizing community members to oppose the rate hike at public hearings. In *YES! Magazine*'s fall 2015 issue, Laura Gottesdiener wrote a feature story on Nobody Leaves Mid-Hudson highlighting its members' experiences and work to relieve utility debt ("When Energy Bills Skyrocketed, These Neighbors Banded Together to Keep the Lights on— and Won").[4]

The report was the main product of the collaboration. *Just Utilities: Organizing for Solutions to the Household Energy Crisis*, which presented statistical data, member narratives, and policy models, was released by Right to the City in July 2016. By September 2016, more than 250 people had downloaded the report through the Right to the City link. Right to the City sponsored a report webinar on July 27, which was attended by more than 130 people from around the country. The release of the report coincided with the Right to the City Alliance's interest in building a utility justice committee of organizations interested in duplicating Nobody Leaves' work. The report was also a tool to bring utility issues faced by working-class people of color into the emerging New York Energy Democracy Alliance.

Changing Unfair Fees and Policies

NLMH mobilized members to testify in rate-setting cases. In 2014–2015, NLMH mobilized individuals, organizational allies, and elected officials to public hearings in Newburgh, Kingston, and Poughkeepsie and submitted official public comments online. In 2015 the Public Service Commission denied Central Hudson's proposal for an increase of $5 a month in basic electrical and $3 for basic gas service charges for residential customers after interventions by PULP, Ulster County–based Citizens for Local Power (CLP), NLMH, and others, but it approved increases in electricity and gas delivery rates. In August 2017, as the next Central Hudson rate case began, NLMH was appointed to the rate hike proceeding as an official representative of the interests of the public and low-income utility users and was working closely with Citizens for Local Power. NLMH mobilized its base, allies, and aligned elected officials to submit public comments and attend direct actions; delivered more than fifteen hundred petitions from customers; and secured media coverage amplifying its position. Central Hudson again proposed to increase the regressive flat fee that every customer pays each month regardless of usage. However, because of NLMH and its allies' advocacy, instead of increasing its flat fee, Central Hudson agreed to decrease its flat fee by about 19 percent over the next three years. This was the first time a utility in New York State had reduced its flat fee charge in over a decade. Central Hudson also originally proposed to increase its rates by more than 11 percent but agreed to reduce its rate hike to 1.04 percent in 2018–2019, 2.99 percent in 2019–2020, and 4.41 percent in 2020–2021.

The campaign also limited arrears and shut-offs facing Poughkeepsie-area residents. Despite Central Hudson's recurring mistrust and rejection of NLMH, Central Hudson facilitated a meeting in April 2015 between ten member-leaders and staff and four senior CH staff, and they designated a staff member as a direct line to deal with cases. CH agreed to recognize NLMH as a third-party negotiator on individual service matters when members had completed authorization forms. After a year and a half of the campaign, NLMH had prevented power shut-offs for about fifty members' households and restructured more than $140,000 of household debt. Early in the campaign and through its meetings and casework, NLMH strengthened member understanding of legal rights. However, mounting a campaign to strengthen HEFPA's protections from shut-offs, even protection for households with children, proved to be much more difficult.

In June 2015, NLMH, with low-income members of Energy Democracy Alliance organizations, interrupted and demanded input at a meeting of the PSC in Albany that was considering the state's low-income energy assistance program. That action won statewide public hearings regarding inadequate low-income energy assistance at multiple sites around the state, including in Poughkeepsie, to which NLMH again mobilized. As a result of these efforts, the assistance program's funding was expanded by $69 million, and eligibility was expanded by 550,000 more households, compared to the original proposal.

In December 2015, NLMH petitioned the Public Service Commission to investigate formally the collection practices of Central Hudson. The organization had observed a high rate of terminations, possible racial discrimination in shut-offs, and illegal utility debt transfers, and they had received a letter from an employee identifying internal company practices pointing in these directions. On December 29 the commission's general counsel sent a letter to Central Hudson indicating that it was opening an investigation. The PSC ordered Central Hudson to make significant changes to its collection practices. Central Hudson agreed to modify its termination practices to consider a reduction of terminations, especially in winter, and prioritize accounts with the oldest and largest debt and not to rely so heavily on convenience and efficiency of its field crews, which resulted in disparate negative impacts on low-income, predominantly black neighborhoods. It agreed to improve training of customer service representatives, including in matters of transferred debt. It urged Central Hudson to continue to work with NLMH to secure assistance for NLMH members.

Democratizing New York's Plan for Energy Efficiency and Renewable Energy

The Reforming the Energy Vision process was initiated by the New York Public Service Commission to accelerate the transition to energy efficiency and renewable energy resources. NLMH works with the New York Energy Democracy Alliance to fight for energy democracy and cleaner energy, with special attention to household and community affordability of utilities; for independent rather than private corporate control of a changing energy grid; for more decentralization and community control of energy; and for a just and equitable transition to renewables. In May 2016 the governor of New York announced a collaborative effort among state agencies, acting as a low-income energy task force to consolidate and expand strategies to ensure that the state's 2.3 million households at or below 200 percent of the federal poverty line had greater access to clean energy and were better serviced by the state's energy efficiency programs. The announcement included commitments from the Clean Energy Fund to focus on affordable housing programs, utility referrals to energy efficiency programs for low-income households, community solar initiatives, and microgrid development in low- and middle-income communities.

Conclusion

The collaboration between Nobody Leaves Mid-Hudson and two academic researchers aimed to produce positive social change through knowledge and action. The partnership responded to the needs and organizing activities of an emerging community organization, augmenting its capacity. The academic contribution was community-responsive, multimethod research and writing that often followed and didn't lead the community organization. Academics were not in direct contact with community members but with organizational leaders who themselves were embedded in the community. The main tangible product of the collaboration, a report completed in June 2016, became a key campaign and organizing tool for NLMH and a resource for introducing household energy insecurity into larger housing justice and environmental movements.

This case of collaboration suggests that academic-community collaborations are dependent upon biographies and relationships—in this case, receptivity to and relationships of founding organizers with academic faculty, the organizers' openness to academic support, and their understanding of the importance of some of the advanced academic skills that could serve their project. It also suggests that academics can play a useful role within a constellation of allies, collaborators, and specialists outside the community organization itself and that these multilateral collaborations are sometimes key to the growth and success of emerging community projects. The breadth of movement and advocacy ties distinguish place-engaged and broad-movement relevant organizations from purely local, often service-oriented nonprofits.

Nobody Leaves Mid-Hudson has added an immigration justice campaign to its work while continuing its utility justice campaign. It has hired new organizing staff, engaged in new types of work, and created new relationships. However, both the previous focus of its work and its experience of academic-community partnership may remain relevant. As Nobody Leaves Mid-Hudson has now expanded its membership beyond Poughkeepsie to include cities in the service territory of Orange & Rockland Utilities, NLMH has entered that company's current rate case to advocate for a reduction in its fixed service charge. Utility companies also frequently deny service to or shut off undocumented customers when they cannot produce social security numbers. However, the Public Service Commission has ruled any such requirement discriminatory and not legal. As NLMH (as a steering committee member of the Green Light NY: Driving Together campaign) strengthens its current work to expand access to driver's licenses for undocumented immigrants statewide, as it organizes and advocates for municipal IDs in cities across the Hudson Valley, and as it demands nondiscriminatory utility practices and energy security for immigrant households, it is considering whether and how academic research and writing skills might bolster these campaigns.

Notes

1   See http://homesforall.org/wp-content/uploads/2016/07/Just-Utilities-Report
    -FINAL.pdf.
2   The Public Utility Law Project (PULP) was an indispensable and generous ally
    throughout the campaign. PULP advances the interests of low-income and rural
    consumers in energy, telecommunications, and other utility matters by appear-
    ing before regulatory agencies, working with social services departments, offering
    educational consulting and support services to other groups and institutions, and
    appearing in courts. A PULP expert reviewed sections of the *Just Utilities* report.
3   The firm Fisher, Sheehan and Colton (FSC) specializes in legal and economic
    consulting, with a strong line of work on the Home Energy Affordability Gap.
    In 2003 they introduced a model that calculated the dollar amount by which
    "actual" home energy bills exceeded "affordable" home energy bills (6 percent
    of household income) on a county-by-county basis. They have continued to
    update the Home Energy Affordability Gap methodology and data; http://www
    .homeenergyaffordabilitygap.com/01_whatIsHEAG2.html.
4   See https://www.yesmagazine.org/issues/the-debt-issue/when-energy-bills
    -skyrocketed-these-neighbors-banded-together-to-keep-the-lights-on-and-won
    -20151019.

Part II

Worker Rights Activism

• •

Labor struggles are a major dimension of activist research. This part is about fighting poverty collectively as opposed to paternalistic efforts to retrain and resocialize individuals. The importance of data and convincing analysis in waging arguments and winning in court and politically is a principal theme, along with the two-way importance of knowledge in building consciousness and skills.

6

Shaping Organizing Strategy and Public Policy for an Invisible Workforce

• • • • • • • • • • • • • • • • • • •

Restaurant
Opportunities Center

VERONICA AVILA,

CHRISTINA FLETES-ROMO,

AND TEÓFILO REYES

Americans now spend the majority of their food budgets eating outside the home (Economic Research Service 2016). This trend began in the previous century, a reflection of an economy built on longer work hours, multiple jobs, and increasingly precarious work conditions. Eating out is so widespread that restaurant workers make up nearly 10 percent of the private sector workforce, totaling more than fourteen million jobs. In fact, the restaurant industry is growing on pace to surpass manufacturing as the fourth-largest employer by 2020. The industry is resilient and was one of the few to grow through the Great Recession, quickly bouncing back from a short employment dip. However, employment growth has not meant greater prosperity for workers.

Restaurant workers live in poverty at more than twice the rate of the rest of the workforce; they are a plurality of minimum wage workers and more than half of workers earning below minimum wage[1] (Bureau of Labor Statistics 2018). A segment of the restaurant workforce is subject to a subminimum wage. More than one-third of all restaurant workers live in states where the hourly subminimum wage for tipped workers is only $2.13, and nearly three-quarters live in states where the subminimum wage falls below the federal minimum of $7.25. As a result, five of the ten lowest-paying occupations in the country are in the restaurant industry.[2]

The Restaurant Opportunities Centers (ROC) United grew as a necessary and organic response to the restaurant industry's power imbalance. ROC works to raise wages and improve working conditions for the nation's restaurant workforce. ROC organizes workers and employers and supports an ambitious policy agenda. The model also weaves in a forceful participatory research strategy that captures and draws on the collective knowledge of restaurant workers around the country. ROC believes that restaurant workers need to take the lead in research on their industry to get the best picture of what's really happening in their communities and workplaces and so that knowledge can be used to create policies that address restaurant workers' needs.

The impact of these low wages and adverse conditions is far reaching. One in two Americans has worked in the industry, and one in three had his or her first employment experience in a restaurant.[3] For many, the industry is their introduction to the workforce and is where ideas about acceptable workplace treatment and behavior are shaped. The industry sets a low bar. The restaurant industry is responsible for more than one-quarter of all cases of wage theft (Cooper 2017). It also has the highest rate of sexual harassment, accounting for more than 14 percent of all sexual harassment complaints to the Equal Employment Opportunity Commission (Frye 2017). The industry also has one of the lowest rates of unionization.

ROC's research has demonstrated the far-reaching impact of low wages and poor working conditions. It has revealed the pervasiveness of occupational segregation in the industry as well as the correlation between the subminimum wage and the prevalence of sexual harassment in the industry. As Saru Jayaraman (ROC cofounder) noted, ROC's work has "re-framed issues that tend to be seen as economic issues, as also race and justice issues," and has led to the adoption of paid-sick-days benefits around the country and multiple increases to the minimum wage. ROC's programs promote mobility of historically disadvantaged communities and aided in the 2017 withdrawal of the nomination of openly antiworker Andrew Puzder for labor secretary under the Trump administration. ROC's organizing model and particularly its research methodology have come under scrutiny, and ROC's advocacy and evolving research methodology have led industry trade groups to spend millions of dollars opposing its research, attempting to undermine its legitimacy. In a turn on a well-known phrase, ROC has found that research gets results.

A History of ROC

The ROC of New York was born out of the struggle of restaurant workers who worked at Windows on the World, one of the top-grossing restaurants in the country (Grimes 2001). The Twin Towers at the World Trade Center collapsed after the terrorist attack on September 11, 2001. Seventy-three Windows on the World workers died in the collapse of Building One; 371 of their colleagues survived, alive due to the serendipity of their shift (Grimes 2001). Windows on the World was one of the few unionized restaurants in the country, and Fekkak Mamdouh was both a server and a shop steward for what was then the Hotel Employees and Restaurant Employees Union (HERE), Local 100. Mamdouh banded together with Jayaraman, then an organizer with the Workplace Project on Long Island, to form ROC New York to support the displaced workers and their families (Jayaraman 2013). The collapse of the north tower dissolved the union contract, and so a workers' center was formed to benefit the surviving restaurant workers.

David Emil, the owner of Windows on the World, had promised the survivors jobs at any new restaurant enterprise but reneged on his promise. The picketing members of ROC NY quickly won many of their jobs back, and restaurant workers across the five boroughs learned there was an organization to represent them. ROC NY grew to represent thousands of workers and led major campaigns to transform working conditions in the industry, eventually winning more than $10 million in misappropriated tips and wages and discrimination penalties. In 2008 the Restaurant Opportunities Center became the Restaurant Opportunities Centers United and grew to a national organization with chapters in the top metropolitan markets, building a presence in Chicago; Washington, DC; Los Angeles; New Orleans; Miami; Houston; Philadelphia; Boston; Seattle; the San Francisco Bay Area; Maine; Michigan; and Minnesota.

Over the years, ROC developed a three-pronged theory of change: (1) workplace justice, organizing workers to demand justice at their workplace; (2) high road, uniting like-minded employers and a workplace development program; and (3) research about policy, to have the necessary foundation to advance policy changes that would transform restaurant workers' lives.

First in New York and then across the country, research became a tool for action and an outgrowth of action. ROC's organizing efforts led to relationships with workers that allowed ROC to take a deep dive into their work and life experiences, and it also helped develop relationships with workers. Jayaraman recalled that research "was one of the first things we did when we founded the organization. . . . In 2002, it was a combination of participatory research, government data analysis, and qualitative interviews that proved so fruitful in so many ways. It helped us recruit, put us on the map, and get press."

Research as a Platform for Organizing

Since its inception, ROC United adopted an ambitious research agenda as a tool for worker organizing and as an effective means of pushing an assertive policy agenda. An early mentor of ROC United advised that to really get off the ground and take effective action, it needed a comprehensive understanding of the restaurant industry. And so began the planning stages for ROC's first multimethod study, *Behind the Kitchen Door (BKD)*, which was conducted in New York in 2002.

Prior to the study, ROC United consulted with experts on research methods such as Annette Bernhardt, an economist at the University of California, Berkeley; Rosemary Batt, a professor at Cornell University; and Marc Bendick, a widely known expert on employment discrimination. Lanie Romero-Alston, a program officer at the Ford Foundation, also helped create a rigorous research methodology that ROC would develop over time. ROC adopted a research model that is worker controlled, participatory, and rigorous and that leads to action. ROC's goal was to ensure research did not sit on a shelf somewhere but rather could incite change and challenge misinformation about the restaurant industry.

The ROC community works collectively to carry out the research process and analyze the findings to come "to an understanding that generates insights that can be used to create [workplace] change" (Illinois Caucus for Adolescent Health 2017). ROC's research ensures a worker's expertise is valued and that his or her leadership and research skills are enhanced through participatory research.

ROC United is also committed to producing academically rigorous research that is sound, has integrity, and is adequately objective. Academic researchers review, guide, and participate in all major research projects.

ROC United has maintained and developed a multimethodology, action-oriented research framework. ROC United engages its membership and its deep connections to workers in the industry to conduct large-scale worker survey projects, employer and employee interviews, worker focus groups, and matched pair audit testing. These methods allow ROC United to capture the collective knowledge of restaurant workers around the country to push forward an aggressive policy agenda. ROC United publishes reports documenting workers' voices, overall industry analyses, occupational segregation, gender issues, and health and safety. Research findings then shape local policy initiatives.

Using Research to Engage Members and Build Leaders

By conducting participatory research, ROC has recruited new worker and employer members and developed current members as leaders. In ROC United's experience, when members become involved in the data collection process, they are likely to become more involved in the organization overall, become politically engaged with their personal and workplace experiences, and feel included in the ROC community as well as their local communities. In one instance, a member trained to be a surveyor later became coordinator for the entire project for a partner organization. In another, a member initially trained to support the data collection process later became the director of the ROC Chicago office.

When it comes to recruiting new members, participatory research, particularly surveys, can be an effective tool to gain insight about people's experiences and turn a conversation into an organizing opportunity.

Focus groups, also proven to be a powerful organizing tool, allow workers to vocalize and conceptualize experiences they have had at work. ROC United's research employs unique methods that place the principles of empowerment and social change at the core of the research. Also unique is its industry focus. No organization or academic has conducted the level of research about the restaurant industry that ROC United has done. As a result, ROC has filled a research and knowledge void. One example is establishing the links between the subminimum wage and sexual harassment, a connection not made by mainstream news outlets until very recently (Einhorn and Abrams 2018; Judkis and Heil 2017).

ROC United's research in this industry is multilayered and intersectional, focusing on wage issues, race, ethnicity, and gender equity. It is an organization led by women and people of color that has been able to gather evidence to reframe issues viewed by many as solely economic and demonstrate their race, ethnicity, and gender equity. For example, ROC United has gathered evidence to demonstrate the racist underpinnings of the subminimum wage. After the Civil War, tipping as a practice spread as newly freed slaves were hired as hospitality workers dependent on the customer for their wage. By adding a race and gender lens to this work, ROC United has been able to engage new partners and gather new attention to the issues plaguing the industry. Two studies illustrate the way research illuminates action strategies to improve conditions for workers.

Case Study 1: Occupational Segregation in the Restaurant Industry

Tipped workers live in poverty at higher rates than the overall workforce, but those who can earn decent wages are concentrated in the industry's fine dining segment, where check averages are frequently three figures. Workers of color and women tend to be "locked out" of these opportunities; occupational segregation is a pervasive industry issue (Restaurant Opportunities Centers United 2014a).

To investigate occupational segregation in the industry, ROC conducted a multiyear, multifaceted, multicity investigation culminating in the 2014 publication *Great Service Divide: Occupational Segregation & Inequality in the US Restaurant Industry (GSD)*. GSD was an in-depth study of occupational segregation and discrimination based on race and gender that analyzed the hiring practices and promotional policies of fine-dining establishments located throughout three principal majority-minority cities: Metro Detroit, Chicago, and New Orleans. Affiliates in those areas conducted matched pair audit testing, demographic canvassing, and worker and employer focus groups. ROC received guidance from Mark Bendick, an expert on employment discrimination who conducts research on disparate treatment in hiring (Equal Employment Opportunity Commission 2011). Bendick pioneered quantitative measures for instances of employment discrimination, which include matched-pair audit testing, sending equally credentialed pairs of white testers and testers of color to apply for the same position. This methodology was the crux of the research project.

Testers in the three cities underwent a rigorous selection and training process. First, testers were screened, and a "match" had to consist of two people of the same gender with similar traits and physical characteristics. The training involved creating personality profiles together, learning industry lingo, and interview training. "By the time I finished the training I felt like he [the 'match'] was my twin. One day we even came to the office wearing the same thing," recounts Felipe Tendick-Matesanz, former tester and director of ROC Chicago. The pairs then went off to apply, in person and within an hour of each other, for open positions at fine-dining establishments. The three ROC affiliates conducted 273 tests. To supplement the testing, affiliates also conducted demographic canvassing to measure the extent of visible occupational segregation in 133 fine-dining restaurants, focus groups with workers, and interviews with employers.

GSD found that the industry had a glass ceiling: workers of color, with equal qualifications compared to white workers, are granted living wage opportunities only 73 percent of the time. Research also revealed a lower floor: workers of color face a race tax of 56 percent lower earnings compared to white workers. Additionally, workers face a locked door: among bartenders and servers currently on the job market, 22 percent of black workers are unemployed, compared to 10 percent of white workers (Restaurant Opportunities Centers United 2014a).

Case Study 2: Sexual Harassment in the Restaurant Industry

In 2014, ROC United released the report *The Glass Floor: Sexual Harassment in the Restaurant Industry*. The report received national attention and widespread press coverage, including *USA Today*, MSNBC, the *Washington Post*, the *Guardian*, *Al Jazeera*, and *Cosmopolitan*. It revealed that sexual harassment was endemic in the restaurant industry, particularly affecting tipped women workers in subminimum wage states.

Available data suggested that restaurants were the largest source of sexual harassment charges, yet survey questions that simply asked about "sexual harassment" had a low response rate. ROC worked with K. C. Wagner at the Worker Institute at Cornell University and other experts to devise a survey instrument that asked about experiences with a spectrum of sexual behaviors, the frequency of occurrence, and how workers felt about those experiences. ROC found that more than 80 percent of restaurant workers experience sexual harassment and that there was a direct link between the subminimum wage and sexual harassment.

For years, ROC United supported raising the minimum wage without eliminating the two-tiered wage system. The two-tiered wage system allows restaurants to pay their tipped workers as little as the federal tip minimum wage of $2.13 per hour. As a result, workers depend entirely on the customer to pay a living wage. ROC's analysis of census data found that women compose more than two-thirds of the tipped workforce. ROC's survey data discovered that tipped workers are often forced to tolerate inappropriate behavior from customers on whose tips they depend, from coworkers who control the quality of the food they serve, and from management that has control over shifts and hours. Therefore, simply raising the minimum wage without addressing the two-tiered wage system would not be enough to address the sexual harassment faced by tipped workers. *The Glass Floor* found that states with a $2.13 subminimum wage have twice the rate of harassment as the seven states without a subminimum wage and that workers in those $2.13 states experience three times the rate of managers telling them to dress "sexier, show more cleavage, and wear tighter clothing" to make more money from tips.

Understanding the link between sexual harassment and the tipped minimum wage provided ROC United a policy solution to dramatically reduce sexual harassment. ROC understands that the subminimum wage is the root cause of several issues plaguing the restaurant industry. The National

Restaurant Association's (NRA) power stems not only from its ability to pay workers a subminimum wage and require them to live on tips but also from its ability to shape young workers' expectations of appropriate workplace behavior. Restaurant work is the first job for millions of young women either in high school, college, or graduate school; in fact, one in two Americans work in the restaurant industry at one point in their life. Working in the restaurant industry—the industry that is the single largest source of sexual harassment charges—is how young women are introduced to the world of work and where they learn what is acceptable and tolerable in the workplace. Those lessons may affect workers for a lifetime and in future employment opportunities.

ROC's analysis of sexual harassment in the seven states that have eliminated the two-tiered system compared to subminimum wage states found that when women are paid one fair wage, the extent and intensity of harassment is reduced by half, presumably because women no longer need to rely on tips to feed their families. Solutions like education, training, litigation, monitoring, and codes of conduct, all of which are important, do not address the power imbalance women face on the job. ROC United proposes that by eliminating the two-tiered wage system, restaurant workers will no longer be required to tolerate harassment, as they will no longer have to depend on tips.

The Glass Floor's findings and the experiences of the membership pushed ROC to realize that if the organization was to continue to fight for gender justice in the workplace, that meant pivoting to fight for the elimination of the subminimum wage, One Fair Wage (OFW). ROC's work then shifted to make enacting OFW the core of the group's work.

Jayaraman said, "To me, it's a lesson to even the restaurant association on the other side, and to academics, that if your goal is actually change and not just documenting or writing, then you're going to be committed to finding out the truth and even change your position based on the truth."

Opposition to the Research Reveals Structural Racism and Sexism

For nearly ninety years, the NRA's policy agenda and rhetoric went relatively unchallenged; they pushed a narrative of a high-earning meritocracy on the one hand and of a teenage or transient workforce on the other, and they threatened the demise of both at any hint of regulation. The NRA has devoted particular attention to excluding tipped workers—more than two-thirds of whom are women—from minimum wage laws. In 1996 the minimum wage was raised, but the NRA pressured Congress to freeze the subminimum wage at $2.13, where it has stood ever since (Restaurant Opportunities Centers United 2014b).

ROC began to produce research to challenge the near century of NRA influence. ROC's research has lifted the veil on the real-life experiences of those employed in America's restaurants, sparking and adding depth to important national conversations on the alarming rates of poverty, discrimination, and sexual harassment in the restaurant industry. The collective body of ROC's work, which includes more than thirty-three studies and two books, has moved a groundswell of workers, employers, and consumers to take action on important industry issues.

ROC's research has placed workers in the center as tellers of their workplace experience and created a new cadre of industry experts, most of whom are people of color, immigrants, and women. Commenting about the importance of research, former ROC Boston member and current ROC legal organizer Yamila Ruiz said,

> I thought that research was this far and away thing that only should be reserved for academia. I didn't think of conducting surveys in our own communities, of workers, of immigrant workers, of women workers, to gather more information about the working conditions in which we participate every day. I didn't see it at the time as something that was available or accessible to me. It was only through the Boston *BKD* [study] that I realized I have the tools to conduct this research and be an active participant in cataloging and collecting data on the industry where I worked and where many of my friends and people I care about work.

The NRA and even members of the media often reject our findings by questioning the integrity of research produced by a campaign-based organization. At the same time, media outlets and legislators seemingly take no issue with the data that come directly from the NRA—a powerful and well-resourced lobbying force. Studies that are released by the NRA are taken at face value and have shaped industry norms for nearly a century.

"Sometimes we're not taken seriously because of who we are. . . . It's a real reflection of racism," states ROC's president Saru Jayaraman. ROC's heavily scrutinized research output has shown that change is needed to create a sustainable restaurant industry in which employers, employees, and diners prosper together. ROC's research investigates restaurant worker issues, exposes the state of the industry, proposes interventions based on findings, and springs workers into action through the research process. Both the output and process of the research help restaurant workers see that the issues they face are sector wide, and this activates them to help change the industry. ROC's research has also influenced public sentiment about restaurant work and raising workers' wages; a recent leaked NRA commissioned poll found that "seven in

10 Americans want to see the minimum wage raised even if it means that they'd have to pay more for meals" (Graves and Jilani 2018).

The NRA has contracted with right-wing public relations firms—in particular, Richard Berman Inc. Berman is the head of several front groups that actively lobby on behalf of the restaurant, hotel, alcoholic beverage, and tobacco industries and have pioneered and deployed "many of the most intentionally deceptive, inflammatory and anti-democratic tactics used in corporate propaganda campaigns today" (Rosenfeld 2013; Eidelson 2014; Austermuhle 2013).

Through the Employment Policy Institute (a Berman public relations shop whose initials are cunningly identical to the renowned economic think tank, the Economic Policy Institute), Berman has released a series of reports that attempt to discredit ROC data. Berman's reports claim that increases to the subminimum wage will cause the collapse of the industry. Berman's efforts are intended both to keep the federal subminimum wage frozen at $2.13 an hour but also to undermine local initiatives to enact OFW. Notably, one of Berman's front groups, the Tips Coalition, was created in DC to funnel corporate dollars to defeat Initiative 77, which calls for the gradual phasing out of the subminimum wage (Rosenfeld 2013).

Berman and the NRA have recently developed more nuanced efforts to oppose the enactment of OFW. Since restaurant workers began local efforts to implement OFW, ROC has seen an increase in organized efforts to keep or reinstate a tip credit through Astroturf groups claiming to speak for restaurant workers. In places like Maine, Minneapolis, and now New York, Michigan, and DC, Astroturf groups are part of restaurant associations' efforts to defend the subminimum wage. The Astroturf organizations consist of owners and managers and the workers that they can galvanize through captive audience meetings.

The local shell groups that were seeded by restaurant associations fall under a national umbrella, the Restaurant Workers of America (RWA). RWA is a 501(c)4, "funded by restaurant owners, that regularly appears with restaurant industry trade groups and Republican politicians" to praise the subminimum wage (Thielman 2018). The group has traveled across the country to testify in support of the subminimum wage and has found corporate partners in various large full-service chains, which at times pay their workers to attend hearings and legislative visits.[4]

Case Study 3: Using Rapid Research to Block Trump's Labor Nominee

ROC's comprehensive goals often yield complex research projects that span months. Yet there are moments when restaurant workers face immediate threats or unanticipated opportunities arise and ROC needs to act quickly. In these moments of rapid response, ROC must investigate and expose an actor or set of issues. The CKE Restaurants survey project highlights how rapid response research served to curb an immediate threat to worker rights at large. CKE is the parent company of Carl's Jr. and Hardee's restaurants.

On December 8, 2016, the president nominated then CEO of CKE Andrew Puzder to be the secretary of labor (Taylor 2016b). His reputation for "believing that the nation's labor laws and regulations hinder the ability of companies to grow and create jobs" made him the ideal choice in the view of the NRA (Patterson 2017; National Restaurant Association 2016). Puzder was known for opposing increased government regulation and wage increases—including subminimum wage increases, the Affordable Care Act (ACA), and the Obama administration's effort to expand eligibility for overtime pay (Puzzanghera and Mascaro 2017). Puzder was also known to be a proponent of automation. "They're always polite, they always upsell, they never take a vacation, they never show up late, there's never a slip-and-fall, or an age, sex, or race discrimination case," said Puzder of replacing workers with machines (Taylor 2016a). Elena Perez, director of ROC Seattle, said, "[The] person you're putting in charge of the department is fundamentally opposed to that department existing as an institution."

While the head of CKE, Puzder released commercials that featured women in bikinis or models eating cheeseburgers. The commercials were met with outrage and public claims of sexism. In 2011 the company shared that they believed "in putting hot models in [their] commercials because ugly ones don't sell burgers" (Carl's Jr. 2011). Puzder defended the ads, claiming that he liked "beautiful women eating burgers in bikinis. . . . I think it's very American" (Carl's Jr. 2011). The nomination of Andrew Puzder for secretary of labor put into focus the priorities of the incoming administration and made clear that Puzder's tenure would be an existential threat for workers' rights.

Throughout Puzder's tenure as leader, CKE struggled with safety violations in its restaurants, creating unsafe working environments for employees and an unsafe dining experience for customers. The company was cited by Occupation Health and Safety Administration (OSHA) ten times between 2009 and early 2017, with several of the citations being for serious workplace hazards (Restaurant Opportunities Centers United 2017). CKE also failed to create fairness for workers of color and women, as evidenced by the history of Equal

Employment Opportunities Commission (EEOC) charges filed against the company. Since Puzder became CEO of CKE in 2000, Carl's Jr. and Hardee's had more federal employment discrimination lawsuits filed against them than any other major U.S. hamburger chain with $1 billion or more in annual sales (Urevich 2017). The sexual harassment and discrimination claims filed against CKE "read like stories from the 1940s or '50s, before civil rights laws were ever enacted" (Urevich 2017).

ROC members were ready to fight the nomination and quickly developed a forty-five-question survey to assess CKE's workplace conditions and learn more about workers' (dis)satisfaction with the company. Only ten days had passed from the point of the announcement of Puzder's nomination to the development of the research plan and instruments to the implementation of the survey in the field. From December 19, 2016, through January 7, 2017, ROC surveyed CKE workers in person in Washington, Texas, Maryland, California, and Tennessee. ROC examined states and regions where CKE's restaurants were concentrated and reached out through social media ads. The response was astounding. CKE workers were eager and ready to share their stories. In just over two weeks, ROC surveyed 890 CKE workers. More than 60 percent of workers were from Carl's Jr. and Green Burrito, and 39 percent were from Hardee's and Red Burrito. ROC also conducted eighteen in-depth interviews with CKE workers.

What began as a rapid response research project to highlight CKE workplace abuses had clearly become a critical awakening for many of the workers ROC spoke with. They began to think critically about their workplace issues. This was their first time being able to share their thoughts on where they thought the company had fallen short. Once ROC administered the survey, many workers realized that things could and should be different. They began to share how they thought the company could do better by its workers.

The report was completed and released within less than a month after the nomination was announced. The report revealed that 66 percent of women at CKE reported experiencing unwanted sexual behaviors at work, a third of respondents worked off the clock, a third experienced a wide range of wage theft violations, and 79 percent of respondents had prepared or served food while sick (Restaurant Opportunities Centers United 2017). These new data highlighting CKE's workplace issues caused a media frenzy.

The report was cited in articles released by Eater, *Forbes*, the *Wall Street Journal*, the *LA Times*, CNN, and so on. Release of the report also bolstered national opposition to Puzder's nomination. ROC was able to participate in a briefing on the hill at which CKE workers testified. For the CKE workers, fighting Puzder's nomination was about acting on the set of values they wanted to see in the workplace and industry at large.

On February 15, the eve of his confirmation hearing, Puzder withdrew his nomination for secretary of labor and in April 2017 resigned as CEO of CKE. Following Puzder's resignation, Carl's Jr. launched a series of ads that pictured "Carl Sr." announcing that he "was back," aware the company had lost its way and committed to placing the company's focus on "food, not boobs" (Stanley 2017). Puzder would not lead the Department of Labor (DOL), and another company had to end its sexualization of women. The workers involved in the organizing were also stronger leaders. Speaking recently about the campaign, Jordan Romanus, ROC national lead organizer in Pittsburgh, said, "They [the workers] take pride in being a part of that campaign, they frequently bring it up and it's something that kinda still goes with us to this day."

Research as a Critical Capacity for Organizing

ROC's research has led to its current fight for One Fair Wage, a steep but necessary climb. Ambitious research projects such as *GSD* and *The Glass Floor* have deepened our understanding and are moving policy around the country. ROC in 2018 has moved three major OFW policy initiatives that have, as of this writing, led to a ballot initiative victory in Washington, DC; a legislative victory in Michigan; and a series of hearings to examine the feasibility of OFW in New York.

But every victory is followed by an equally difficult and pitched struggle. In DC, the city council has threatened to overturn the will of the people and members have introduced legislation to that effect. In Michigan, the Republican-controlled legislature passed One Fair Wage without debate to remove the issue from the ballot and attempt to amend it in a lame-duck session. However, the nomination of Puzder was an existential threat to restaurant workers that threatened to undermine service workers' rights for a generation.

ROC succeeded by pushing its tried and true tactics of an organizing model built on a participatory action research platform. A dramatic and time-sensitive research campaign uncovered working violations and sexual harassment and mobilized CKE workers around the country to oppose Puzder's nomination. One of the first antiworker initiatives of the current administration failed thanks in no small part to the concerted efforts of restaurant workers, mobilized by ROC's participatory action research model.

Notes

1 Poverty, government assistance, and demographic calculations by the authors, examining American Community Survey data for all currently employed

individuals, individuals employed in all restaurant occupations, and individuals employed in customarily tipped occupations (Ruggles et al. 2015).

2 Seven of the ten and ten of the fifteen lowest-paid occupations are either tipped or restaurant occupations. Analysis based on sorting by median hourly wage (Bureau of Labor Statistics 2017).

3 See note 1.

4 For example, internal communications to employees from Team Schostak Family Restaurants, owner of sixty-four Applebee's franchises in Michigan offering employees $20 per hour to publicly oppose One Fair Wage.

References

Austermuhle, M. 2013. "Shadowy Group Jumps into Initiative 77 Fight." WAMU, June 18, 2013. https://wamu.org/story/18/06/13/shadowy-group-jumps-d-c-fight-tipped-wage/.

Bureau of Labor Statistics. 2017. *Occupational Employment Statistics*. National Occupational Employment and Wage Estimates. Washington, D.C.: U.S. Department of Labor (DOL).

———. 2018. *Characteristics of Minimum Wage Workers, 2017*. Washington, D.C.: U.S. DOL.

Carl's Jr. 2011. "Carl's Jr. and Hardee's Offer No B.S. and That's Just the Way It Is." https://www.carlsjr.com/company/releases/carls-jr-and-hardees-offer-no-bs-and-thats-just-the-way-it-is.

Cook, N., and M. Levine. 2018. "Puzder Resurfaces in Trump's White House in Spite of #MeToo Movement." Politico, January 8, 2018. https://www.politico.com/story/2018/01/08/andy-puzder-white-house-administration-328240.

Cooper, D. 2017. *Employers Steal Billions from Workers' Paychecks Each Year*. Washington, D.C.: Economic Policy Institute.

Economic Research Service. 2016. *Food Expenditure Series*. Washington, D.C.: U.S. Department of Agriculture.

Eidelson, J. 2014. "Exclusive: Private Documents Reveal How Big Restaurant Lobby Monitors Fast Food Protests." Salon, May 5, 2014. https://www.salon.com/2014/05/05/exclusive_private_e_mails_reveal_how_big_restaurant_lobby_monitors_fast_food_protests/.

Einhorn, C., and R. Abrams. 2018. "The Tipping Equation." *New York Times*, March 11, 2018. https://www.nytimes.com/interactive/2018/03/11/business/tipping-sexual-harassment.html.

Equal Employment Opportunity Commission. 2011. "Disparate Treatment in Hiring: Written Testimony of Marc Bendick, Jr., Ph.D. Economist, Bendick and Egan Economic Consultants, Inc." June 21, 2011. https://www.eeoc.gov/eeoc/meetings/6-22-11/bendick.cfm.

Frye, J. 2017. *Not Just the Rich and Famous: The Pervasiveness of Sexual Harassment across Industries Affects All Workers*. Washington, D.C.: Center for American Progress.

Graves, L., and Z. Jilani. 2018. "The Restaurant Industry Ran a Private Poll on the Minimum Wage. It Did Not Go Well for Them." Intercept, April 17, 2018. https://theintercept.com/2018/04/17/the-restaurant-industry-ran-a-private-poll-on-the-minimum-wage-it-did-not-go-well-for-them/.

Grimes, W. 2001. "Windows That Rose So Close to the Sun." *New York Times*, September 19, 2018. https://www.nytimes.com/2001/09/19/dining/windows-that-rose-so-close-to-the-sun.html.

Illinois Caucus for Adolescent Health. 2017. "What Is Participatory Action Research?" https://www.icah.org/blog/participatory-action-research.

Jayaraman, S. 2013. *Behind the Kitchen Door*. Ithaca, N.Y.: Cornell University Press.

Judkis, M., and E. Heil. 2017. "Rape in the Storage Room. Groping at the Bar. Why Is the Restaurant Industry So Terrible for Women?" *Washington Post*, November 17, 2017. https://www.washingtonpost.com/lifestyle/food/rape-in-the-storage-room-groping-at-the-bar-why-is-the-restaurant-industry-so-terrible-for-women/2017/11/17/54a1dof2-c993-11e7-bocf-7689a9f2d84e_story.html?utm_term=.14b304463818.

National Restaurant Association. 2016. "NRA Applauds Puzder as Labor Secretary." https://testcms.restaurant.org/News-Research/News/NRA-applauds-Puzder-as-labor-secretary.

Patterson, M. 2017. "Andrew Puzder: The Borking of a Nominee." *Forbes*, January 24, 2017. https://www.forbes.com/sites/mattpatterson/2017/01/24/andrew-puzder-the-borking-of-a-nominee/#2553baf84550.

Puzzanghera, J., and L. Mascaro. 2017. "Andy Puzder Withdraws as Labor Secretary Nominee amid Republican Opposition." *LA Times*, February 15, 2017. http://www.latimes.com/business/la-fi-puzder-labor-senate-20170215-story.html#.

Restaurant Opportunities Centers (ROC) United. 2014a. *The Great Service Divide: Occupational Segregation and Inequality in the US Restaurant Industry*. New York: ROC United.

———. 2014b. *The Other NRA: Unmasking the Agenda of the National Restaurant Association*. New York: ROC United.

———. 2017. *Secretary of Labor Violations? The Low Road Business Model of CKE Restaurants, Inc's Andrew Puzder*. New York: ROC United.

Rosenfeld, S. 2013. "The Corporate Bully Whose Front Groups, Willful Distortions and Hate-Mongering Has Poisoned U.S. Politics: Meet Richard Berman." AlterNet. https://www.alternet.org/corporate-accountability-and-workplace/richard-bermans-propaganda-wars-take-us-politics-gutter.

Ruggles, S., K. Genadek, R. Goeken, J. Grover, and M. Sobek. 2015. *Integrated Public Use Microdata Series: Version 6.0*. Minneapolis: University of Minnesota. http://doi.org/10.18128/D010.V6.0.

Stanley, T. L. 2017. "Burgers, Not Boobs: Carl's Jr. Brilliantly Flips the Script by Tearing down Its Own Smutty Ads." *Adweek*. https://www.adweek.com/brand-marketing/burgers-not-boobs-carls-jr-brilliantly-flips-the-script-by-tearing-down-its-own-smutty-ads/.

Taylor, K. 2016a. "Fast-Food CEO Says He's Investing in Machines Because the Government Is Making It Difficult to Afford Employees." *Business Insider*. https://www.businessinsider.com/carls-jr-wants-open-automated-location-2016-3.

———. 2016b. "What Trump's Labor Pick Andrew Puzder Means for Workers' Rights." NPR, December 29, 2016. https://www.wnyc.org/story/what-trumps-labor-pick-andrew-puzder-means-for-workers-rights/.

Thielman, S. 2018. "One Conservative Group's Successful Infiltration of the Media." *Columbia Journalism Review*, June 21, 2018. https://www.cjr.org/analysis/77-referendum-astroturf-tipping.php.

Urevich, R. 2017. "Civil Rights Suits Plague Corporation Run by Labor Pick Andrew Puzder." *Newsweek*, January 23, 2017. https://www.newsweek.com/civil-rights-suits-plague-corporation-labor-pick-puzder-546327.

7

Worker-Led Research Makes the Case for Labor Justice for Massachusetts Domestic Workers

• •

Social Research and Social Change at the Grassroots

TIM SIEBER AND NATALICIA TRACY

Social research guided by genuine community concerns—and even better if carried out by community members—can promote meaningful social change likely to benefit community participants. Ours is a story of such an effective research experience. A women-led Massachusetts immigrant organization, the Brazilian Worker Center (BWC), engaged in a four-year campaign to advance labor rights for domestic workers. We sought to reverse their historic exclusion from U.S. labor protections dating from the 1930s by advocating for new legislation: a state-level Domestic Worker Bill of Rights (DWBoR) eventually signed into law in 2014.

As in all effective movements for social justice, the Domestic Worker Bill of Rights campaign required years of hard work to build momentum and grassroots power and many organizing tactics, including thousands of gatherings among activists—one-on-ones, house meetings, workers' councils, congresses, training workshops, strategy sessions, and alliance-building encounters (more than eighty organizations endorsed our efforts)—and meetings with legislators in their offices, where workers could give testimony of the need for change. Maintaining a regular presence in the ethnic and mainstream print and electronic media, through interviews and press releases, required constant attention. We also compiled and published a legal manual on domestic worker rights (in Portuguese, Spanish, and English) and trained and certified a board of thirty-one workers and employers in mediation skills to resolve workplace disputes. Constant fund-raising during the campaign was required to support the effort. Over four years, we raised more than a half million dollars of foundation support, mostly awarded in small grants, to fund our effort.[1]

Research was also an important strategic tool in our campaign. We completed a modest research project, a participatory worker-led survey on the working conditions of Massachusetts Brazilian house cleaners. That project and the role it played in our campaign are the specific focus of the present chapter. Supported by a university-community partnership and guided by a nonprofit executive director who is also a professional sociologist, the survey yielded findings of multiple uses. It provided valuable resources for organizing, developing trainings, coalition building, legislative education, advocacy, and fund-raising.

Our story shows that credible, systematic empirical research can inform public messaging and drafting of legislation and legislative testimony and can help generate support for policy change from coalition partners as well as the public at large. Training and engaging workers in participatory field research also aids movement building and efficacy, making critical policy literacy a central feature in the development of worker leadership.

Domestic Workers and Their Historic Challenges

Globally, domestic work is one of the most common jobs for women, an estimated sixty-seven million of them. One out of every thirteen women worldwide who work for pay has this job (International Labor Organization 2017). Domestic workers, by definition, work inside the private domestic sphere and perform a variety of household services for an individual or a family, including caring for children, elderly, or the disabled and/or taking actions that maintain everyday family functioning, such as cleaning, cooking, or household maintenance. Two and a half million now work in the United States, a number expected to grow to four million by 2035, according to the National Domestic Workers Alliance (Poo 2010). The industry always has been mired in the informal economy. Domestic workers labor in isolation from one another in private spaces, and their labor always has been considered women's work, akin to wifely and motherly duties or those of servants. This situation presents many obstacles to organizing the workers as a labor force.

Exclusion of domestic workers from respect and recognition as real workers with standard labor rights has deep, age-old roots in racism, classism, and sexism. In the United States, for the first centuries of the nation's history, only people with less than full citizenship—slaves, indentured servants, disenfranchised minorities, and poor immigrants—furnished the bodies, always mostly women, who did this work.

Labor rights defended by most U.S. workers today originated in the 1930s New Deal labor legislation, especially the National Labor Relations Act (1933) and the Fair Labor Standards Act (1938). Domestic workers—the primary job held then by African American women in the South—as well as farmworkers were excluded from New Deal labor legislation through the infamous "Devil's Bargain" that northern labor-friendly politicians made with Southern Democrats not to disturb Jim Crow labor market segregation. Domestic workers were also excluded from the 1935 Social Security Act (until 1950), the Occupational Safety and Health Act (1970), and the Family Medical Leave Act (1993). Except for social security eligibility, these exclusions all remain today.

It has been a slow process to reverse these exclusions to bring domestic work under the same legal protections as other kinds of labor. Only since 2010 has any progress occurred, through the passage of state-level bills in eight U.S. states and an Obama executive order guaranteeing minimum wage for all hours caretakers spend on the work site. This progress has mainly happened due to grassroots organizing and legislative campaigns promoted by the National Domestic Workers Alliance (NDWA), representing more than twenty thousand nannies, housekeepers, and other caregivers. Today, NDWA's sixty affiliate organizations do grassroots organizing and movement building in thirty cities across nineteen states.[2] This effort is linked to a global movement for domestic worker rights that recently resulted in the passage of Convention 189, or the Convention concerning Decent Work for Domestic Workers, adopted by the International Labor Organization (ILO). Established in 2013, Convention 189 has since been endorsed by twenty-five nations (though not the United States).

Most of the NDWA's efforts have focused on supporting campaigns for a state-level DWBoR, which New York was the first state to pass in 2010. It was later joined by Hawaii and California in 2013 and Massachusetts in 2014.[3] The Massachusetts campaign was the context for our worker-based participatory research, funded by the Sociological Initiatives Foundation during 2013.

The Domestic Worker Movement in Massachusetts

The organizing campaign on behalf of the 110,000 domestic workers in Massachusetts started in the summer of 2010. It began with the visit by Brazilian

Worker Center staff to Domestic Workers United (DWU) in New York, seeking guidance in the wake of the fresh DWBoR win there. The Brazilian Worker Center had been the site of many prior conversations and meetings among domestic workers, trying to make sense of the issues that were plaguing them in Massachusetts. The discussions grew wider in December 2010, when the Massachusetts Coalition for Domestic Workers formed, established by the Brazilian Worker Center, Dominican Development Center, Brazilian Women's Group—Vida Verde Cooperative, Matahari Eye of the Day, and Women's Institute for Leadership Development, with Greater Boston Legal Services soon retained as legal counsel. BWC and the coalition resolved to follow the model set earlier by New York's DWU. The first step would be significant outreach from all the involved organizations to assemble a statewide Congress of Domestic Workers to dialogue and debate over what legal protections were most important but lacking in Massachusetts.

The first Massachusetts Domestic Workers Congress was held on International Domestic Workers Day on June 16, 2012, at the offices of the labor union SEIU 1199 in Boston. More than one hundred domestic workers gathered to define the workplace justice issues to address in a new bill of rights. The congress was funded by the Boston Women's Fund and Berger Marks Foundation of Washington, DC. The gathering was multiethnic and multilinguistic, with four official languages: English, Portuguese, Spanish, and Chinese, with simultaneous translation offered through a headset system.

The congress provided the opportunity for participating organizations to share information on their organizing work and for workers to identify key workplace problems that needed remedies. The congress divided attendees into twelve breakout tables to enable workers to compile their wish lists for how a new Massachusetts DWBoR should address their concerns. Two tables were Portuguese speaking; three, Spanish speaking; one, Chinese speaking; the rest, English speaking. After brainstorming, each table sent two representatives to the front, and to applause and encouragement, they displayed their notes, explaining their table's key recommendations in their own languages. Later, the BWC completed a report of the overall findings and recommendations, which the Employment Law Unit of Greater Boston Legal Services used to draft the formal bill of rights that was submitted to the legislature two months later, in January 2013.

Recommendations of the 2012 Domestic Worker Congress included the following twelve points:

1 **Fair pay and benefits.** This means recognizing the regular workweek and providing for overtime pay. For one group, a $15 per hour minimum is recommended for the hourly wage. Other compensation and benefit

items needed are periodic pay raises, paid holidays, paid sick days, and specified, mandated break times.

2 **Clear expectations and defined work duties.** The specifics of the job assignment should be made clear in writing or in contracts—what is and is not part of the job. Hours, benefits, and other necessary working conditions should be specified as well.

3 **Advance notice dismissal.** Employers should give advance notice if there is no work available instead of letting the worker report for work to be told they are not needed. Similarly, live-in nannies or other workers should not be dismissed immediately since it is tantamount to making them homeless.

4 **Better protection for "the help" who work for schedule owners in housecleaning.** These house cleaners deserve clear work expectations and deserve fair pay, overtime, and meal breaks.

5 **Workers' compensation coverage.** All domestic workers should be covered by workers' compensation insurance so that injuries can be treated with minimum or no cost to the worker. Workers should not be discharged for being out sick or for staying home with sick children or other dependents. Several groups called for the availability of health insurance.

6 **Dignity and respect.** All domestic workers deserve respect and dignity as intelligent people providing much-needed professional services to employers. They should not be subject to employer insults, personal abuse, or harassment.

7 **Training and professional development.** Opportunities should be available for workers to gain professional development training related to their work duties.

8 **Protection from discrimination and harassment.** Domestic workers should not be subject to harassment or discrimination on account of race, sexuality, immigrant status, national origin, accent, or religion. This includes the need for protection against sexual harassment and discrimination against workers on account of pregnancy.

9 **Retirement investment or pension programs.** There should be a way for workers to accumulate some resources for retirement. Many will not be eligible for social security, and 401(k) plans or other arrangements would be beneficial.

10 **Protection from workplace safety and health hazards.** Domestic workers should be protected against dangerous exposures to unsafe and unhealthy working conditions, including toxic cleaning products.

11 **Oversight.** An external, official entity should oversee these arrangements and receive appeals and intervene in cases of violations and abuse.

12 **Path to citizenship.** There should be a pathway to citizenship for those doing this important work, even though this is a federal, not state, prerogative.

Proposing the Domestic Workers Bill of Rights to the State Legislature

The Massachusetts Coalition for Domestic Workers launched a massive lobbying campaign in December 2012 and January 2013. The campaign involved hundreds of hours of personal visits to the state capital for meetings with legislators and organizing efforts to secure support from allies for the bill. The Massachusetts American Federation of Labor and Congress of Industrial Organizations (AFL-CIO) Labor Council unanimously endorsed the Massachusetts DWBoR as a priority item on their 2013 legislative agenda, and it gained support from many other nonprofit, labor, immigrant, and faith-based organizations. When formally submitted as a legislative proposal on January 18, 2013, because of this early organizing, the bill had more than 40 percent of both the House of Representatives (67 of 140) and the Senate (17 of 40) signed on as official cosponsors. Its provisions closely mirrored the recommendations that resulted from the Domestic Workers Congress the previous June.

Gaining sponsorships was not easy, however, since many legislators remained skeptical about the prevalence of workplace problems for domestic workers. We were met with continuing questions about whether the workers were speaking of rarely occurring, individual grievances they had against employers and whether we could really speak with authority about widespread issues affecting the industry. If problems were so bad, some said, why had no one made an issue of this in the state since 1938, when the Fair Labor Standards Act was passed?

Bolstering the Campaign with Research

After submission, the bill of rights required almost another eighteen months of active campaigning to consolidate public and legislative support. Following organizing models elsewhere, we knew results from empirical studies of problematic working conditions can give power and heft to advocacy, public messaging, and testimony used to advance grassroots campaigns for change. Successful organizing efforts and campaigns that won bills of rights in both New York and California had been facilitated by earlier survey research studies conducted by their respective coalitions, resulting in Domestic Worker United's *Home Is Where the Work Is: Inside New York's Domestic Work Industry* (2006) and the Mujeres Unidas y Activas report *Behind Closed Doors: Working Conditions of California Domestic Workers* (2007). More recently, the nation-wide campaign had gained traction from NDWA's widely disseminated sixteen-city study *Home Economics: The Invisible and Unregulated World of Domestic Work* (2012), with 2,086 respondents. Boston was one of the cities sampled, and BWC worker volunteers had formed part of the team that carried out the local survey, but the final analysis for this national survey did not report separate findings for Massachusetts or any other state.[4]

It was clear that for credibility, we needed to produce our own survey data on local conditions. We knew professionally conducted social surveys were the gold standard for accurate information on public policy issues. Even though we were confident that we understood our problems, we knew that workers often shared their stories with legislators and key opinion makers and would be listened to with sympathy but often could not convince them these were more than individual problems. Storytelling by individual workers about their workplace problems can be powerful, but as one anonymous activist put it, "You can talk yourself blue in the face to legislators and other people about the problems you're having, but in the end regular workers who are common people just lack credibility. Even though you have a lot of experience with the situation you're describing and know the truth, society treats your problem as an isolated incident that happened just to you." Credible research could clearly help us ramp up more intense organizing efforts during the critical months ahead when the Massachusetts legislature would be considering our bill of rights.

Forming a Community Research Partnership

Two partnerships were critical for moving ahead on the research component of our campaign. One was between the BWC and the University of Massachusetts Boston, where both authors are members of the faculty. In November 2012, the two parties signed a memorandum of understanding, with the support of the Office of Community Partnerships, to formalize an already long-term relationship in carrying out collaborative projects in research, service, and teaching. The lead university units were to be the Department of Anthropology and the Mauricio Gastón Institute for Latino Community Development and Public Policy. We gained approval from the university's institutional review board (IRB) for our research design and were provided space and facilities to support the project. The university has a long history as a community-engaged, urban university and has more than three thousand community partnerships at present. There was widespread institutional support for this particular initiative in terms of resource sharing—especially space—and attention in university publicity.

Our second partnership was with our funder, the Sociological Initiatives Foundation. One of us (Sieber) already knew of the foundation and its mission and had been a participant in another foundation-funded Boston-based project on immigrant integration. We were greatly encouraged by the foundation's openness to funding research with public policy implications, especially when embedded in community-based organizations and grassroots change. We used the grant to stipend worker surveyors and respondents.

Codesigning the Research Project

Ours was not an exploratory research question into unknown terrain. The key gaps in labor protection and rights for domestic workers were already well known from earlier studies and collective deliberations at large gatherings such as our 2012 congress as well as from smaller meetings and storytelling occurring regularly at the BWC. Our research was more a matter of documenting local Massachusetts conditions so we could convincingly cite them in our campaign messaging. The key conclusions of our earlier congress, in fact, had already informed the design of the bill of rights and its provisions, which were at the time being introduced for legislative consideration at the state capitol.

The Massachusetts Coalition for Domestic Workers, as noted earlier, was multiethnic, and any future bill of rights would cover a domestic workforce made up mostly of Brazilian, Latina, West Indian, Haitian, and Chinese immigrant women. BWC conducted research in only a portion of this wider domestic work labor force, a Portuguese-language survey of an occupational niche quite common in our community: housecleaning. We knew that whatever their educational, professional, or class background, most Brazilian women migrants' first job after arriving in the United States was housecleaning, where they would work at least temporarily before attempting to reestablish themselves professionally.

We planned a forty-question survey, focused on known key problem areas: (1) workplace safety and health issues, especially exposure to toxic substances; (2) wage and benefit issues, especially wage theft; (3) job creep and indefiniteness due to lack of contracts and the informal nature of the work; and (4) economic conditions of workers and their families, especially whether the remuneration from the work afforded a living wage. These perennial topics had emerged as areas of concern at the 2012 congress. We also borrowed survey items from many previous surveys used by the NDWA and from Eduardo Siqueira and Andrea Roche in their study done in 2003 on the Brazilian Worker Center's health and safety training project for construction and domestic workers (Siqueira and Roche 2013). We also took steps to validate our survey. We did snowball sampling in four key state regions where Brazilian immigrant communities are the largest. We sought a sample of 200 workers and would eventually achieve 198. Finally, following past practice in earlier surveys of domestic workers' job conditions, we resolved to train and supervise a team of present and former domestic workers—all Brazilian themselves—to carry out the survey.

Recruiting and Training the Field Research Team

One of us (Tracy) recruited, trained, and supervised the project's field surveyors, ten mature women in their thirties and forties with domestic work experience. All the women were involved in the movement, understood well what doing domestic work entailed, and were eager to learn research methods. A few had been participants in the 2012 NDWA-sponsored Boston segment of the national survey. All were first-generation Brazilian immigrants bilingual in Portuguese and English, and the survey instrument and the interviews with respondents were to be in Portuguese. Training involved survey methodology and interviewing techniques and ethics, and each field surveyor became certified in human subject research through the university's institutional review board. It was important for them to understand informed consent and the right of respondents to refuse participation, given that the surveys would be conducted at dispersed locations in the state and could not be supervised directly.

Author Tracy, who regularly teaches sociological research methods at the undergraduate level, found the surveyors to be quick learners who could absorb the applied, practical dimensions of research methodology and were systematic in their work. They also had no problem in understanding the need to be neutral in questioning and not to lead respondents in their answers. Training also involved two hours of rehearsed interviewing and, for each surveyor, three pilot administrations of the survey, after which they returned for a postmortem on how things had gone. The surveyors helped modify the wording of some questions toward more everyday, colloquial Portuguese. Some reported that they encountered respondents with serious problems—severe workplace abuse, depression and other mental problems, and domestic violence from partners at home. The surveyors equipped themselves with referral information to agencies and resources that could give help to respondents in whatever region they were living.

From the outset, we clearly understood why community-based participatory research involving workers has been an important part of leadership training and movement building. Those doing the surveys, as well as the respondents, can gain from the research process a sense of efficacy in creating useful knowledge relevant to public policy issues affecting them. They began quickly to see that the quality of the survey information and its reference to broader population samples made their findings more compelling. As one of the surveyors reported later, remembering that her personal stories had earlier been doubted in contact with legislators, "It was interesting to do because it allowed us women to understand the power of research, to show that what we knew was happening was really true." Others responded that they knew how strong the information was going to be in the campaign in convincing skeptics and how compelling the repeated stories were to them on a human level.

> I saw the research was important. It made the information seem more valid because it provided numbers and more information about how necessary it was to protect domestic workers.
>
> I'm a house cleaner, and I thought my life was complicated, with being a mother, but to hear from some of these women what are some of the issues out there for mothers is just crazy. There's so much they are dealing with. They had so many complaints, it's hard to digest all of them. I thought my life was complicated!
>
> I never had the chance before to think of myself as a worker. There's so much that we have in common I never recognized before.
>
> I was so shocked that what they told me during my interviews with them kept me up all night. I realized how important it was what they were telling me, how important this survey was.

Being able to connect research findings with advocacy made it easier for workers to develop a greater stake in activism about the policy issues involved. Particularly for the surveyors, the research experience enhanced their policy literacy, allowing them to see how individual workers' private troubles reflected their profession's broader, structural vulnerabilities. After the research, most of the surveyors went on to play active leadership roles in the campaign— testifying with their stories at meetings with legislators or before relevant legislative committees, being present to speak at press conferences or other events, and recruiting and encouraging other workers to join the movement.

As for the respondents, after finishing the survey questions, the surveyors asked if they were interested in more information about becoming active in the campaign (such responses were recorded separately from the survey questionnaires). The survey provided an impetus for many workers to join the movement and later attend meetings and actions in support of the bill of rights. Almost every respondent gave contact information and expressed interest in further involvement. This was yet another way the survey became a tool in building the movement.

Survey Shows the Need to Protect Domestic Workers

The survey results showed a pattern of stressful work, unclear expectations, considerable wage theft, mistreatment by employers, gender discrimination, and exposures to toxic substances without protection or training, among other problems. Overall the findings pointed to several key problem areas:

Violations of employment laws governing most workers. The survey revealed a high level of wage theft related to poorly defined job duties and hours, chronic "job creep," and lack of written contracts. In fact, 59 percent of the respondents reported being confused about the scope of their job duties. When employers routinely added new requests to be done, leading to job creep, 66 percent of the workers noted they did not get paid for the extra hours expended on work as a result. Also contrary to standard workplace time rules for most workers, a slight majority of the worker respondents (53 percent) indicated they were not granted any break time at work, even to eat.

Insecure, poorly remunerated employment. Although most house cleaners are providers or coproviders for family dependents—true both in the United States and abroad—they are often discharged suddenly, without notice. It is not uncommon for them to be left without work for several weeks when families go on vacation without notifying them. Their income is not secure. Employers do not always recognize that these are real jobs for people through which they support themselves and others; 44 percent of the respondents said that what they earn does not give them enough money to meet basic expenses.

Poor workplace safety and health protections. House cleaners have a high level of exposure to toxic cleaning products in intense concentrations due to multiple uses each day, but they have little knowledge or practice regarding greener, healthier alternatives. Sixty percent reported that they seldom or never used personal protective equipment. Very few (14 percent) said they ever received professional training in safety or health or other matters related to their job duties.

Abusive, discriminatory treatment by employers. The responses revealed a modest level of unacceptable harassment, disrespectful treatment, and arbitrary and punitive employer decisions that affected job security. Workers reported being fired for being pregnant (12 percent) or asking for a raise or for needing to stay home with a sick child or parent. Many reported having their pay reduced if something was broken in the house. Eleven percent of the women said they had been verbally abused by an employer, and 10 percent were falsely accused of stealing something—items that frequently were later discovered simply misplaced by the employers' families.

Rallying the Public and Convincing Legislators

In addition to positive effects on leadership development and campaign engagement of the surveyors themselves, we used the survey findings in public advocacy for the bill. We released a report of our findings at a press conference at the University of Massachusetts in November 2013. It was widely covered by the mainstream and ethnic media. Boston's main daily, the *Boston Globe*, covered the release, as did several local ethnic media outlets. Interestingly, as was the case with the previous year's Domestic Worker Congress and the proposed bill of rights legislation, the release of findings received a great deal of attention from the Latin American media: television crews were present from the *O Globo* television network broadcast from Brazil, the Latin American Telesur network based in Venezuela, and Univision's popular network in Mexico and the United States. Our efforts garnered this Latin American attention because of the visibility and strength of the global domestic worker movement in Latin America (fourteen of the twenty-five nations endorsing Convention 189 are in Latin America) and because emigrants from the region living in diasporic communities in New England are leading the campaign here in the United States.

In November 2013, author Natalicia Tracy offered testimony before the legislature's Joint Labor and Workforce Development Committee. Her remarks in favor of the legislation were informed by our research results. She was joined on the panel by the president of the Massachusetts AFL-CIO statewide federation, the legislative director of health workers union SEIU 1199, and the president of the Boston NAACP chapter.

During the campaign to build support among legislators for the bill of rights, we and our coalition partners and allies made literally hundreds of additional visits to state house offices to speak with elected officials and their aides about why we needed the bill of rights. We also held dozens of what are called "in-district meetings," events in the community or at district offices throughout the state where we would invite legislators to meet, within their home districts, our allies from a range of faith, labor, legal, women's, and immigrant organizations supporting the bill of rights. In many of these meetings for educating legislators, we found it effective to use our survey findings documenting serious workplace abuse problems. This was particularly the case when skeptical legislators claimed there was no proof that worker abuse was so common in the state that it required going to all the trouble of moving a new bill at the state level. Some even made the argument that workers were already well protected under current laws. Another key senator in a leadership position even asserted to us, "I talked to my house cleaner and she does not want this bill!" Our survey findings allowed us to counter doubts about the need for the bill of rights.

Building Tools, Resources, and Supports for Domestic Workers

We also used the findings, especially on workplace safety and health dangers, to design a safety training course for domestic workers in collaboration with the New England Regional Occupation Health and Safety Administration (OSHA). We have subsequently offered the course to groups of workers in Massachusetts, Connecticut, and New Jersey. Among the topics covered are bed bugs, blood-borne viruses, safe body movement and ergonomics, toxic chemicals and green product replacements, and violence and discrimination at the workplace. The training also offers information on the provisions of the new bill of rights and locations where workers can find more help and information. We also have included the same information in audio recordings available on a new domestic worker hotline and in text files within a new telephone app designed for domestic workers to install on their mobile phones.

Reflecting on the Past and the Future

In October 2014, we published a broader analysis reporting our survey results but also situating our own current efforts into the long-forgotten history of domestic worker organizing and considering what we can learn from the Massachusetts experience that can be extended to organizing in other states. We released *Invisible No More: Domestic Workers Organizing in Massachusetts and Beyond* at a gathering of more than one hundred labor leaders and activists at a large labor policy breakfast sponsored by our university's Labor Resource Center and SEIU 1199 in Boston (Tracy, Sieber, and Moir 2014). This report has had wide distribution and has been presented at many conferences and meetings, particularly in New England, where it is also used as assigned reading in university courses in labor studies and sociology and at community-level trainings and workshops.

Of course, this particular story has a happy ending. The Domestic Worker Bill of Rights passed both houses of the Massachusetts legislature by wide bipartisan margins and was signed into law by then governor Deval Patrick on June 26, 2014. It remains the strongest bill of rights yet to pass in any state in the nation. In Massachusetts, it is virtually unheard of for such a significant labor bill to secure passage in a single legislative session as ours did. The BWC and other grassroots organizations representing workers got almost everything we initially asked for in terms of the bill's provisions. The bill attracted the support of wide segments of the public—labor, faith, legal, immigrant, women's, and university groups—who agreed this shameful labor law exclusion should finally be ended.

The bill guaranteed many new labor rights for Massachusetts domestic workers:

1 Earned sick time (unpaid but job protected)
2 Pay for all time worked
3 Days of rest/vacation, including five paid vacation days after one year of full-time work or one after three months
4 Food/lodging: costs must not be deducted from pay
5 Privacy: employers cannot enter workers' living space without their consent
6 Protection against trafficking
7 Right to a written employment contract if the domestic laborer works sixteen-plus hours weekly
8 Records/notice of rights: workers must receive notice of their workplace rights
9 Termination: a written explanation required if fired; prior notice required if let go without cause; special protections for live-ins who lose their homes when fired
10 Domestic workers brought under the protection of the Massachusetts Commission against Discrimination and thus can file discrimination and sexual harassment complaints for the first time ever

Worker-based participatory research was crucial, helping the campaign move beyond anecdotes, hearsay, and gossip about unfair and abusive working conditions and document hard facts about a state-wide sample of nearly two hundred workers. Because this was community-based research, we had a clear grassroots sense of the problem and what was needed to solve it and were following a pathway involving research and action already pioneered by domestic worker activists in New York and California.

Our study gained outside legitimacy not only from its professionalism but also from its sponsorship from a local university. While opposition certainly existed to honoring the dignity, equality, and rights of domestic workers under the new legislation, we never once encountered a single question from anyone about the validity of our research-generated account of problematic working conditions among the workers. The research made our claims about injustice and abuse credible to legislators, the media, allies, and the public. It is critical to recognize that the community participatory dimension of the research set the stage for the close integration among the diagnosis of our problem, information that validated our concerns and informed advocacy and messaging, and a responsive action plan to correct the problem. The feedback loop among planning, research, and action is especially dynamic and intense when these are all being carried out by the same set of activists.

Notes

1   Among the funders supporting our campaign were Boston Women's Fund, Herman & Frieda L. Miller Foundation, Hyams Foundation, Miller Innovation Fund, Anna B. Stearns Foundation, Berger Marks Foundation, Lenny Zakim Fund, Episcopal City Mission's Burgess Urban Fund, Universalist Unitarian Funding Program, Foley Hoag Foundation, Sociological Initiatives Foundation, and National Domestic Workers Alliance.
2   Founded at the first U.S. Social Forum held in Atlanta in 2007, the NDWA has rapidly grown. Its present sixty affiliate organizations are located in all regions of the country, with especially large concentrations in New York (fourteen), California (ten), Texas (eight), and Massachusetts (five). Affiliates are also working in Washington, Illinois, Hawaii, Oregon, Alabama, Georgia, New Mexico, Connecticut, Arizona, Colorado, Florida, Maryland, Minnesota, North Carolina, New Jersey, and Tennessee.
3   Since that time, as of 2018, another four U.S. states (Oregon, Illinois, Nevada, and Connecticut) have passed legislation to end domestic worker labor law exclusions.
4   In any case, the NDWA sampling was done on a national scale, and the sample of 120 Boston workers was small, stratified for ethnicity and job type (house cleaner, nanny, eldercare worker, etc.) and not geographically representative of the state. The data would not have been suitable for our purposes.

References

Domestic Workers United and Data Center. 2006. *Home Is Where the Work Is: Inside New York's Domestic Work Industry*. New York: Domestic Workers United and Data Center.
International Labor Organization (ILO). N.d. "Domestic Workers." http://www.ilo.org/global/topics/domestic-workers/lang--en/index.htm.
Mujeres Unidas y Activas, Day Labor Program, Women's Collective of La Raza, Centro Legal, and Data Center. 2007. *Behind Closed Doors: Working Conditions of California Household Workers*. Oakland, Calif.: Mujeres Unidas y Activas, Day Labor Program, Women's Collective of La Raza, Centro Legal, and Data Center.
National Domestic Workers Alliance and the University of Illinois at Chicago Data Center. 2012. *Home Economics: The Invisible and Unregulated World of Domestic Work*. Chicago: National Domestic Workers Alliance and the University of Illinois at Chicago Data Center.
Poo, Ai-jen. 2010. "Organizing with Love: Lessons from the New York Domestic Workers Bill of Rights Campaign." *Left Turn—Notes from the Global Intifada*, December 1, 2010. http://www.leftturn.org/Organizing-with-Love.
Siqueira, C. Eduardo, and Andrea Roche. 2013. "Occupational Health Profile of Brazilian Immigrant Housecleaners in Massachusetts." *New Solutions* 3 (3): 505–520.
Tracy, Natalicia, Tim Sieber, and Susan Moir. 2014. *Invisible No More: Domestic Workers Organizing in Massachusetts and Beyond*. Boston: University of Massachusetts at UMass Boston, Labor Studies Faculty Publication Series. https://scholarworks.umb.edu/laborstudies_faculty_pubs/1.

8

Power Sharing through Participatory Action Research with a Latino Forest Worker Community

•••••••••••••••••••••••

VICTORIA BRECKWICH VÁSQUEZ,
DIANE BUSH, AND CARL WILMSEN

Workers who plant trees, thin forests, and do all the other tasks required in forest restoration have very high rates of job-related injury, illness, and fatality, but they rarely receive safety training. They also typically endure wage theft and substandard working conditions. To improve safety and health on the job as well as working conditions overall for Spanish-speaking immigrant forest workers in southern Oregon, the Northwest Forest Worker Center (NFWC) collaborated with the Labor Occupational Health Program at the University of California, Berkeley, and the Pacific Northwest Agricultural Safety and Health Program at the University of Washington to initiate a community health worker (*promotora*) program through participatory action research (PAR). The research has built leadership in the community and informed NFWC's outreach and advocacy. Challenges to PAR included the social positionality and life circumstances of community members, the time needed for skill and confidence building among community members, and worker fears of retaliation for seeking improved working conditions.

Power Sharing and Participatory Action Research

Power sharing between professional researchers and community members lies at the core of participatory research. Collaborating as equal partners is essential to conduct research relevant to community issues and produce results that can benefit the community. This ideal is not easy to achieve. Differing motivations and objectives of researchers and community members collaborating on the research as well as their differing social positioning may lead to token participation, in which researchers include community members in the research process but retain major decision-making power for themselves (Cooke and Kothari 2001). Participation of community members in the research process does not in itself lead to their empowerment. Empowerment also requires developing relations of reciprocity and trust (Walters et al. 2009; Hankins and Ross 2008; Wilmsen 2008a).

In 2010 the Northwest Forest Worker Center (NFWC; then called the Alliance of Forest Workers and Harvesters); the Labor Occupational Health Program (LOHP) at the University of California, Berkeley; and the Pacific Northwest Agricultural Safety and Health (PNASH) Center at the University of Washington began collaborating on what would become a series of PAR projects with Latino forest workers in southern Oregon's Rogue Valley. The development of this partnership illustrates challenges to power sharing in university-community partnerships as well as the benefits for research, researchers, and community members.

Gathering the Stories of an Invisible Workforce

Most people who work in the woods are an "invisible workforce." In 1997, a group of forest workers and harvesters founded the Alliance of Forest Workers and Harvesters (presently known as the Northwest Forest Worker Center) to address issues of racial and economic injustice that directly affected them and the land. The NFWC focused on community organizing. As one of the thirteen Community-Based Forestry Demonstration Projects supported by the Ford Foundation from 1999 to 2005, NFWC assisted forest communities in northern California, Oregon, and Washington with community-based ecosystem restoration projects, trained workers in ecosystem restoration, engaged leaders of harvester communities in multiparty monitoring of nontimber forest products (NTFPs), and educated policy makers and the public about the realities of working conditions in the forest.

NFWC began outreach to Latino forest workers in the Medford, Oregon, area (the Rogue Valley) in 2004. Medford is a hub of the forestry services industry, with some forty firms located there that contract with federal, state, and private landowners all over the western United States. They thin trees to reduce wildfire risk, fight wildfires, and do all the other tasks necessary in tending America's forest lands. Workers employed by these firms are largely Spanish-speaking, immigrant men (Sarathy 2006). Most are probably undocumented (Sarathy 2012), although the numbers being hired in the Pacific Northwest on H-2B ("guest worker") visas have risen steadily over the past several years. The occupational segregation so common in U.S. industry (Mann 2007; Quesada, Hart, and Bourgois 2011; Marable 2015) figures prominently in forestry services, with Latino workers performing the more labor-intensive, dangerous work and white workers tending to do better-paying technical work (Moseley 2006). Funded participatory research by the Sociological Initiatives Foundation (SIF) in 2005 led to long-term relationships with forest workers in the local area, resulting in meetings with officials in the U.S. Forest Service and Department of Labor and presentations to members of Congress.

With a second grant from the SIF in 2010, NFWC interviewed twenty-seven more forest workers in southern Oregon and revealed a leading concern for occupational safety and health. To address this concern, NFWC collaborated with LOHP to initiate a *promotora* program. Promotora programs involve training members of local communities in the skills and knowledge they need to provide culturally appropriate health education and information to their peers. Promotoras, who are commonly called community health workers in English but are sometimes also called peer health educators, lay health advisors, and other similar titles, conduct formal training on priority health topics in their communities, assist community members with accessing the health care they need, and advocate for individual and community health needs. They are trusted members of their communities and thus have greater credibility and reach. Promotora programs have been used for health education in farmworker communities for more than thirty years. NFWC's promotora program is the only one we know of that focuses on forest workers. Its focus on occupational safety and health is also unusual because most promotora programs deal with obesity, diabetes, HIV-AIDS, women's health, prenatal care, and other such public health issues.

NFWC initially recruited three women who had been volunteering with the organization for many years to be promotoras. These women are married to forest workers, are native speakers of Spanish, and are respected leaders in the community. Subsequently, we recruited two more promotoras, Gladis García and Martha Valle, and they collaborated on the project we describe in this chapter.

With funding from the PNASH Center, the National Institute of Occupational Safety and Health (NIOSH), and the Occupational Safety and Health Administration (OSHA), and using the results of the SIF-funded study to inform the project, our first step was to conduct a survey of forest workers to identify priority issues and training needs. We convened a project advisory committee consisting of forest workers, the promotoras, and other project staff. Advisory committee members assisted with development of the questionnaire, analysis of the results, selection of training topics, and program evaluation. We trained the promotoras in interviewing techniques, and they interviewed 150 forest workers in the Rogue Valley about injuries sustained on the job and working conditions in general. We developed training materials based on the results of this survey. The promotoras played a crucial role in revising and testing drafts. We trained the promotoras in popular education and training techniques for adult learners. They then used the materials to train hundreds of workers (Bush et al. 2014).

The survey results suggested higher rates of injury among forest workers than official estimates and that a large proportion of the registered local forest labor contractors may not be in compliance with laws requiring rest breaks, potable water, protective equipment, and safety training. And consistent with the two previous SIF-supported studies, the workers interviewed reported high levels of fear of retaliation (Wilmsen, Bush, and Barton-Antonio 2015; Moseley 2006). These results raised questions that informed our fourth project, a partnership between NFWC, LOHP, and PNASH on a three-year NIOSH-funded PAR project and the one we describe and analyze in the remainder of this chapter.

Job-Related Injuries and Illnesses and Experiences Advocating for Better Working Conditions

Working together, the project planners—including academics, forest workers, promotoras, and other NFWC staff—developed the research questions for the new project. Although workers had said they were afraid of being fired or retaliated against if they reported injuries to their supervisors, 76 percent of those interviewed had indeed reported injuries. So under what circumstances do forest workers report their injuries to their supervisors? The high levels of fear of retaliation survey respondents reported led NFWC's promotoras and worker advisors to recommend finding and sharing examples of workers who were successful in attempting to improve working conditions and to understand the question "Under what circumstances will workers make such attempts?" Finally, we corroborated other studies that have found high rates of job-related injuries and illnesses among forest workers; the research partnership wondered, "What conditions contribute to the occurrence of injuries and illnesses?"

NFWC adopted participatory research as a regular part of its programming in support of its advocacy. This choice resulted from a need for accurate and reliable information that would withstand scrutiny and from interrelated desires to empower forest workers to advocate for themselves and establish democratic processes within the organization itself. NFWC's approach is rooted in the knowledge production, participation, and social change elements common to the many orientations and methodologies in participatory (Wilmsen 2008b) and action (Boog et al. 2008) research.

The academic partners shared a commitment to, and experience with, participatory research. LOHP had participated in several long-term formal community-based participatory research (CBPR) projects focused on workplace health and safety where workers played key roles in planning and conducting the research and became spokespeople in sharing the results (Chang, Minkler, et al. 2013; Chang, Salvatore, et al. 2013; Lee et al. 2008). PNASH also shared values inherent in community-based participatory research and has more than twenty years of experience working closely with rural Latino communities throughout the Pacific Northwest region to address disparities in worker health.

NFWC's approach acknowledges that workers have intricate, detailed knowledge of production processes and experience with the forces of oppression that affect their communities. Therefore, a collaboration between researchers and workers produces better accounts of the world (Haraway 1991), and collaboration in knowledge production builds the capacity of community members to take action to improve the well-being of their communities.

With these principles in mind, project partners addressed the questions raised by the previous research with a goal to incorporate actionable information in educational materials to train forest workers to prevent job-related injuries and illnesses and engage constructively with management to improve their working conditions. A further objective was to use the information to advocate for better worker protections and inform government policies and improve enforcement of existing labor laws. Project partners—workers and academics—were in agreement about these goals. Specifically, they sought to do the following:

- describe the kinds of injuries forest workers sustain and conditions that contribute to them
- investigate circumstances under which forest workers report their injuries to supervisors, their experiences getting medical treatment, and outcomes of that experience
- investigate circumstances under which forest workers try to help improve safety and health at work
- develop new training materials to help forest workers avoid the most common types of injuries as well as help them successfully improve safety and health at work
- train workers using these new training materials

Sharing Power, Negotiating Roles

Sharing power in this project occurred in three distinct but overlapping social settings: the relationships (1) among NFWC, LOHP, and PNASH; (2) among staff in NFWC itself; and (3) between NFWC and forest workers in the community at large. The mechanism for shared decision-making was consultation, interaction, and sharing tasks among members of four groups: the core research team, NFWC's staff, an expert working group (EWG) composed of forest workers, and a technical advisory group (TAG) composed of forestry and occupational safety and health professionals. Members of the core research team included faculty from the University of Washington Bothell and University of Washington PNASH Center, LOHP, and NFWC's program coordinator and executive director. NFWC and PNASH led the research phase of the project, and LOHP took the lead in developing the educational materials and training NFWC's promotoras in their use. In addition, faculty obtained institutional review board approval at their respective universities.

The core research team managed implementation of the project. The team held monthly conference calls in which we shared progress reports, discussed challenges, and planned our next steps. Engaging NFWC's promotoras and members of the EWG was crucial to developing solutions to problems and planning.

Power sharing within the NFWC was more complex due to the differing social positionalities of the staff. The promotoras are monolingual, Spanish-speaking immigrant women from the forest worker community. NFWC hired them because of their expert knowledge of the local forest worker community, their extensive social networks in the community, and their connections to forest work through their spouses. Traditionally promotoras are often volunteers (U.S. Department of Health and Human Services 2007), but NFWC sought and acquired funds to hire them as employees.

NFWC's other staff involved in the project are not from the local forest worker community but are bilingual, including the coordinator, who is Mexican American, born in Los Angeles, and the director, a third-generation German/Irish American, who has a PhD in geography.

NFWC was founded by forest workers and harvesters of nontimber forest products, and its board of directors remains largely composed of such workers and harvesters. Multiculturalism is a deeply held value of the organization's founders and is written into NFWC's articles of incorporation. In addition, democratic processes are woven into the everyday operations of the organization. Each employee has a say in setting priorities, identifying issues to work on, addressing challenges, and making needed adjustments in the work. The goal is to live by the collaborative principles in participatory research and popular education (Freire 1981), much as Magdalena Avila has described participatory research as being a way of life (Muhammad et al. 2015, 1052).

In addition to employing members of the forest worker community as staff, NFWC has a long-standing worker advisory committee composed of forest workers that contribute to leading the organization. Members of this worker advisory committee, which we originally assembled as the advisory committee for our earlier PAR projects, compose the EWG for the project analyzed in this chapter. The role of the EWG was to identify priority issues to cover in the interviews with workers, provide guidance in developing interview questions, assist with the analysis of the interview data as well as with the development of the educational materials, and provide direction to NFWC based on project results. We also held joint meetings of the EWG and TAG (at the beginning, midpoint, and end of the project). The TAG's role in the project was to provide technical advice in developing interview questions, data analysis, and educational materials development.

The focus of the project arose from combined interests of core research team members, the promotoras, and worker advisory committee members who were stimulated by results of the previous PR project. Core research team members designed the project in the process of writing the NIOSH grant proposal. The promotoras, the EWG, and the TAG all participated in development of the interview guides. The promotoras also assisted with the recruitment script and securing informed consent from interviewees.

We adopted a case study approach in the project, initially conducting preselection interviews with ninety-nine workers and selecting twenty-five of these interviewees with whom to conduct second, more in-depth case study interviews. To be included in the study, the worker had to be (1) currently employed as a forest worker, (2) eighteen years of age or older, and (3) injured on the job within the previous two years or involved in a proactive attempt to improve working conditions within the previous five years.

Recruitment involved nonrandom sampling, including chain-referral (snowball) and convenience sampling. First, promotoras and other project staff interviewed workers within their own social networks and solicited names of others who met the inclusion criteria. In addition, NFWC staff visited trailer parks, housing projects, and motels in Medford and surrounding communities where forest workers are known to live and knocked on doors. Workers received a small financial incentive for their participation.

All interviews were conducted in Spanish by teams of two, including NFWC and PNASH staff. Research staff trained the interviewers in protection of human subjects and qualitative interviewing techniques.

The preselection interview guide included many closed questions with prewritten responses that the note taker could check off. The twenty-five case study interviewees were selected based on whether their stories involved one of the priority hazards or organizational factors previously identified by the EWG and TAG (lack of training, inadequate personal protective equipment, bullying, pace of work, and employer response) and whether the interviewee had achieved success in an attempt to improve working conditions and was judged to be a good storyteller.

The questions were about the interviewee's experience in the forestry services industry, working conditions where he was currently employed, and demographics. Interviews also elicited details about the type of injury the worker had experienced, how the accident had occurred, and experience getting medical treatment for the injury. A similar set of questions was included to elicit details about any attempts the worker had made to improve working conditions.

Interviews were transcribed in Spanish and translated into English. Three members of the research team participated in coding the interview transcripts for the key themes and extracting quantitative data. Coders were bilingual; they referred back to the original Spanish versions as needed to assure that they were capturing the full meaning of the interviewee's words.

Threats to Health and Safety

The transcripts revealed the relationships of power through which forest workers in southern Oregon negotiate their workday lives. Workers described environments where production pressure and bullying are high and relations with direct supervisors are often antagonistic. Fears of retaliation for being injured on the job or speaking out about working conditions, including attempting to improve safety, were widespread and not unfounded. U.S. immigration law exacerbates those fears. By criminalizing undocumented immigrants and tying foreign temporary workers who are in the United States on H-2B visas to a single employer, the law creates vast power imbalances favoring employers (Griffith 2009). Undocumented workers fear deportation, workers on visas fear not being rehired the following season, and workers with legal permanent residency or citizenship may fear the deportation or denial of rehiring a loved one also working in the area. The leverage this gives employers over their employees is reinforced by threats and actual retaliation.

These power relationships had profound impacts on the interviewees' injuries, injury outcomes, and attempts to improve working conditions. Many workers we interviewed (29 percent) thought that production pressure or bullying contributed to their injuries. Two-thirds of the interviewees struggled with receiving medical care and workers' compensation benefits. These struggles included (1) not being taken to the hospital and having to seek alternative treatment or treat themselves with home remedies (35 percent); (2) not knowing that they had the right to choose an interpreter at the medical exam, which was associated with poorer injury outcomes (35 percent); (3) being fired for being injured on the job (30 percent); and (4) being told to lie at the hospital about their injuries being work related (13 percent). In contrast, about one-third reported that their employers provided safety training, inspected worksites for safety hazards, held safety meetings, and/or provided rest breaks. These workers were more likely to have better injury outcomes than the other case study interviewees (Wilmsen et al. in press).

Yet workers do exert some limited agency (Mitchell 2011). In our full sample of ninety-nine workers, seventy-nine had made proactive attempts to improve working conditions. Most of these involved requests for tools or safety equipment in good working order, but 25 percent were requests for more substantive changes such as rest breaks or being permitted to work at a slower pace. Workers were more likely to have a request granted if they acted collectively and were assertive. For example, one group of workers did not simply ask for a rest break after working seven hours without stopping. They insisted on resting, and there was nothing the foreman could do to stop them. Another group of workers decided among themselves to work at a safer distance from each other, and the foreman did not interfere with their action.

Creating Policies and Tools to Protect Workers

The NFWC strategy to empower workers to improve working conditions included training to prevent job-related injuries and illnesses and, when possible, to engage constructively with management to create a safer, nonabusive workplace. After deliberation with the EWG, the group decided to develop video stories from some case studies as core educational tools. We selected five that illustrated the types of accidents that occurred as well as issues with getting medical treatment. We invited these workers to a two-day workshop facilitated by the Story Center of Berkeley, California, in which they each created a three- to four-minute digital story, a video that describes and depicts the story of their injury and follows the seven-step process of digital storytelling (Lambert and Hessler 2018). NFWC's promotoras also created videos describing why they became promotoras. (Readers may view five of the videos at http://deohs.washington.edu/pnash/forestry-services-videos.)

We created training materials to accompany the digital stories and guidelines for leading a training session with these videos. They use a popular education approach (Freire 1981; Wallerstein and Weinger 1992) to engage workers in discussing how the workers' stories resonate with their own experience and to prompt discussion about how the injury depicted in the video could have been prevented—including what the employer should have done—and what workers can do themselves to work more safely. The promotoras were instrumental in designing the training guides, formulating discussion questions that would elicit responses from the workers based on their experiences, and formatting them for easiest use.

During the final year of the project, the promotoras used the videos to train 237 workers in exercising their rights to a safe workplace as well as preventing being struck by a falling object (the leading cause of injury in our study). Using an outreach model they developed on their own, the promotoras went to workers' homes, H-2B worker motels, laundromats, grocery stores, and other places forest workers gather and did impromptu field trainings. They showed the videos on android tablets and then used the training guides to engage the forest workers in discussions.

The second component of our strategy to address forest worker issues was to present the research results to policy makers and agency officials. NFWC had been participating in a partnership with the U.S. Department of Labor, the Forest Service, the Bureau of Land Management, Oregon OSHA, and the Oregon and Washington labor bureaus since 2009. NFWC's executive director presented the results to this group. In addition, we held a picnic in a park in Medford with the members of this group and invited forest workers as well. This was an opportunity for government officials and forest workers to meet and talk with each other directly. While this was a useful exchange in which government officials heard firsthand from participants about working conditions, no specific actions resulted from this meeting. Two forest workers traveled to Salem at the invitation of the Interim Committee on Workforce of the Oregon State Senate to testify before the committee and present recommendations for new legislation on safety training, retaliation, enforcement of labor laws, and improving worker safety. The workers' testimonies marked the first time that many committee members had heard about working conditions in the forestry services industry. While it did not result in any immediate policy changes, presenting the testimony was an important first step, and NFWC has stayed in contact with the committee chair discussing possible future policy development.

The Benefits and Challenges of Sharing Power

Forest workers face formidable barriers to overcoming their structural vulnerability (Quesada, Hart, and Bourgois 2011). Was our power sharing in this project effective in empowering forest workers to begin to overcome these barriers? The strength of a community-university partnership lies in all the partners pooling their respective skills and resources and working together to break down hierarchies and redistribute power.

Participation of the university partners in the project broadened the set of skills available to the community and project for engaging in research and popular education. The executive director of NFWC is a trained social scientist, but bringing in university partners expanded the skills, knowledge, and technical expertise available to the project. The university partners brought attentiveness to the PAR process as well as strategies for research and developing and deploying the educational materials. Their involvement imparted greater legitimacy to the work, both inside and outside the community. This was important because a worker advocacy organization may be dismissed as too partisan to produce trustworthy findings. NFWC's advocacy is enhanced because organization representatives can point to peer-reviewed research to support their claims. University partners also brought access to different sources of funding, which NFWC could not have obtained on its own.

The community members—the promotoras and the worker advisory committee members—brought intimate knowledge of the community, its language and culture, extensive community social networks, and experiential knowledge of forestry services work. Their contributions led to successful recruitment of workers for this and previous studies. Facing numerous challenges in reaching this hidden and fearful population, the promotoras innovated and developed the convenience sampling method described earlier. Knowledge of the community and Spanish language that promotoras and worker advisors brought to the study also led to additional insights into the analysis of the interviews and to culturally and linguistically relevant interview guides and training materials. The EWG contributed insights on how pressure to work faster contributes to injuries, incentives foremen have for pressuring workers, and specific hazards workers commonly face.

NFWC served as a bridge between the community and academia, with a staff that includes community insiders as well as outsiders. The different social positioning of its staff better enables it to connect with community members and academics.

Participating in this research project also has helped build the capacity of the community to engage in advocacy and mutual support. The community members who were directly involved in the research gained confidence in their role as resources for the community. Through interviewing ninety-nine workers, promotoras enhanced their outreach skills and gained clarity about the systemic roots of the issues workers faced. Members of the EWG also gained insights into the power relations that shape working conditions and became more invested in NFWC's advocacy work. In fact, participating in interviews motivated three forest workers to join the EWG.

The promotora-led outreach and training had a positive effect on workers. Evaluation of the training sessions revealed that the vast majority of workers (82 percent) found the information useful, especially the information about their rights. Most workers (78 percent) contacted three to six months after participating in a training said that they then worked more safely and felt more confident knowing their rights. One worker said that since the training, he has become a foreman, and he now knows how to treat his workers well. Eighty-nine percent of the workers said that they shared the information they learned in the training (about their rights, how to work safely, and the employer's responsibility to provide a safe workplace) with family, friends, and coworkers.

Although it is hard to measure broader community impacts, the promotoras offer anecdotal reports that working conditions are improving, albeit slowly—less bullying in some crews and some foremen more often providing rest breaks and access to clean drinking water (as opposed to requiring workers to drink untreated water from mountain streams). In addition, more workers now contact NFWC seeking assistance with workplace issues.

It is important to note that these changes in the community are not just the result of the latest three-year project. Rather, individuals and the whole community have been working on this issue for years and have developed increased confidence, new understandings, and shifts in consciousness as a result. The longevity of the program and engagement in multiple PAR projects have been key. In addition, the educational materials developed in the many projects are public resources and have changed, and will likely continue to change, community dialogue about forest worker health and safety.

Participatory action research is invaluable in redistributing power to oppressed peoples, even if progress is slow. The positionality of varied partners in a PAR project brings benefits and opens opportunities but also creates challenges. Overcoming these challenges is part of the learning process, and the partners in the project gain new knowledge and skills as they engage in these types of partnerships. Community capacity building advances with each project, leading in small steps to workers' empowerment to protect themselves from injury and mistreatment and to advocate for better workplace conditions. More actionable information is needed, and more action must be taken. Participatory action research is thus a way of life.

Meaningful participation in research can strengthen research evidence and build community capacity. However, we encountered significant challenges arising from the very social structures we were trying to change—namely, challenges in sharing power. The positionality and life circumstances of the workers and promotoras inhibit, but do not prevent, power sharing.

Forest workers must support their families, and economic stress is understandably their top priority. While many of the workers on the EWG have been committed members for many years, and the workers who were newly recruited to the committee during this project are equally committed, their participation was hampered by work schedules and familial responsibilities. Although we held meetings on weekends and in the evenings to accommodate their schedules, they were not always able to attend. Moreover, while they contributed valuable ideas, insights, and questions during many phases of the project, it was unrealistic to expect them to commit time beyond meeting attendance. For example, when we took two workers to testify before the Oregon State Senate, they had to take the day off from work. This meant losing wages. NFWC reimbursed them for the lost wages, but it is challenging for NFWC to raise funds for this purpose. The workers are also limited in the amount of time they can take off without arousing the displeasure of their employers.

There were also educational challenges in working with the promotoras. Their limited formal education impeded their participation in parts of the project that involved writing. The working poor in Mexico and other Latin American countries face barriers to formal education of class, race, gender, family income, and geographic isolation. In our previous research, for example, we found that the average level of education attained by the workers we interviewed was the sixth grade (Alliance of Forest Workers and Harvesters and Labor Occupational Health Program 2012). One of NFWC's promotoras explained her education as follows: "It was a two-hour walk to school, and in Mexico, education is seen as something for boys. So after the sixth grade, I just stopped going." The other promotora completed high school in Mexico. Both promotoras were not comfortable engaging in specific project tasks such as grant writing (in which the details of project design were hashed out) and writing up results. To engage them in developing other written materials, we had initial conversations about content and design and asked them to review drafts of interview guides, recruitment materials, and training materials and provide feedback on their content and appropriateness of language and culture. They sometimes provided written comments. At other times, they shared their comments in conversation. For this chapter, the promotoras wrote out their thoughts and ideas as if they were writing a letter to a friend. They wrote about how the power imbalance between workers and their employers works to the advantage of the latter. For example, "Interviewing all these workers was one way we managed to learn several reasons why workers allow themselves to be mistreated and humiliated. We know workers come to this country out of necessity. And that is why they allow themselves to be humiliated: they know that if they defend themselves, the employers will not bring them back."

They also pointed out the positive impact of participatory research: "Since the interviews began, there has been a change in the workers—a little more security, a little more confidence, and they are a little more open to us. We have even had a positive impact on the supervisors. We have had calls from supervisors and they have told us, 'There are some workers in this hotel, go give them the talks.' It is huge, because the supervisors are the main challenge, our main obstacle. That we are gaining ground with the supervisors is pretty good."

Another observed that "the research has had a positive impact in the community as well, not only the people who work in this [forestry services] industry, all the people feel benefited. Other people come to us from agriculture, from hotels, from restaurants and ask us for help. And people are talking about everything related to the supervisors—accidents, how and why they happen."

Language was a barrier too, as all but two of the workers on the advisory committee as well as the promotoras were monolingual in Spanish. The other project partners varied in their command of Spanish from very little to bilingual. This prevented direct involvement of the promotoras and workers in writing the research proposal, writing up research results, and developing educational materials, because most of the writing was done in English (although later translated into Spanish). The promotoras did play an important role, however, in assuring that Spanish translations used the vocabulary and phraseology of the Spanish dialect spoken by forest workers.

By far the biggest challenge NFWC faces is workers' fear of retaliation, which directly affected the research and action phases of this project and the organization's long-term empowerment goals. Fear of retaliation affected worker participation in the promotoras' training sessions. Most workers were open to participation in training sessions, but promotoras encountered some who were clearly uncomfortable participating. This most often occurred when a job foreman was present and workers did not want to risk displeasing their supervisor. One supervisor was openly hostile to the promotoras, shouting insults at them and saying that the information they wanted to give the workers was incorrect. He did this in the presence of the crew that the promotoras had approached about participating in a training session. The promotoras had been trained in precautions against threats and followed these guidelines to protect themselves.

Fear of retaliation affects the long-term empowerment of workers beyond the duration of this project. The intent of training workers with the materials developed in this and other projects is to empower them to advocate for themselves in improving working conditions. Our evaluation of the trainings confirmed their effectiveness in helping individual workers prevent job-related injuries and illnesses. Workers quietly change their behavior to work more safely and share safety information with their coworkers. However, fear of retaliation limits group-based actions that challenge social structures and institutions that maintain workers' vulnerability to structural violence. Overcoming this structural violence will not be accomplished overnight, and empowering workers through informing them about their rights is crucial but not sufficient. Organizing to increase the collective bargaining strength of workers is also necessary.

References

Alliance of Forest Workers and Harvesters and UC Berkeley Labor Occupational Health Program. 2012. "Healthy Forests, Abused Workers: Safety, Health and Working Conditions among Forest Ecosystem Restoration Workers in Southern Oregon." Berkeley, Calif. https://www.coursehero.com/file/10694582/HealthyForestsAbusedWorkers/.

Boog, Ben, Julia Preece, Meindert Slagter, and Jacques Zeelen. 2008. *Towards Quality Improvement of Action Research: Developing Ethics and Standards*. Rotterdam, Netherlands: Sense Publishers.

Bracho, America, Ginger Lee, Gloria P. Giraldo, and Rosa Maria De Prado. 2016. *Recruiting the Heart, Training the Brain: The Work of Latino Health Access*. Berkeley, Calif.: Hesperian.

Bush, Diane, Carl Wilmsen, Tim Sasaki, Dinorah Barton, and Andrea Steege. 2014. "Program Evaluation of a Pilot Community-Based Promotora Program for Latino Forest Workers in Southern Oregon." *American Journal of Industrial Medicine* 57:788–799.

Chang, Charlotte, Meredith Minkler, Alicia L. Salvatore, Pamela Tau Lee, Megan Gaydos, and Shaw San Liu. 2013. "Studying and Addressing Urban Immigrant Restaurant Worker Health and Safety in San Francisco's Chinatown District: A CBPR Case Study." *Journal of Urban Health* 90 (6): 1026–1040. https://doi.org/10.1007/s11524-013-9804-0.

Chang, Charlotte, Alicia L. Salvatore, Pam Tau Lee, Shaw San Liu, Alex T. Tom, Alvaro Morales, Robin Baker, and Meredith Minkler. 2013. "Adapting to Context in Community-Based Participatory Research: 'Participatory Starting Points' in a Chinese Immigrant Worker Community." *American Journal of Community Psychology* 51 (3–4): 480–491. https://doi.org/10.1007/s10464-012-9565-z.

Cooke, Bill, and Uma Kothari, eds. 2001. *Participation: The New Tyranny?* London: Zed Books.

Freire, Paulo. 1981. *Pedagogy of the Oppressed*. Translated by Myra Bergman Ramos. New York: Continuum. First published 1970.

Galvin, Kit, Jen Krenz, Marcy Harrington, Pablo Palmández, and Richard A. Fenske. 2016. "Practical Solutions for Pesticide Safety: A Farm and Research Team Participatory Model." *Journal of Agromedicine* 21 (1): 113–122.

Griffith, Kati L. 2009. "U.S. Migrant Worker Law: The Interstices of Immigration Law and Labor and Employment Law." *Comparative Labor Law and Policy Journal* 31:125–162.

Hankins, Don L., and Jacquelyn Ross. 2008. "Research on Native Terms: Navigation and Participation Issues for Native Scholars in Community Research." In *Partnerships for Empowerment: Participatory Research for Community-Based Natural Resource Management*, edited by Carl Wilmsen, William Elmendorf, Larry Fisher, Jacquelyn Ross, Brinda Sarathy, and Gail Wells, 239–257. London: Earthscan.

Haraway, Donna. 1991. "Situated Knowledges: The Science Question in Feminism and the Privilege of Partial Perspective." In *Simians, Cyborgs, and Women: The Reinvention of Nature*, edited by Donna Haraway, 183–201. New York: Routledge.

Heckathorn, Douglas D. 2002. "Respondent-Driven Sampling II: Deriving Valid Population Estimates from Chain-Referral Samples of Hidden Populations." *Social Problems* 49:11–34.

Kim, Nicole Jung-Eun, Victoria Breckwich Vásquez, Elizabeth Torres, R. M. Bud Nicola, and Catherine Karr. 2016. "Breaking the Silence: Sexual Harassment of Mexican Women Farmworkers." *Journal of Agromedicine* 21 (2): 154–162.

Lambert, Joe, and Brooke Hessler. 2018. *Digital Storytelling: Capturing Lives, Creating Community*. 5th ed. New York: Routledge.

Lee, Pam Tau, Niklas Krause, Charles Goetchius, Jo Marie Agresti, and Robin Baker. 2008. "Participatory Action Research with Hotel Room Cleaners in San Francisco and Las Vegas: From Collaborative Study to the Bargaining Table." In *Community-Based Participatory Research for Health: From Process to Outcomes*, edited by Meredith Minkler and Nina Wallerstein, 544. San Francisco: Jossey-Bass.

Mann, Geoff. 2007. *Our Daily Bread: Wages, Workers, and the Political Economy of the American West*. Chapel Hill: University of North Carolina Press.

Marable, Manning. 2015. *How Capitalism Underdeveloped Black America: Problems in Race, Political Economy, and Society*. Chicago: Haymarket Books.

Minkler, Meredith, and Nina Wallerstein. 2005. "Improving Health through Community Organization and Community Building: A Health Education Perspective." In *Community Organizing and Community Building for Health*, edited by Meredith Minkler, 37–58. New Brunswick, N.J.: Rutgers University Press.

Mitchell, Don. 2011. "Labor's Geography: Capital, Violence, Guest Workers and the Post–World War II Landscape." *Antipode* 43 (2): 563–595. https://doi.org/10.1111/j.1467 -8330.2010.00855.x.

Moseley, Cassandra. 2006. "Ethnic Differences in Job Quality among Contract Forest Workers on Six National Forests." *Policy Sciences* 39:113–133.

Muhammad, Michael, Nina Wallerstein, Andrew L. Sussman, Magdalena Avila, Lorenda Belone, and Bonnie Duran. 2015. "Reflections on Researcher Identity and Power: The Impact of Positionality on Community Based Participatory Research (CBPR) Processes and Outcomes." *Critical Sociology* 41 (7–8): 1045–1063.

Quesada, James, Laurie K. Hart, and Phillippe Bourgois. 2011. "Structural Vulnerability and Health: Latino Migrant Laborers in the United States." *Medical Anthropology* 30 (4): 339–362.

Sarathy, Brinda. 2006. "The Latinization of Forest Management Work in Southern Oregon: A Case from the Rogue Valley." *Journal of Forestry* 104 (7): 359–365.

———. 2012. *Pineros: Latino Labour and the Changing Face of Forestry in the Pacific Northwest*. Vancouver: University of British Columbia Press.

U.S. Department of Health and Human Services. 2007. *Community Health Worker National Workforce Study*. Rockville, Md.: Health Resources and Services Administration, Bureau of Health Professions.

Vawter, Ed. 2017. "Oregon Forest Industry: A Comparison of Occupational Safety and Health Measures, 2016." In *Statistical Reports*, 1–3. Salem, Ore.: DCBS. https://www .oregon.gov/dcbs/reports/Documents/osha-activities/safety-health/16-4840.pdf.

Wallerstein, Nina, and Merri Weinger. 1992. "Introduction: Health and Safety Education for Worker Empowerment." *American Journal of Industrial Medicine* 22 (5): 619–635. https://doi.org/10.10002/ajim.47002205.

Walters, Karina L., Antony Stately, Teresa Evans-Campbell, Jane M. Simoni, Bonnie Duran, Katie Schultz, and Deborah Guerrero. 2009. "'Indigenist' Collaborative Research Efforts in Native American Communities." In *The Field Research Survival Guide*, edited by Arlene Rubin Stiffman, 146–173. New York: Oxford University Press.

Wilmsen, Carl. 2008a. "Extraction, Empowerment and Relationships in the Practice of Participatory Research." In *Towards Quality Improvement in Action Research: Developing Ethics and Standards*, edited by Ben Boog, Julia Preece, Meindert Slagter, and Jacques Zeelen, 135–146. Rotterdam, Netherlands: Sense Publishers.

———. 2008b. "Negotiating Community, Participation, Knowledge and Power in Participatory Research." In *Partnerships for Empowerment: Participatory Research for*

Community-Based Natural Resource Management, edited by Carl Wilmsen, William Elmendorf, Larry Fisher, Jacquelyn Ross, Brinda Sarathy, and Gail Wells, 1–22. London: Earthscan.

Wilmsen, Carl, Diane Bush, and Dinorah Barton-Antonio. 2015. "Working in the Shadows: Safety and Health in Forestry Services in Southern Oregon." *Journal of Forestry* 113 (3): 315–324.

Wilmsen, Carl, A. Butch De Castro, Diane Bush, and Marcy Harrington. 2019. "System Failure: Work Organization and Injury Outcomes among Latino Forest Workers." *Journal of Agromedicine* 24 (2): 186–196.

9

Making Injustice Visible

• •

National Day Laborer
Organizing Network's
Research and Action

PABLO ALVARADO, CHRIS NEWMAN,

BLISS REQUA-TRAUTZ, AND

NIK THEODORE

The National Day Laborer Organizing Network (NDLON) was founded in 2001 as an alliance of twelve community-based organizations and worker centers dedicated to improving the lives of day laborers in the United States. Over the years, NLDON has grown into a nationwide organization, with more than fifty member organizations. It engages in community organizing, strategic litigation, media communications, arts and cultural expression, and other activities to defend the rights of day laborers. Through its mission and activities, NDLON remains committed to authentic, grassroots support of its base of member organizations and the wider day laborer community.

From the beginning, NDLON has used social science research to advance its program of leadership development, worker organizing, and policy reform. With roots in popular education praxis, NDLON's research has sought to help day laborers and their organizations protect and expand the civil, labor, and human rights of workers by identifying problems in low-wage labor markets, including failures of labor standards enforcement and unjust immigration policies. This chapter begins by briefly describing the evolution of NDLON's approach to action-oriented research, which dates to the early days of day laborer organizing in the 1990s. We then present the findings of a survey of 188 day laborers seeking work at informal hiring sites located in store parking lots, major intersections, and other public spaces in Las Vegas. Survey questions were designed to document widespread wage theft and health and safety problems on the job. The survey was complemented by a series of in-depth interviews with day laborers that elaborate the key findings. The chapter concludes by reflecting on the role of research in community building and social change.

Research for Popular Education

The origins of NDLON's research program date back to the early 1990s and the beginnings of immigrant day laborer organizing in the United States. In 1992, a group of activists and low-wage workers in the Los Angeles area began the process of founding the Institute of Popular Education of Southern California (IDEPSCA), a social change organization that was an early proponent of day laborer organizing. Grounded in popular education praxis, IDEPSCA began with efforts to systematically understand the conditions facing day laborers and their families so that day laborers could analyze the sociopolitical and economic conditions that give rise to their marginalization as immigrants and as contingent workers in the United States.

The first study was undertaken by organizers who surveyed community members to identify issues that resonated most deeply, an approach with direct links to rebel social activism during the Salvadoran civil war (see Theodore 2015). Several day laborer organizers had been popular educators in El Salvador during the protracted conflict, and after migrating to Los Angeles, they incorporated community research into worker organizing. In conducting this open-ended, inductive investigation, organizers had respondents articulate their key concerns to identify the issues to be addressed by the organization. Several years later, in 1996, organizers from IDEPSCA, the Coalition for Humane Immigrant Rights of Los Angeles (CHIRLA), and approximately thirty day laborers who were participating in a leadership development school initiated a second, more systematic research process. This too was directed by popular educators/organizers. During the leadership school, the question was posed, "Who *is* the day laborer? Who are we?" Day laborers took turns describing their individual identities and characteristics. This provided an intimate, inward look at the lives of day laborers that immediately led to the question "Who are we *collectively*?" In the subsequent sessions, each worker developed a profile that delved deeper, posing questions about housing and homelessness; occupational skills; demographics; and civic engagement.

When the opportunity arose to collaborate with the University of California, Los Angeles (UCLA) Center for the Study of Urban Poverty for the first formal survey of day laborers at informal hiring sites in Los Angeles (Valenzuela 1999), the key research questions had already been identified because workers had developed them in their profiles. Once day laborers were able to say, "This is who we are," the next question became "Who do we want to be?" So day laborers used the survey research to collectively assess what it would take to change their circumstances. Within a popular education framework, the survey helped day laborers develop their abilities to conduct critical analysis, understand power relations, and undertake campaigns to defend workers' rights.

In 2004, NDLON initiated a partnership with researchers from UCLA, the University of Illinois at Chicago, and the New School in New York City to jointly design and implement the National Day Laborer Survey (NDLS). University-based researchers were tasked with refining the survey instrument, developing a survey methodology, monitoring the fielding of the survey, and inputting data. Eight teams, composed of roughly equal numbers of organizers and college students, traveled to preselected cities to administer the surveys at informal hiring sites and worker centers. The results were analyzed by the university-based researchers in consultation with an advisory committee composed of worker center representatives. In total, a random sample of 2,660 day laborers was surveyed in twenty states and the District of Columbia (Valenzuela et al. 2006). The NDLS built on the earlier research projects and offered an unprecedented look at the day laborer workforce, including its demographics; labor market experiences; interactions with residents, police, and merchants; and health and safety on the job. This information was used to educate worker leaders, policy makers, the media, and the general public about labor-standards violations and other abuses in day labor markets. It also helped catalyze an upsurge in day laborer organizing in many parts of the country. Through a worker-initiated inquiry and with guidance and access provided by organizers, systematic information was collected and made widely available about a previously hard-to-reach population.

The NDLS marked a rigorous methodological advance in surveying day laborers. Randomization was employed at all stages of sampling, including selecting a random sample of metropolitan areas for the survey, identifying a random sample of informal hiring sites within each metropolitan area, and surveying a random sample of workers present at hiring sites (see Valenzuela et al. 2006). Subsequent day laborer surveys have sought to solve the problem of small sample sizes in single-city surveys through the implementation of census-style, time-location surveys in which all workers present at a hiring site at the time of survey implementation are surveyed (Theodore 2016, 2017). The use of social-scientific techniques in the service of NDLON's applied and activist-oriented research goals resulted in robust and reliable data. This rigor insulated the research process from potential accusations of bias and demonstrated that scholar-activist research can implement the methodological and analytical standards of professional social-scientific research. In late 2017, in collaboration with day laborers in Las Vegas, Nevada, NDLON initiated a survey of day laborers as a prelude to opening the first worker center in the city. The aims of the survey were to contribute to the development of worker leaders who would shape the design and objectives of the center and to elevate the issue of wage theft. We now turn to the findings of this survey—an example of NDLON's action research.

Day Labor in Sin City

Las Vegas was the epicenter of the 2007–2009 Great Recession; its housing market had collapsed, it led the nation with nearly one in ten homes in foreclosure, many major construction projects were scuttled, and the effects of plummeting consumer spending rippled through every sector of the local economy. According to the state's Department of Employment, Training and Rehabilitation, Nevada was "the hardest-hit state during the Great Recession, with employment impacts arriving later and lingering longer than in the U.S. as a whole" (Sun Staff 2017). Even after the recession had officially ended, the Las Vegas-Paradise metropolitan area continued to shed jobs, with the unemployment rate climbing to 14.1 percent in September 2010.

By mid-2017, eight years after the end of the Great Recession, the Las Vegas economy had finally recovered. The unemployment rate had fallen to 4.8 percent, housing markets had stabilized, and several major construction projects were under way. There was even talk of labor shortages in the construction sector, with government officials estimating a shortage of ten thousand construction workers in southern Nevada alone (Millward et al. 2017).

Informal hiring sites are a key source of temporary workers who are employed on a just-in-time basis for construction, landscaping, and moving jobs. Day laborers are hired by construction contractors, private households, landscaping companies, and other businesses to perform a range of short-term, manual-labor jobs. These jobs may last a few hours or a few days, though some projects can span several weeks or longer. The conditions of work also vary, with some day laborers earning decent wages for physically demanding work. Too often, however, workers' rights are violated, wages are not paid, and day laborers are unduly exposed to worksite hazards.

To document the employment conditions of day laborers in Las Vegas, NDLON implemented an in-person survey using a written survey questionnaire and conducted in-depth interviews with two dozen workers. The survey team, which was composed of day laborer organizers, used a time-location methodology and attempted to survey each day laborer who was looking for work at a hiring site on the day the survey was administered. In total, 188 surveys were collected. Surveys were conducted in English and Spanish during the early morning hours at informal hiring sites. Each survey took approximately fifteen minutes to complete. Respondents received a $10 incentive. For the in-depth interviews, day laborers, including several worker leaders of Arriba Las Vegas Worker Center, were asked whether they would be willing to share some of their experiences working in Las Vegas.

The survey focused on day laborers' employment, wages, and on-the-job injuries. To determine employment rates and hourly wages by occupation, respondents were recruited by organizers and asked a series of questions for each day in the previous workweek: (1) Did the worker look for employment at the hiring site? (2) Was a job secured? (3) If a job was secured, what was the occupation, total pay, and total hours worked? This information was used to compute hourly wage and unemployment rates. This generated a data set of 870 workdays that was used to analyze hourly wage rates and other aspects of employment. Data analysis was conducted at the University of Illinois at Chicago and reviewed by worker leaders from the Arriba Las Vegas Worker Center and organizers from NDLON. This analysis and review yielded a set of topline findings. We now turn to a presentation of those findings.

A System That Fails to Protect Workers Employment and Wages

Day laborers in Las Vegas are employed on an as-needed basis by construction contractors, landscaping companies, and other businesses, as well as by private households, for a range of manual-labor jobs, primarily those related to construction, landscaping, and moving. They are paid in cash, and in most instances, terms of employment are hastily arranged at one of the eighteen informal hiring sites in the city. About half (49 percent) of day laborers seeking employment on a given day found work. Moving (37 percent) and landscaping (31 percent) jobs were most common, followed by construction (11 percent) and cleanup (8 percent) jobs. Moving jobs are likely overrepresented, while construction jobs and other occupations are underrepresented, because the survey was conducted at the end of the month when the number of moving jobs increases substantially.

Average hourly wages for most day laborer jobs in Las Vegas appear to be adequate. The average hourly wage across all jobs worked in the week prior to the survey was $20.33. Moving jobs had the highest average hourly wages ($24.72), followed by construction ($23.81), painting ($19.82), and landscaping

($18.83) jobs. Cleanup and excavation jobs paid the lowest, with average hourly wages of $14.73 and $13.62, respectively. However, many workers are employed for less than a full day, resulting in poverty-level earnings. The median hours worked on moving jobs is just three, while on landscaping jobs, it is five, and on cleaning and painting jobs, it is six. Only construction and excavation jobs provide median hours of eight. Furthermore, the impact of low and variable hours on workers' earnings is exacerbated by the widespread problem of wage theft, an issue to which we now turn.

Wage Theft

Wage theft—the nonpayment of wages for work completed—is a common problem in day-labor markets (Theodore et al. 2008; Meléndez, Theodore, and Valenzuela 2010; Fussell 2011), and day laborers in Las Vegas report that it is frequent and widespread. One-third (33 percent) of respondents experienced at least one instance of wage theft in the two months prior to the survey. The average amount of the most recent instance of nonpayment was $224 (the median amount was $160; the maximum was $2,000).

Employers use various tactics to withhold wages: (1) refusing outright to pay wages; (2) evading responsibility for wage payments—for example, by casting doubt about the person responsible for making the wage payment; (3) making false promises to pay workers at a later date; and (4) requiring workers to perform additional, unpaid tasks in order to receive their pay. Often an unscrupulous employer will engage in several of these tactics to extract additional unpaid labor or avoid payment as agreed, and these violations of employment laws may be accompanied by threats of immigration-based retaliation.

Outright Refusal to Pay Wages

The most blatant form of wage theft occurs when employers refuse to pay workers any wages for work completed. Amounts may vary, ranging from a day's pay (approximately $100) to wages for several days or more. In other cases, employers flatly refuse to pay workers the agreed-upon rate, instead offering a lower amount. Workers may reluctantly accept the lower wage because they fear that if they protest too vociferously, they will be paid nothing at all. This usually results in wage theft amounts of $80 or less. Omar, who has more than ten years working as a day laborer, explained, "You make an agreement with someone looking to hire you. For example, you agree on $20 per hour, but they end up paying you $10 per hour. And they tell you it's because they know you don't have papers to work."

Miguel explained how a work crew he was on was forced to leave a job site without pay:

On that day, four of us were working together to move a four-bedroom house, including a full garage. We had an agreement with the owner for each of us to be paid $150. We had been working more than three hours when one of the workers dropped a box and broke something. It was an accident. Of course, no one wants to break something during a job. But the homeowner got upset and told us all to leave. Even though we had already done half the work, he refused to pay us anything. We didn't have a written contract. What could we do?

Juan, who has been working in Las Vegas for more than twenty-three years, shared a recent case of wage theft: "The agreement we made with the employer was $120 each for a moving job, and that included the use of my truck. When it came time to settle up, he only gave us $50 each. This employer spoke Spanish. When I complained about the lack of payment, he told me 'You're on the corner to work, not to make faces at someone more educated than you.'" The employer then threatened to call a friend who is a police officer, and so the two workers left. They each were still owed an additional $70 based on the initial agreement.

Employers may also abandon day laborers at worksites, tell workers they can only pay with a personal check (which turns out to be bogus), claim that clients have not paid for the work completed, or falsely tell workers they will employ them the next day, at which time wages will be paid in full. In September 2016, Armando experienced his first case of wage theft. He and another day laborer accepted a job with a homeowner who had rented a U-Haul truck for a move. They agreed on $120 each for the job and, at the request of the employer, climbed into the truck, leaving their own vehicles in the parking lot. They spent the morning fully loading the twenty-seven-foot truck with beds, sofas, and boxes. On the way to the second location, the homeowner stopped at a gas station, and while he pumped gas, he told the workers to run in and get some lunch. They went into McDonald's for takeout. When they returned, the U-Haul and driver were gone. "At first, we waited, in case he was coming back. After a while, it was clear that he had left us there on purpose. I lost the whole day. I wasn't paid, I had to pay for bus fare, and it took hours to get back to my car. I bet he went to another corner [informal hiring site] and did it all over again with other workers." The practices of repeat offenders who avoid payment are well known among workers, and it is not uncommon for workers to report that an employer who stole their wages also owed payment to other day laborers at the same hiring site.

Evading Responsibility for Wage Payments

A second tactic to avoid paying workers is to cast doubt about who is responsible for making the payment. Although by law the employer is the person who hired the worker, contractors frequently tell workers that they themselves were not paid for the work. Rodolfo explains how he was denied his wages for several days of work. "The last time I didn't get paid, I felt like a ball the homeowner and contractor kicked back and forth." In July 2017, he was recruited from an informal hiring site in front of a Home Depot to remove and replace floor tiling. After assessing the scope of the job, the contractor agreed to pay Rodolfo $1,500 plus expenses for equipment and materials. Rodolfo rented a jackhammer from Home Depot and started the project. After removing the tile, a full two days of work, the relationship between the contractor and the homeowner soured. The contractor left the job site, telling Rodolfo to "figure it out with the homeowner." The contractor told Rodolfo that he had not been paid for the job, and when Rodolfo approached the homeowner for his wages, she told him the contractor had already been paid for the work. "She offered me $100 to leave, but I was owed $120 for the jackhammer rental alone. The value of the work I completed was at least $500. When I pressed, asking to be paid for my work, she threatened to call the police. I was furious that day, but I didn't react. I didn't want any problems, so I decided it would be better to lose my time and money rather than end up in some kind of trouble."

False Promises to Pay Workers Later

In cases where wage theft occurs over several workdays or longer and unpaid wages rise to hundreds or even thousands of dollars, employers may begin by paying workers a partial amount. Day laborers return to work the following morning with the expectation that the previous day's wages will be paid in full along with wages for the current day's work. The longer this continues, the greater the amount of cumulative unpaid wages and the costlier it becomes for the day laborer to walk away without being paid for work completed. Under this scenario, the day laborer is in a bind: either risk the further accumulation of unpaid wages by continuing to work for an employer or count whatever wages remain unpaid as a loss and seek alternative employment. Because of the economic insecurity that accompanies day labor employment as well as the illegality of wage theft practices, workers are loath to refuse continued employment with a business that owes them money, even though this may mean that wage theft amounts may increase substantially.

Francisco was employed by a construction contractor offering steady work. At first, he was paid daily and everything seemed fine. The contractor then stopped making daily payments and switched to monthly payments. This continued until the final month of work, when the contractor failed to make an agreed-upon payment of $4,000. Francisco recounted, "I went to the Labor Commission, and they told me . . . that they couldn't help. So I took him to small claims court. But he hired an attorney, and I didn't. In the end, he offered me just $800 of the $4,000 he owed me."

Requiring Workers to Perform Additional Tasks

In addition to the outright nonpayment and underpayment of wages by employers, day laborers often are required to undertake tasks for which they are not paid. While the survey did not quantify these amounts, the practice of assigning workers additional duties is widespread. Sixty percent of day laborers reported that while working in Las Vegas, they were required to complete tasks beyond what was agreed without receiving additional pay. Workers frequently feel compelled to perform work that is beyond the scope of the tasks initially described because if they refuse, they risk not being paid for work they have already completed.

On July 8, 2017, Jose accepted a job to move boxes from two locations to a FedEx store so they could be shipped. He agreed to load and unload the boxes, and he provided the use of his truck. He then followed the employer to several locations, first to load boxes into the truck and then to another location where there were boxes, but no items had been packed. He explained that he had been hired to load and unload boxes, not to pack them. The employer appeared not to understand and left him alone with the items. After a while, he began to pack the various items since he had already invested time and gas money in the job. After packing and loading were completed, the employer returned, and Jose followed him to the FedEx store for shipping. Upon arriving at the store, FedEx staff requested that the boxes be repacked. Again Jose stated that it wasn't his job. One of the FedEx staff was bilingual and served as an interpreter between Jose and the employer. The employer held up the $100 they had agreed on, insisting that Jose repack the boxes if he wanted his pay. Thoroughly frustrated, Jose stated again that this was not the agreed-upon arrangement. The employer responded by threatening to call immigration authorities and have Jose, a Honduran, "deported to Mexico." Seeking to avoid conflict, Jose left. After he departed, the employer called asking him to return to tape the boxes. When he refused to do so, the employer accused him of stealing her keys and said she would file a police report. After several promises to pay Jose for the work completed, the employer can no longer be found.

Missing Resources for the Recovery of Wages

Wage theft directly reduces earnings of day laborers and contributes to their economic insecurity. When wage theft is not redressed through the wage-recovery activities of workers, government enforcement agencies, or workers' rights organizations, it can depress wages and working conditions across the construction and landscaping labor markets.

A major obstacle to the reduction of wage theft and the effective recovery of unpaid wages is the lack of information about redress mechanisms. In our study, 80 percent of day laborers indicated that they do not know where to report the nonpayment of wages or other workplace abuses. In Nevada, the Office of the Labor Commissioner (OLC) is responsible for administering and enforcing the state's wage and hour laws. However, given the prevalence of wage theft reported and the large number of workers who indicate that they do not know where to report wage and hour violations, the OLC clearly must do more to ensure that day laborers are receiving employment protections.

Furthermore, worker interviews indicate that simply expanding outreach to informal hiring sites will not be enough to effectively address the problem of wage theft. Day laborers reported various experiences with the OLC. Although some indicated they were able to resolve wage theft cases through the OLC, these cases mainly involved work for larger, licensed companies that are required under Nevada law to have a surety bond. Those employed by smaller construction contractors, homeowners, or unlicensed businesses, however, have encountered major obstacles when redressing wage theft. Berto's experiences were similar to those of other workers:

> People told me about the Labor Commission so when I had an employer who refused to pay, I went. They asked me for all kinds of proof that I didn't have. That's not how this industry works. We have very little time in this industry to gather the kind of information they were looking for. I had the basic information: what I was owed, the time I had worked, phone number, name, license plate number, and the address where I worked, but that wasn't enough. When you've only worked for someone for two or three days, you don't know about their business license, for example. Not only that, but when I went to the [OLC] office, they told me it would have had to have been a week or more of work in order for them to act. That's not how this industry operates.

Marco's experience was similar: "I had worked one day for a homeowner removing old tile and he didn't pay. When I went to the Labor Commission, they asked me for a pay stub. I didn't have one, and that was that. I didn't bother going back."

Even in cases where there are written employment agreements, the OLC is rarely able to recover unpaid wages. For example, Carlos was recruited from an informal hiring site by a local contractor. He began working regularly for this employer, performing a variety of jobs ranging from tiling to landscaping. Over time, the employer fell behind on the payment of wages. Carlos addressed the situation in a forgiving manner, and he met with the employer to negotiate a payment amount and payment plan. Carlos and the employer both signed a note of payment due totaling $1,842. When the employer failed to make any payments, Carlos went to both local the Las Vegas Metropolitan Police Department (LVMPD) and the OLC. He submitted documentation to the labor commissioner, including the signed payment note; work logs with hours, dates, the types of work performed, and the location of the jobs; and text message exchanges with the employer who was promising to pay back wages. Nevertheless, the agency declared there was insufficient evidence to make a ruling.

In cases where the OLC rules in favor of a day laborer, workers report that judgments rarely result in actual wage collections. Following the completion of the survey, several workers provided documentation of cases filed with the OLC that had been in the collections process for several years. When a case is placed in collections, it is transferred to the Nevada Attorney General for collection and the possible prosecution of a delinquent employer. One worker who provided documentation of his case stated, "The Labor Commission awarded me $5,955. They told me to call every week for an update. I have called almost every week since I filed the case in 2013, but there is never any new information." The limited ability of the OLC to enforce court decisions further reduces the likelihood that workers will report wage theft when it occurs and that wages will be recovered after receiving judgments in their favor.

On-the-Job Injuries and Illnesses

More than one-quarter (28 percent) of day laborers report that they have been injured on the job in the past twelve months and nearly one-third (31 percent) report they have become ill in the past year because of conditions on the job. However, 74 percent of those who were injured or became ill on the job did not receive medical attention for these injuries and ailments. Antonio describes the injuries he sustained working as a day laborer:

> I was doing a landscaping job at a local wedding chapel, trimming more than thirty palm trees. I was not provided with a harness or bungee [cord] for safety. When I got to one of the trees in the back, I called over an employee of the chapel, and said I was uncomfortable going up the tree. It looked to me to have a section that had rotted. He told me to "just get up there." As I feared, I fell more than fifteen feet from a rotten section of the palm near the top of the tree. My hand and wrist were swollen for more than a week. I had splinters in my hands, arms, and legs that became infected. When I reported the incident to my employer, I was provided with a safety harness, although I was still not provided with a respirator or hardhat. . . . At no point was I asked to make a report, offered support with health care costs, or offered a workers' compensation claim. The landscaping company has still not paid me for the time worked.

Seventy-one percent of day laborers reported that they have not received health and safety training. Of those who were injured on the job, 81 percent reported that they have not received health and safety training. Fewer than one in five day laborers (18 percent) reported that they have received the basic ten-hour training course designed by the Occupational Safety and Health Administration (OSHA) for entry-level construction workers. Of those workers who suffered injuries on the job, 87 percent reported that they have never participated in OSHA's ten-hour safety training.

Difficulties with Local Law Enforcement

A substantial segment of the day laborers in our survey reported having had problems with the police while looking for work in Las Vegas. Thirty percent indicated that they have been insulted or harassed by police while looking for work, 60 percent have been forced to leave a hiring site, and 17 percent have been arrested. Among foreign-born day laborers, 12 percent indicated that police had inquired about their immigration status while they were looking for work. The LVMPD's policy is to ask for a social security number to ascertain a person's identity, though it publicly states that officers are not required to inquire about immigration status during routine stops. For many immigrants, however, asking for a social security number is tantamount to asking about one's immigration status. Workers also reported that some officers had directly asked about their immigration status.

The Las Vegas day laborer workforce is composed largely of immigrants (94 percent), and the problems these workers experience with police are exacerbated by police involvement in federal immigration enforcement. The LVMPD signed an agreement with U.S. Immigration and Customs Enforcement (ICE) that delegates authority to LVMPD to pursue a range of immigration-enforcement activities. Such policies have been found to increase the "social distance" between local police and Latino residents, increasing reluctance to contact police (Theodore 2013; Theodore and Habans 2016). This also is the case in Las Vegas; 47 percent of immigrant day laborers indicated they worry that by reporting a crime to police officers, they risk being asked about their immigration status or that of someone they know. Such fear undermines public safety and erodes the trust that immigrant workers have in law enforcement authorities. It also negatively impacts a range of crucial worker support systems, like accessing wage-recovery assistance in the event of wage theft or receiving medical care for on-the-job injuries (see Boyas, Negi, and Valera 2017).

Making Injustice Visible

In January 2018, the Arriba Las Vegas Worker Center was founded, the first worker center to open during the Trump presidency. During its first year, the worker center has engaged in wage recovery, provided occupational safety and health training, and advocated on behalf of residents from El Salvador, Nicaragua, Haiti, Guinea, Liberia, and Sierra Leone who have been stripped of their temporary protected status by the Trump administration. Worker leaders have used the day laborer survey to highlight conditions in the local economy and to call attention to a workforce too often overlooked by policy makers and the public.

The type of scholar activism in which NDLON has been engaged "always begins with the politics of recognition" (Gilmore 2008, 55). In the case of day laborers, the struggle for recognition centers on the quest for collective identity formation, one that rejects the alienation of contingent work and embraces dignity and solidarity. It involves a reimagining of community so that day laborers see themselves as a potent force for social change. That is why, ever since the earliest days of day laborer organizing, NDLON's activist research has sought to better understand the individual and collective conditions facing day laborers. NDLON's research thus simultaneously faces inward to inform day laborers about their shared circumstances and outward to policy makers and other stakeholders in the form of demands for recognition and reform. NDLON's research program therefore involves a series of interventions that call into question the systemic marginalization of low-wage immigrants by making injustice visible.

References

Boyas, Javier Francisco, Nalini Junko Negi, and Pamela Valera. 2017. "Factors Associated to Health Care Service Use among Latino Day Laborers." *American Journal of Men's Health* 11 (4): 1028–1038.

Fussell, Elizabeth. 2011. "The Deportation Threat Dynamic and Victimization of Latino Migrants: Wage Theft and Robbery." *Sociological Quarterly* 52 (4): 593–615.

Gilmore, Ruth Wilson. 2008. "Forgotten Places and the Seeds of Grassroots Planning." In *Engaging Contradictions: Theory, Politics, and Methods of Activist Scholarship*, edited by Charles R. Hale, 31–61. Berkeley: University of California Press.

Meléndez, Edwin, Nik Theodore, and Abel Valenzuela Jr. 2010. "Day Laborers in New York's Informal Economy." In *Informal Work in Developed Nations*, edited by Enrico Marcelli, Colin C. Williams, and Pascale Joassart, 135–152. New York: Routledge.

Millward, Wade Tyler, Todd Prince, Nicole Raz, Eli Segall, and Richard N. Velotta. 2017. "Will Las Vegas Have Enough Workers for Major Construction Projects?" *Las Vegas Review-Journal*, June 9, 2017. https://www.reviewjournal.com/business/will-las-vegas-have-enough-workers-for-major-construction-projects/.

Sun Staff. 2017. "How Much Better Is the Economy, Really?" *Las Vegas Sun*, July 17, 2017. https://lasvegassun.com/news/2017/jul/17/how-much-better-is-the-economy-really/.

Theodore, Nik. 2013. *Insecure Communities: Latino Perceptions of Police Involvement in Immigration Enforcement*. Chicago: Department of Urban Planning and Policy, University of Illinois at Chicago.

———. 2015. "Generative Work: Day Labourers' Freirean Praxis." *Urban Studies* 52 (11): 2035–2050.

———. 2016. *Day Labor in Seattle: Casa Latina's Impact on Wages and Earnings*. Los Angeles: National Day Laborer Organizing Network.

———. 2017. *After the Storm: Houston's Day Labor Markets in the Aftermath of Hurricane Harvey*. Chicago: Great Cities Institute, University of Illinois at Chicago.

Theodore, Nik, and Robert Habans. 2016. "Policing Immigrant Communities: Latino Perceptions of Police Involvement in Immigration Enforcement." *Journal of Ethnic and Migration Studies* 42 (6): 970–988.

Theodore, Nik, and Bliss Requa-Trautz. 2018. *Day Labor in Las Vegas: Employer Indiscretions in Sin City*. Chicago: Great Cities Institute, University of Illinois at Chicago.

Theodore, Nik, Abel Valenzuela, Edwin Meléndez, and Ana Luz Gonzalez. 2008. "Day Labor and Workplace Abuses in the Residential Construction Industry: Conditions in the Washington, DC Region." In *The Gloves Off Economy: Workplace Standards at the Bottom of America's Labor Market,* edited by Annette Bernhardt, Heather Boushey, Laura Dresser, and Chris Tilly, 91–109. Ithaca, N.Y.: Cornell University Press.

U.S. Immigration and Customs Enforcement. 2017. *Delegation of Immigration Authority Section 287(g) Immigration and Nationality Act*. Washington, D.C.: Department of Homeland Security, United States Government. https://www.ice.gov/287g.

Valenzuela, Abel. 1999. *Day Laborers in Southern California: Preliminary Findings from the Day Labor Survey*. Los Angeles: UCLA Center for the Study of Urban Poverty.

Valenzuela, Abel, Nik Theodore, Edwin Meléndez, and Ana Luz Gonzalez. 2006. *On the Corner: Day Labor in the United States*. Los Angeles: UCLA Center for the Study of Urban Poverty and UIC Center for Urban Economic Development.

10

Milking Research for Social Change

● ●

Immigrant Dairy Farmworkers
in Upstate New York

CARLY FOX, REBECCA FUENTES,
FABIOLA ORTIZ VALDEZ, GRETCHEN
PURSER, AND KATHLEEN SEXSMITH

The dairy industry in New York—and indeed nationwide—has increasingly turned to undocumented immigrants as its primary workforce. Though living in conditions of isolation and invisibility, these workers have helped the state earn the title of number-one yogurt producer in the nation. This chapter introduces a community-based participatory action research (PAR) project that we carried out to expose the working and living conditions of farmworkers as well as build their strategic capacity to organize for change. We describe how the research process served as a tool for conducting outreach, building worker solidarity, and developing worker leadership. We then describe how the research product is being mobilized, or "milked," for the purposes of effecting policy change.

New York's dairy industry has undergone several dramatic transformations in recent decades. The phenomenal popularity of Greek yogurt has turned dairy into the star sector of the state's agricultural economy and New York into one of the leading dairy-producing states in the country. Farms have consolidated, becoming fewer, larger, and more efficient. And in conjunction with consolidation, the composition of the workforce in dairies has changed. Dairy farmers have increasingly turned to undocumented immigrants from Mexico and Guatemala to milk the cows, tend the calves, and clean the increasingly mechanized, fast-paced, and round-the-clock milking parlors.

In the wake of these changes, organizers and outreach staff at the Workers' Center of Central New York (WCCNY) and Worker Justice Center of New York (WJCNY) learned of the growing number of workplace injuries and fatalities suffered by immigrants employed in the dairy industry. One such fatality occurred in February 2013, when Francisco Ortiz, originally from Veracruz, Mexico, was crushed to death by a skid-steer loader while working on a small dairy farm in Ithaca, New York. In response to this preventable fatality, the organizers ramped up health and safety trainings on farms around central, northern, and western New York, where they witnessed firsthand the dangerous conditions and inadequate protections workers face each day. Through these trainings, they began mobilizing workers to advocate for greater health and safety protections on dairies. In July 2013, they organized a delegation of immigrant dairy farmworkers to meet with Occupation Health and Safety Administration (OSHA) representatives in Syracuse to testify about these workplace hazards and to lobby for the implementation of a Local Emphasis Program (LEP), a special enforcement strategy employed by OSHA to target industries where there are high numbers of workplace fatalities and injuries. In February 2014, they helped workers draft letters to the editor, published in the *Syracuse Post-Standard*, calling for greater health and safety protections on dairies. Collectively, these efforts proved successful, and OSHA began implementation of the LEP program in July 2014.

This juxtaposition of booming sales and broken bodies in the dairy sector set the stage for the collaborative research project that we undertook with the generous support of the Sociological Initiatives Foundation (SIF), resulting in the publication of the report *Milked: Immigrant Dairy Farmworkers in New York State*. Throughout the campaign for the LEP, we were understandably frustrated by the lack of reliable data and rigorous research on this vital sector of the economy. We struggled to answer even the most basic questions, such as "How many immigrants are employed on New York dairies?" or "How prevalent is wage theft on the farms?" We were impressed by the emergent leadership of farmworkers and the powerful impact of their testimony on the public and policy makers alike. This fueled the decision to pursue SIF funding to design and carry out a participatory action research project on the working and living conditions of immigrant dairy farmworkers throughout Upstate New York.

This chapter presents an overview of our project and the ongoing ways in which we are milking research to promote progressive social change. After introducing our report, we discuss our research team, our research process, and the uses to which we have put our research product. It is our hope that this chapter illustrates both the extraordinary opportunity presented by the SIF funding and the extraordinary potential of community-based participatory action research projects for workers' rights campaigns.

The *Milked* Report: Filling a Research and Advocacy Gap

The principal output of this SIF-funded project was the advocacy report *Milked: Immigrant Dairy Farmworkers in New York State*, published by WJCNY and WCCNY in June 2017. The seventy-three-page report describes the findings of our participatory action research with eighty-eight immigrant workers on fifty-three dairy farms across western, central, and northern New York, carried out in 2014 and 2015. We focused on these regions because they are the most important dairy-producing regions of the state and therefore are the locations of a majority of the state's immigrant dairy farmworkers. The report had several objectives: to identify trends in employment conditions, health and safety risks, and social isolation on dairy farms; to tell farmworkers' stories about workplace abuses to the public, bridging the language barriers that separate them from consumers and their communities; to analyze structures of power in the dairy supply chain; and to provide evidence-based policy recommendations to the New York State government, dairy-processing companies, and consumers. Separate sections of the report were dedicated to these topics.

Each of these sections makes important contributions to the analysis of power relations in the dairy industry. The overarching finding of the report is that dairy workers are being "milked" by a supply chain that concentrates power in the hands of the largest cooperatives and manufacturers, a process that is helped along by the political and economic support of the New York State government. The first major section analyzes the economic importance of the dairy industry to the rural upstate economy and the crucial contributions of immigrant farmworkers to the viability of these farms. This analysis is followed by an explanation of the division of labor between immigrant and nonimmigrant workers on dairy farms, which often relegates Spanish-speaking workers to less-well-paid positions working directly with animals in milking parlors and barns. We present the striking finding that 88 percent of workers feel their boss cares more about the cows than their immigrant employees. The core of the report follows and is divided among three sections: work, safety and health, and social life. Each thematic section provides significant detail from our quantitative analysis, complemented by short worker profiles. We document how dairy farmworkers are overworked and underpaid and note in particular that wage theft is prevalent in the industry (28 percent of all workers knowingly experienced wage theft); that a majority experience injury on the job, which may be related to the fact that a significant share work on farms outside of OSHA jurisdiction; and finally, that workers feel "stuck in place," unable to leave the farm for more than a short visit to the store due to their heavy work schedules and fear of immigration enforcement. In our concluding section, we provide detailed recommendations to the government of the State of New York and to dairy processing companies and consumers, which arise directly from our findings. The path we recommend toward meaningful social change includes specific examples of legislation that must be passed to provide decent and safe conditions of work, housing, and community integration. We also advocate a worker-driven social responsibility program for New York dairy farms, the campaign for which is discussed in more detail in the following section.

Setting Up the Research: Blurring the Lines between Organizers and Scholars

The project was designed and carried out by five principal researchers: Carly Fox, senior workers' rights advocate with the WJCNY and board member of WCCNY; Rebecca Fuentes, lead organizer at the WCCNY; Fabiola Ortiz Valdez, a PhD candidate in anthropology at the Maxwell School of Syracuse University, former staff organizer of the WCCNY, and current organizer for the New York Immigration Coalition; Gretchen Purser, an associate professor of sociology at the Maxwell School of Syracuse University and chair of the board of the WCCNY; and Kathleen Sexsmith, then a PhD candidate in development sociology at Cornell University and now an assistant professor of Rural Sociology at Pennsylvania State University. WCCNY is a worker member–led organization that uses community organizing, leadership development, popular education, and policy advocacy to empower low-wage workers to combat workplace abuses and improve wages and working conditions. WJCNY promotes justice for agricultural and other low-wage workers across New York State by providing them with legal representation, rights training, community services, and advocacy. Both organizations work with members across low-wage sectors in the Upstate New York economy, with a special focus on dairy farmworkers.

Many community-based, participatory research projects are conceptualized as "collaborations" among differing and distinct academic and community partners. Our project veered from this model insofar as the lines between the "academic" and the "community" were already quite blurred. Thus two of the three academic collaborators (Purser and Ortiz Valdez) served in formal roles—respectively as chair of the board and staff organizer—with the WCCNY. In that respect, this was neither a fleeting nor an opportunistic collaboration but rather the manifestation of an already established partnership and a shared commitment to the struggle for immigrant and workers' rights. *Milked* was not a product of a collaboration between distant and distinct "academics" and "community" but rather a project among "scholar activists" and "activist scholars" committed to crossing these lines, minimizing these divides, and collectively producing knowledge for the express purpose of effecting social change.

Immigrant farmworkers—including Crispin Hernandez, Lazaro Alvarez, Agustín Omar Rodríguez Juarez, and others who wish to remain anonymous—were involved in almost every step of the research project, including establishing the goals of the project, designing the survey questions, conducting surveys, contributing photographs, transcribing interviews, selecting stories for inclusion in the report, and publicly presenting the study's findings. We relied heavily on workers' expertise particularly in the initial stages of the project to design and pilot the survey instrument. Workers drafted many of the questions and corrected the phrasing of others so that participants would understand the questions and feel comfortable participating in the research, particularly when we were trying to get sensitive information, such as on the often abusive practices of *contratistas* (labor contractors). Admittedly, we did not rely as heavily as we had initially hoped on workers' expertise in the actual analysis of data and drafting of the report. This was largely due to language barriers, since our farmworker colleagues spoke limited English, and to time constraints in getting our report published. Throughout the project, we were mindful about not letting the academic nature of the project overshadow the long-standing work and goals of the advocacy organizations. For that reason, the eventual report was stamped with the names of WCCNY and WJCNY instead of being marketed with our academic institution affiliations.

The collaboration took different forms over the course of the project, and the contributions of each collaborator varied. For the academics involved, the nationally recognized SIF grant helped legitimize the kind of community-based scholarship to which they were deeply committed but for which there is limited institutional support. The academic researchers received no material compensation from the SIF grant for their involvement in this study and so had to maintain all other research and teaching commitments while doing this work. But securing the competitive external SIF grant did provide a kind of symbolic currency that is prized within the academy. Moreover, for two of the scholars (Ortiz Valdez and Sexsmith), this study contributed valuable data to their dissertation research.

For one of the organizers involved, the SIF grant provided limited salary support and, for both organizers, the rare opportunity to focus on research and develop a deeper understanding of the targeted workforce. Typically, under pressure from service-oriented grant deliverables, they felt it was a privilege and honor to simply sit down with workers, listen to their stories, and have those stories and perspectives inform the direction for advocacy and organizing. In addition, as coauthors of the report, the organizers felt that they gained local and national recognition among their peers, as well as the credibility to speak as "experts," a privilege that problematically is typically reserved for those in the academy.

For the worker leaders involved, the SIF-funded study facilitated the cultivation of new skills, including survey design, audio transcription, and public speaking. It also provided workers the opportunity to deepen their connection to, and leadership within, WCCNY and WJCNY and to develop strong relationships with other dairy farmworkers across the state. This networking was the most impactful result of the research process.

The Research Process: Survey-Based Field Research as an Organizing Tool

As a participatory action research project, our goals for the study extended far beyond traditional knowledge production, whereby research results constitute more privileged output than the methodology. From the start, we recognized that the *research process* was as vital to the organizations' needs and objectives as would be the *research product*. The primary way the research process served the purposes of WCCNY and WJCNY was through the establishment of a statewide network of farmworkers interested in fomenting solidarity in the workplace and mobilizing for policy change.

We thus used the survey as a tool for outreach and membership recruitment. Many of the eighty-eight workers surveyed had not previously had access to the legal and other support services for farmworkers offered by WCCNY and WJCNY. Via the survey questionnaire, researchers learned of dozens of cases of wage theft, uninhabitable living conditions, unaddressed workplace hazards and injuries, and other injustices. The survey therefore served as a tool for making legal referrals to WJCNY, whose attorneys could immediately begin to redress wage, health and safety, and/or housing violations or connect the worker to appropriate service providers. Moreover, these lengthy one-on-one, face-to-face surveys often resulted in the worker inviting an organizer to come back to the farm to lead a "know your rights" or health and safety training, which benefitted not just the interviewee but the entire immigrant workforce of that farm.

Importantly, the survey provided an opportunity to gain workers' trust and gauge their interest in connecting with other dairy farmworkers to discuss strategies for improving working and living conditions. Workers were asked if they wanted to join a group text-messaging service and/or Facebook group for the purposes of both communicating with other immigrant dairy farmworkers across the state and keeping abreast of WCCNY meetings, trainings, and campaign activities. From these responses, we built an extensive network of workers across New York, many of whom began participating in weekly conference calls to discuss working conditions and brainstorm goals and strategies for a worker solidarity campaign. Through these calls, workers were able to identify commonalities in the conditions they had been experiencing in relative solitude. Week by week, we had a consistent group of workers participating in the calls but also many newcomers. Workers recounted the challenges they were facing on their farms and came up with strategies for how best to deal with these challenges. On a few occasions, service providers and advocates joined the calls and reported on the latest immigration- or labor-related news. Worker leaders eventually formed what they called the "May 1st committee," a subcommittee of WCCNY that took on much of the role of presenting and publicly disseminating the eventual *Milked* report. The network generated through the research also laid the groundwork for the establishment of the Alianza Agricola, a group of farmworker leaders in western New York supported by WJCNY.

Given the extremely isolating conditions in which farmworkers live and work, establishing this statewide network and expanded WCCNY membership was arguably the single most important outcome of this project. Indeed, we cannot overstate the level of isolation and fear experienced by undocumented workers toiling on New York dairies, who are extremely vulnerable to aggressive immigration enforcement activity. A large portion of dairy farms are located within one hundred miles of the U.S.-Canadian border. Within this expansive zone, Border Patrol has the authority to set up immigration checkpoints on roadways and to aggressively seek out and detain those in the country without legal authorization. This renders day-to-day life for farmworkers quite precarious since all forms of travel are risky. Combined with workers' grueling, round-the-clock work schedules and inability to secure driver's licenses, these conditions mean that workers go for long periods of time without ever leaving the farm; they leave the farm as infrequently as every eleven days, on average.

The research thus not only helped ameliorate social isolation but provided workers the opportunity to share their experiences and give voice to their concerns. It also ensured that a great many workers across dozens of farms are familiar with our work and know where to turn in the event of some form of workplace injustice. Furthermore, the weekly calls and the group messaging system gave us a way to engage in ongoing political education about injustices toward farmworkers inscribed in labor and immigration laws, and they ensured that workers themselves helped shape campaign strategy and decision-making.

The Research Product: A Farmworker Rights Advocacy Tool

In addition to the local- and state-level impacts of the research process, the research product helped generate national support and solidarity for dairy farmworkers. On June 1, 2017—the first day of National Dairy Month—we held a well-attended press conference at the offices of the WCCNY to launch the *Milked* report. The release of the report garnered extensive media attention, from local, state, national, and even international sources, including the *New York Times*, the *Nation*, and Mexico's *La Jornada*. This media attention was pivotal in raising the public's awareness about the issues facing the largely invisible immigrant workforce on dairies, another key goal of our research. Much of the media coverage directed audiences to the MilkedNY website to freely download the report, and traffic on our website—where we also listed updates and carefully thought-out action items—spiked in the days, weeks, and even months following the release.

The report—the first in New York State to focus on the plight of immigrant dairy farmworkers—secured attention and support of organizations across the country, especially workers' centers, immigrant rights groups, and unions. National organizations such as the Food Chain Workers Alliance, the National Employment Law Project, the National Council for Occupational Safety and Health, Farmworker Justice, and Interfaith Worker Justice distributed our report to their organizational affiliates and/or via social media. So too did New York–based organizations such as the New York Immigration Coalition and the New York Civil Liberties Union. Moreover, our report garnered the attention and support of groups in California, Washington, Wisconsin, and Vermont. Migrant Justice, who had launched the Milk with Dignity campaign targeting Ben & Jerry's, began meeting with us to discuss common goals and their campaign strategy. SEIU 32BJ, the property services workers union, provided myriad support after learning about ongoing organizing work through the report. They not only picked up the tab for the initial print run of the report (the cost of which far exceeded our SIF grant budget) but invited us to launch the report at their national headquarters in New York City. They have continued to provide crucial assistance to WCCNY's work.

In addition to the public release of the report in Syracuse and New York City, we presented the study in many other locations, including Ithaca, Baltimore, and Mexico City. Each of these public-speaking opportunities presented an occasion for workers' leadership development, as workers helped present the results of the study, personally testified to what they have seen and experienced on farms, and advocated publicly for policy change. One worker leader, Agustín Rodríguez, who had returned to Mexico by the time of the study's release, presented the report along with Kathleen Sexsmith at the National Autonomous University of Mexico (UNAM). These speaking opportunities also helped in promoting the ongoing work of WCCNY, soliciting organizational and campaign support, and modeling the power of academic-community collaborations in participatory action research.

Beyond garnering the public's attention through the media and presentations, the report has also been used as an important tool for popular education with dairy farmworkers around the state. The report was written in English, but we created a Spanish-language presentation that compiled its central claims and findings. WCCNY and WJCNY use this presentation during trainings with farmworkers so they can become cognizant of the prevalence of workplace injustices in the industry. Awareness of the systemic nature of the conditions they face is an important step in building motivation and capacity to organize for change.

Over the course of this research and our ongoing organizing and advocacy, we gained a firmer understanding of structures of power in the dairy industry and how they reinforce the marginalization of undocumented workers. This knowledge then reinforced our strategy by helping us develop well-targeted recommendations in the conclusion of our report. For example, our power analysis helped us gain a better appreciation of the role of large dairy cooperatives in controlling the supply chain. While cooperatives could play a critical role in demanding improved working conditions from individual farm suppliers, they often deflect these concerns, impeding progressive change. We also learned how the zealous subsidization of the industry by the state government has helped it grow and consolidate, yet the New York legislature continues to deny New York farmworkers basic rights such as overtime pay and collective bargaining. This broader power analysis guided our decisions regarding the targets of the recommendations that we ultimately included in the report. Thus after much collective discussion, we decided to focus our recommendations not on individual farm owners but rather on policy changes to be implemented at the state level.

We also focused our recommendations in the report on powerful dairy purchasers such as Chobani. We called for purchasers to comply with a worker-driven and independently monitored social responsibility program for New York dairy farms. Upon the report's release, we set up a link on the MilkedNY website so readers could send a message directly to Chobani requesting attention to the concerning contents of the report and its implications for social responsibility in the supply chain. Following the New York City release of the report, we held a widely attended action at the Chobani café in Manhattan, where worker leaders delivered copies of the report along with a letter demanding a meeting with Hamdi Ulukaya, the celebrated founder and CEO of the number-one selling Greek yogurt company. Thanks to the media attention generated by the report and the letters to Chobani sent by readers, we secured a seat at the table with company executives the very next month. During this meeting, worker leaders presented findings of the study, asked questions about the company and its operations, and urged Chobani to take responsibility for the working conditions not just in its processing plants but throughout its supply chain. We are hopeful that our ongoing negotiations will lead Chobani to agree to join a worker-led and independently monitored fair food program for the New York dairy industry, one that privileges workers' right to organize.

Only one year since its release, it is still far too early to assess the full impact of the report. Nevertheless, its findings provide ample support for several ongoing campaigns for immigrant and labor rights with which we are involved. Given the extreme degree of isolation and immobilization documented in the report, one of the main recommendations we put forward is for New York State to pass legislation that would enable all eligible residents, regardless of immigration status, access to driver's licenses, as is currently possible in twelve states throughout the nation. *Milked* is regularly used and cited in meetings and rallies for the New York Green Light campaign, which advocates for this legislation. The report also makes a strong recommendation for the immediate passage of the Farmworker Fair Labor Practices Act, which would provide farmworkers with the basic labor rights that all other New York workers enjoy, including a day of rest, overtime pay, disability pay, and the protected right to organize.

Finally, the report highlights the historic lawsuit *Hernandez v. State of New York*, currently pending before the appellate division third department of the state supreme court. This lawsuit was filed by the New York Civil Liberties Union (NYCLU) on behalf of lead plaintiff Crispin Hernandez, one of the worker leaders who assisted with this project and who had been fired for organizing while working at Marks Farm, one of the state's largest dairies. Crispin now works as a staff organizer for WCCNY. We prominently included his story and testimony in the report to raise awareness of this lawsuit, which seeks to extend to farmworkers the protected right to organize. While the state has declined to fight the lawsuit, the New York Farm Bureau has stepped in as the defendant. The findings in our report, along with other studies of immigrant farmworkers, have been cited in amicus briefs filed with the court.

Challenges and Lessons Learned

This project was an enormous and challenging undertaking. Some challenges were, in retrospect, avoidable, since they had to do with decisions we made regarding study design or with the limitations of time, energy, and funding.

Given the profound lack of information about working and living conditions among immigrant dairy workers, we ended up designing a lengthy and admittedly unwieldy questionnaire. Although we had piloted the survey instrument with five workers, the varied practical, academic, and organizational interests of our research team and the strong collaborative spirit of the undertaking made it difficult for any one of us to insist on which questions could be eliminated. Wanting to take full advantage of our capacity and the opportunities that this project offered, we included as many questions as we thought relevant, resulting in a 225-question survey instrument. One unfortunate result of the length of the instrument was that the interviews were sometimes rushed or questions were left unaddressed. Although we were strategic about wanting to capture both quantitative data on the workforce as well as qualitative stories of workers' experiences, we could have done a more effective job on both fronts.

Additionally, we went into the field to conduct surveys without having adequately thought through the time requirements to enter the data from a 225-question survey with more than eighty participants. As a result, we had to engage in a painstakingly laborious process of jotting down responses to survey questions by hand in the field and then entering that data into an online survey platform (Qualtrics) in the office. Real-time data entry via cellular-enabled tablets in the field would have been far more practical. Another downside of this approach was that researchers could not always record workers' lengthier responses to open-ended questions, with the result that some poignant stories never made it into our database. Fortunately, many had been recorded and were later transcribed, although this added an enormous layer of unanticipated work. Finally, once the report was drafted, we circulated it to at least a dozen experts and supporters from a variety of organizations. This too took a long time, as the feedback we received sometimes conflicted with and required further discussion to reconcile the views. But ultimately, the feedback was invaluable for strengthening the quality of the report, and it helped us forge a collaborative relationship with an even broader network of academics, union officials, activists, service providers, and lawyers.

In retrospect, we all believe that we went into this project drastically underestimating the challenges involved. If we were to do it over, we would spend even more time carefully thinking through the survey design, survey execution, data entry, and data analysis.

The other challenges reflected the difficult conditions on dairy farms that form the subject of our research. First and foremost is the fact that dairy farms are geographically dispersed across Upstate New York; we had to travel long distances through rural areas of the state to carry out this research. Carrying out one ninety-minute interview often took a total of four and a half hours when taking into account travel time from Ithaca, Rochester, and Syracuse to remote rural farms. This reality made the project far more expensive and time consuming than anticipated. We had underestimated the logistical challenges involved in this undertaking, especially considering that none of us could dedicate ourselves full time to the project. Visiting with and interviewing workers at fifty-three different dairy farms across the state, traversing thousands of miles across more than twenty counties, our data collection efforts lasted a full two years. These challenges of geographic distance and dispersal were compounded by the no less significant challenge of scheduling. As we documented in our report, dairy farmworkers typically work twelve-hour shifts six—and sometimes even seven—days a week. Given such circumstances, finding a time when workers could sit down with us for a lengthy interview was often enormously challenging.

Moreover, access to farmworkers was complicated by the fact that they live on—and almost never leave—the farms where they work. Some farms are laid out in such a way that visitors must pass management offices before reaching farmworker housing, and on some farms, owners' houses are within a few meters from workers' living quarters. Therefore, it is easy for farm employers to monitor who is visiting their workers. Moreover, farms tend to be located along roads where there is not much commuting traffic, meaning that researchers' visits to the farms were often quite conspicuous, and our presence raised the possibility of suspicion and/or conflict. Certainly, most farmers were undisturbed by our presence. However, some workers feared retaliation from farmers, particularly those who had previously witnessed occasions when the owners called the police on visitors. This informed one of the recommendations we put forward at the end of our report: that the New York attorney general's office should update Formal Opinion No. 91-F7 (1991) concerning the common law right of visitor access to migrant farmworker labor camps to extend to dairy farmworker housing. Additionally, because workers typically live in cramped and overcrowded quarters, it was sometimes difficult to find private space in which to carry out one-on-one conversations. We were often stuck with the less-than-ideal situation of carrying out interviews outside, which rendered workers vulnerable to being seen and overheard, or carrying out interviews in farmworkers' bedrooms, which created discomfort for interviewers.

As a team of female-identified researchers, we were carrying out this research in very masculine spaces. Indeed, nine out of ten workers we interviewed were male. On many occasions, we were traveling alone and visiting farms we had never been to before. Arriving at a house sheltering as many as ten men generated for some of us a certain degree of anxiety. Our concerns for our own safety gave us a deeper understanding of the much more acute vulnerability of undocumented female farmworkers, a subject that, in retrospect, we should have explored in more depth in the report by purposively sampling female workers.

Finally, the network of worker leaders established through this research has proven difficult to sustain given the relatively high degree of transiency experienced by this transnational workforce. In the wake of the increased immigration-enforcement activities ushered in by the Trump administration, many of the strongest leaders—including contributors to the research—have been deported or have voluntarily returned to their home countries. This turnover of worker leaders is a stark reminder of the fact that our organizing needs to be sustained over the long haul. While it is admittedly far too soon to know the full impact of this project, it is our hope that the *Milked* report demonstrates the need for a well-funded and sustained organizing campaign among dairy farmworkers.

Participatory Action Research as a Standard

Community-based PAR is a direct challenge to the individualist, positivist, and self-referential production of knowledge for knowledge's sake (Brydon-Miller, Greenwood, and Maguire 2003). PAR starts from the premise that those directly affected are experts on matters that affect and shape their own lives and that researchers pursue projects that are vital to the interests of the community and oriented to the goal of social change. In this regard, much of the power of participatory action research lies in its afterlife as it is put into action. We have discussed the ways in which we are endeavoring to milk this research for social change. But we also want to address the change that this project produced in us.

As our first foray into community-based PAR, a methodology in which none of us had any formal training, we drastically underestimated the logistical, personal, and financial challenges involved. While we have little interest in romanticizing this approach, each of us found this project to be not just valuable but, indeed, transformational. Each one of us is eager and committed to pursuing this kind of research again in the future thanks to the very tangible and positive outcomes we saw arise from our work. The organizers found the research to be an effective tool for outreach and mobilization and the report to be an invaluable resource for generating public awareness and support. While they already knew many of the findings presented in the report, given their extensive outreach to and engagement with immigrant farmworkers across the state, the project demonstrated to them the power of systematic documentation via research, the role research can play in building workers' confidence and leadership, and the benefit of collaborating with solidaristic trustworthy academic partners. The academics came to recognize that PAR methods should be the baseline standard for all research with low-wage workers and other socially marginalized populations. The participation of workers greatly improved the quality of the research and the relevance of the report. And the collaboration with community groups rendered this a far more meaningful and personally rewarding (if not institutionally rewarded) experience, a way of utilizing our academic skills and resources for our activist commitments.

Finally, the workers involved felt empowered as advisors and contributors to the project. Workers whom we surveyed, for instance, were asked what they would want to say to the public. Countless workers used this opportunity to claim their self-worth and the import of the contributions that they make to society, typified by statements such as "I just want people to know about us"; "People should know who we are, that we are the basis of agricultural products like milk. People need to know who works hard, and that is not the farm owners who are working hard"; "We immigrants do the dirty, heavy, and low-paid work behind the gallons of milk that you and your family consume"; and "It is because of me that you are drinking milk." Workers involved in the research itself also expressed feeling recognized and validated. Crispin Hernandez, one of our core worker leaders, articulated the value of community-based PAR projects in these terms:

> It is very important to include workers [in research]. Sometimes we feel uncomfortable stepping into this role . . . because people work and have no time, or they are afraid. But we know we have to participate because we are the work experts. No one else knows but us. Farm owners never give us credit for our work. They make us feel like we are worthless, so it is important that projects like this one do not do the same. Farmers take advantage of us and make us feel invisible. Being part of this project made us feel the opposite. And that's important.

References

Brydon-Miller, Mary, Davydd Greenwood, and Patricia Maguire. 2003. "Editorial: Why Action Research?" *Action Research* 1 (1): 9–28.

Fox, Carly, Rebecca Fuentes, Fabiola Ortiz Valdez, Gretchen Purser, and Kathleen Sexsmith. 2017. *Milked: Immigrant Dairy Farmworkers in New York State*. New York: Workers' Center of Central New York and the Worker Justice Center of New York.

11

Building a Better Texas

• • • • • • • • • • • • • • • • • • • •

Participatory Research Wins
for Texas Workers

RICH HEYMAN AND EMILY TIMM

This is a David and Goliath story about a small group of construction workers frustrated with the abuses they saw on the job who fought back against
the construction industry—one of the most powerful sectors in the Texas
economy and with major influence on Texas politics. Ultimately the research
study is just one act in the story; not only did it prove to be a powerful tool
for validating the lived experiences of Texas construction workers and launch-
ing successful policy campaigns, but it also was transformative for all the
actors—construction workers, organizers, and academics alike. The *Building Austin, Building Injustice* project empowered Workers Defense Project
(WDP) members to take control of the narrative of their working conditions
and build power in a sector where they often were viewed as powerless. Organizers learned new ways to arm the community with the expertise and respect
commanded by an academic study. And academics saw how they could contribute to meaningful social change.

This chapter will discuss the collaboration of WDP members and staff
with the Academic Advisory Committee (AAC) of professors at the University of Texas (UT) and the University of Illinois at Chicago. The project
brought together partners with vastly different experiences and social stations.

We explore the challenges and successes from two perspectives: Emily, the community organizer who works with, and is directly accountable to, WDP's construction worker members, and Rich, the academic who faces the pressures of the ivory tower to publish, teach, and build a career in academia. This is the story of a participatory research project *Building Austin, Building Injustice*. One would think that the story starts when researchers from the University of Texas team up with a community organization, Workers Defense Project, but the real story began several years before on construction sites in Austin, Texas.

Where the Story Begins (Emily)

In 2007, Pedro Hernandez was replacing the roof on a house in East Austin when he fell twenty feet, severely injuring his back. Pedro was hospitalized for four days and incapacitated for months with no financial support because his employer didn't carry workers' compensation insurance. On another site a few months later, Ramiro Mora and seven other workers were cheated out of more than $8,000 in back wages for their work building houses in a KB Home subdivision in Austin. On yet another worksite that year, sisters Dominga and Martha Hurtado's employer refused to pay them $1,800 for painting work on commercial worksites across central Texas.

By the spring of 2008, these workers and hundreds of others had found their way to the Workers Defense Project. They began to meet weekly to discuss what they could do about the rampant wage theft and dangerous conditions that had brought them together. WDP had fought alongside each of them to right the injustice in their individual cases. Pedro eventually received $4,000 from his employer for his injury, Ramiro and his coworkers recovered their $8,000 by filing liens on the property and protesting outside of KB Home corporate headquarters, and Dominga and Martha negotiated with their employers to pay them the $1,800 they were owed. But these workers continued to come to WDP every single week, fueled by the righteous indignation that you shouldn't have to fight to be paid for honest work and because they realized that what had happened to them at work was not unique. They knew that it was happening to construction workers all over central Texas, that these dishonest practices were business as usual in the industry. However, they also saw that when WDP tried to raise these concerns with local elected officials or in the media, the most common response was "These are just a few bad-apple employers, right?" Unfortunately, the anecdotal, firsthand experiences of construction workers were not enough proof to get policy makers or the public to take notice of the rampant abuses in the construction industry. Therefore, these workers—and others—continued to collaborate with WDP and eventually became the members of WDP's Construction Worker Committee.

I had joined WDP as a volunteer organizer in 2004, and after a few years of working on wage-claim cases and providing know-your-rights education to day laborers, I was excited to work with these construction worker leaders to win some real improvements in conditions. There were just two of us on staff at that time—Director Cristina Tzintzún and myself—and we had discussed how we could have a greater impact on improving working conditions for Texas's immigrant workers. We saw that the Restaurant Opportunities Center in New York had systematically documented labor violations experienced by New York restaurant workers and had won major improvements in that sector. We thought about focusing our limited resources on dry cleaning workers or Austin restaurant workers, but attendees at our weekly wage claim meeting made it clear we were surrounded by the leading experts on the Texas construction industry—if only we could collect the data to prove that their experiences were not outliers in the sector. In conversations with the Construction Worker Committee, we agreed on a plan to leverage our relationships with University of Texas academics (Cristina was a recent University of Texas graduate) to do a systematic survey of the Austin construction industry to document the problems that our construction committee members saw every day on the job.

Act 1: The Actors

The Construction Workers

WDP had formed in 2002 in response to the widespread problem of wage theft in many lower-income sectors, providing direct assistance in recovering unpaid wages. Realizing that assistance in individual wage theft cases was not in itself empowering to workers, WDP began to provide ESL (English as a second language) and leadership development classes. At its core, WDP was about building power for low-wage workers through community organizing and strategic campaigns to win stronger protections for Texas workers, not just deliver a useful social service. The Construction Worker Committee formed to figure out how to go beyond individual wage claim victories and take on the systemic causes of wage theft and the deadly conditions in the construction industry.

Throughout 2007 and 2008, WDP's Construction Worker Committee grew to roughly fifteen members—men and women either who worked in construction or whose family members worked in construction. We met every Sunday at borrowed space at a Salvation Army community center. Most of the members, like Dominga, Martha, Ramiro, and Pedro described previously, had come to WDP because of their own experiences with injuries or wage theft. Some members had been professionals in their home countries (lawyers, engineers) but had been forced to migrate to the United States because of economic or political pressures largely due to U.S. free trade or foreign policies. Other members had only received rudimentary education or were barely literate. Committee members hailed from Mexico, Guatemala, Honduras, El Salvador, and Nicaragua and had varying immigration statuses from undocumented to guest worker visa to legal permanent resident and U.S. citizen.

At Workers Defense Project, our central theory of change is that our fight must be led by those who are experiencing oppression—that our members are the ones who must lead that fight. This organizing philosophy draws heavily from the theory of popular education and Freirean pedagogy, which led us to see our members as the experts through their lived experience regardless of education and to see our role as organizers to facilitate a process where members' experiences and knowledge are prioritized and given the weight and expertise that they deserve. As an organizer, it was my role to facilitate dialogue with and between our members to develop a shared analysis of the powers and pressures that lead to abusive labor conditions. WDP members are, in Antonio Gramsci's sense, organic intellectuals who come by their knowledge not by study and books and earning degrees but by living their lives and reflecting on the larger forces that shape their individual experiences (Gramsci 1971, 15). This philosophy is central to the research model that we developed to undertake the *Building Austin, Building Injustice* study.

The Community Organizer (Emily)

I would be remiss not to explain a bit about who I am. My own background and experiences put me in a unique position to navigate the space between the academic world and our construction worker members. Originally from a small town outside of Baltimore, both of my parents are teachers. I grew up in a white, liberal, middle-class household that valued tolerance and education. I graduated from Brown University in 2003 with a degree in international development studies. Since graduation, I had worked at Casa Maryland (a worker center that recovered wages for immigrant workers just outside of DC) and then lived in Brazil for a year before I realized that my heart was in the fight back at home in the United States to take on the deep inequality that plagued our country—particularly the discriminatory treatment that immigrant workers faced and that I had witnessed firsthand during my time in college (as an ESL teacher) and at Casa Maryland. My international travel and my time working in U.S. immigrant communities had made abundantly clear that the privileges I had enjoyed growing up were not shared by most in the United States (much less so in the developing world) and that that inequality had everything to do with the privileges I enjoyed as a white, middle-class, cisgender woman.

When I began to organize with the Construction Worker Committee, I had been working with Texas immigrant workers for four years, had led our

Day Labor Committee to our first policy victory—defeating an antisolicitation ordinance that would have criminalized looking for work in public—and had assisted dozens of construction workers to recover their wages through community-based direct action tactics.

When we began to approach professors to put together the Academic Advisory Committee, I was able to put my Ivy League education and my college experience as a research assistant for a sociology professor to the service of our community organizing. My privilege allowed me to navigate the space between construction worker members, many of whom had no more than an elementary education, and the academics we needed to buy into the project. Throughout the project and throughout my organizing career, my role often has been to bridge the intentionally inaccessible spaces of academia and policy making in order to fully engage our members in those processes.

Institutional and individual racism have everything to do with the fact that my role is even needed: academia has a long history of devaluing the perspectives of communities about themselves and asserting that outside experts are needed to observe, document, and give meaning to the experiences of regular people. It was critically important to WDP that the *Building Austin* study didn't fall into that traditional dynamic of the passively studied community and the researchers as experts. We would approach the research with the same philosophy that we approached community organizing—that the movement must be led by those who are experiencing oppression.

The Academic Advisory Committee: More Than One Way to Be an Academic (Rich)

One key to the successful collaboration between WDP and UT academics was that all involved shared a fundamental understanding that real, progressive social change comes from people who are organized to fight against their own oppression. Traditional academic work (such as books, articles, and conference presentations)—however much it might impact conversations in the academy—on its own will not produce real social change. Real social change requires a different way to think about how to make the tools and resources of academic work meaningful. It needs to connect directly with everyday struggles of men and women and allow them to make their own knowledge and meaning using those tools. Typically, academics see themselves as producing new knowledge and having the final say about the meaning. Academics traditionally see their "expert" knowledge and meanings as superior and expect policy makers to pay deference to their views. They work with policy makers and other academics as their primary audience. This mode of knowledge production prevents most people from having influence and silences their voices. This is especially troublesome because history is littered with examples where "expert" views worked against the interests of oppressed people.

I and my colleagues who collaborated on this project tried to make the tools and resources of the academy available to people in their everyday struggles in ways that allow them to produce knowledge on their own. This is what the collaboration between academics at the University of Texas and WDP was designed to accomplish through the Academic Advisory Committee.

As Emily discussed, construction workers at WDP realized that they would need more than anecdotal information to expose the issues they were facing and the systematic nature of dangerous and poor working conditions in the construction industry. They needed credible data on the scope of problems in construction, and they needed systematic knowledge of the industry to understand the causes of, and therefore the solutions to, these problems. They needed research. Through college-educated staff, they contacted faculty at UT who were likely allies.

Perhaps knowing my background might help explain why I joined the *Building Injustice* project. I am a first-generation college graduate from a working-class family in northern California. My father made and sold slipcovers for a living, just as his parents had done. My mother worked at numerous entry-level jobs while I was growing up, including selling ads for newspapers and working as a bank teller. Eventually, she got a civil service job with the county, working in the local welfare office. We were lucky. My dad was a good salesman, and we were able to move to an affluent suburb, where I and my siblings got great educations that propelled us toward college.

At the same time, I was deeply aware of the class differences between the two places we had lived, feeling that we didn't quite "belong" in the affluent suburb—we weren't the "right" kind of people. Part of this feeling was that my parents weren't professionals, like so many of our neighbors, but part of this feeling was also because we were the only Jewish family in town and faced some mild discrimination and prejudice. As a child, these circumstances had a lasting impact on me, beginning a lifelong concern about social inequality and injustice. It was clear to me from an early age that just because someone was well educated and affluent does not mean that he or she had the only valid perspective on the world.

I went to UCLA as an undergraduate and eventually got my PhD in geography at the University of Washington (UW). At UW I became deeply involved in several social justice movements, including protests against the World Trade Organization in 1999 and a campaign to organize a union for student workers (which was ultimately successful). Even though I was working toward a career in academia, I did not accept the dominant idea that traditional academic work itself produces social change. Instead, I firmly believe that only by organizing regular people does real change occur. Part of this belief carries over into my teaching, which I view less as a forum where I tell students what to think than as an opportunity to show students how the tools of academia can be made useful to everyday struggles. Therefore, I viewed my position in the academy as somewhat at odds with the traditional idea of an academic. I wanted to make change possible—not in a top-down way by working directly with other academics and policy makers but in a bottom-up way by working with people engaged in social struggle.

When I came to the University of Texas in 2006, I began looking for community organizations working on social justice issues as partners for a class that I was teaching. I found WDP on a list of organizations willing to work with students on service learning projects. When I contacted them, they invited me to join their AAC, and I accepted.

Act 2: The Field Research

Critical Pedagogy: Community Ownership of Knowledge (Emily)

WDP staff and members knew the importance of our partnership with the University of Texas. We knew that if we were going to undertake a survey of construction working conditions, it had to be representative of the sector as a whole and that it had to meet all standards of academic rigor, including human subjects' protections and sound sampling methodology. Just like our members' lived experiences were disregarded as "outliers" and "a few bad-apple employers," our data would be disregarded as unsound or biased if we didn't ensure academic rigor in our methodology. But we also knew that the data had to belong to our members rather than be held and interpreted by our academic partners. We knew how previous academic-community partnerships had produced rich data sets for an initial report developed with community input but academic partners went on to use the data to publish additional reports that did not serve community priorities and in some cases even undermined them. Thus when we began to approach UT professors, we had an unusual proposal—we wanted them to be our full partners in developing the surveys, the interviews, and the sampling methodology; to work with us to collect the data in the field; and to interpret and analyze the resulting data, but in the end, we wanted the data to belong to WDP members, which meant that it couldn't be used without our permission.

Designing the Best Possible Methodology

Rich. WDP members identified the problems that needed investigation and defined the goals of the project, which was to produce knowledge that was useful to them in their struggles. Academics who wanted to partner with WDP agreed that the data and knowledge produced through the research project would be owned by WDP and not the academics (although they could use it, with the approval of WDP). This was not an academic-initiated project.

The academics primarily provided their methodological expertise—their experience of how to do research in ways that make valid and credible knowledge. The academics worked extensively with WDP to ensure that the research was carried out in a way that made findings both valid and useful. For example, WDP members wanted a comprehensive understanding of working conditions in the construction industry in Austin, but how to do that? Through conversations with members of the AAC, the research team recognized that the best way to find out what was happening on construction sites was to ask construction workers themselves, to systematically survey construction workers to get a picture of the industry as a whole. How were we to do that when construction sites are scattered across the city, some of them large commercial sites with many workers, some small residential sites with few, and so on? Academics were able to help identify a city database of all construction permits, listing location, scope, type, and size of project. Through this database, the team was able to create a "stratified random sample" of worksites that ensured that different parts of the city were covered and that different types and sizes of projects were covered. The academics helped identify and explain this type of approach, which matched the goals of WDP members. Through conversations with WDP and academics, we determined that three hundred surveys along with twenty in-depth interviews with workers and employers would suffice to give us a good picture of practices in the construction industry as a whole in Austin.

Because they had access to databases and extensive research libraries, the academics also helped gather existing data on the industry and other relevant information about the region. Several groups of students working in my geography courses pulled together and mapped demographic data, data on construction activity, economic data on cost of living, and reported violations of Occupation Health and Safety Administration (OSHA) regulations by construction companies. Other classes gathered policy and legal information about Austin and Texas as well as "best practices" examples from elsewhere.

Emily. The construction worker committee identified the research questions for the study. They determined what topics we should ask about, including wages, safety, training, access to breaks, immigration status, and so on.

As we set about designing the methodology with our worker members and academic partners, we realized that the construction industry posed a unique challenge to data collection. Sampling was based on the plan devised by the AAT, using permit data to randomly select construction sites. Construction sites themselves vary by size and complexity, from single-family residential sites with only a handful of workers to massive commercial sites with thousands working for different contractors. Safely approaching workers on these different sites and navigating contact with a hostile employer or high security on a larger site proved added challenges for the methodology.

Our construction worker members piloted the draft survey to each other and helped craft the questions in language that was accessible and current. When the formal word for scaffold (*el andamio*) in Spanish got us weird looks during the pilot study, our members gave us the best alternatives, including the more commonly used Spanglish term *escaffold*. When we tried to explain what prevailing wage was in one of the survey questions, they helped us craft the definition that would make sense to the average worker. It was our construction worker members who fine-tuned the protocol to approach workers on their lunch break or at the end of their shift to take the fifteen-minute survey. They tested the script to invite workers to participate and made tweaks to inspire confidence and trust while fully disclosing the study purposes. They worked with us to make sure the in-depth interview asked the right questions in the right way that would get interviewees to share key details about their experiences.

Rich. Some students also helped pilot test and administer the survey, conduct and transcribe interviews, and analyze data. Students did these activities as service learning classes, independent studies, parts of honors theses, internships, and as volunteer work. While they were learning discipline-relevant content (in geography, urban studies, anthropology, sociology, law, and others), students also learned how to work with community members to further social justice goals, learning that academics don't have all the answers—or even all the questions. When asked about their experiences, many said that working with real people on real problems in the "real world" made the work more compelling, relevant, meaningful, and memorable than other coursework.

Throughout the course of the study, WDP continued to consult with members of the AAC to make certain that the background research, survey, interviews, and so on were handled in ways consistent with the highest academic standards to ensure that the results would be valid and defensible against anticipated attacks by the construction industry. Members of the AAC spoke publicly to news organizations, on the radio, and to policy makers to explain both the credibility of the study and its significance, often urging specific policy outcomes, such as the rest break ordinance discussed by Emily in the following section.

Emily. In addition to student researchers, WDP members also administered the survey. They helped us to scope the randomly selected construction sites to make sure they were active before sending a research team out. Worker members were trained by the academic team to administer the surveys and were some of the most effective at convincing workers to participate in the survey. Conducting the survey proved to be transformative for many of our members who stepped into leadership and advocacy roles in their own communities by going out to talk to other workers about their experiences. Once the anonymous surveys were put away, members could also inform participants of their rights and let them know how they could come forward to report wage and safety violations. WDP construction worker members who participated in the survey became skilled educators and agitated other workers to join their efforts to create good construction jobs. They even recruited new members to the organization through their conversations at worksites. Equipped with the perspective of their own lived experiences, our members who participated as researchers in the study came to recognize their own expertise and leadership. Interview participants were selected through contacts at worksites but also from WDP members who had experienced many of the challenges revealed in the survey data.

Finally, when the surveys and interviews were completed and the AAC had produced the data tables, WDP members reviewed the aggregated findings and had the opportunity to interpret them and give meaning related to experiences in their workplaces. They discussed the findings and considered recommendations that could address those problems. The study found that one out of five construction workers experienced wage theft, less than half had workers' compensation coverage, 64 percent never had a formal safety training, and 41 percent did not get rest breaks. Presented with undeniable data supporting their own experiences, WDP members were energized to fight back. But one finding from the study shocked even our worker members. They had not realized just how deadly their sector was; Texas had 142 construction worker fatalities just in the year *Building Austin* came out. And the survey found that one in five workers had been injured on the job, requiring medical attention. Even our members were shocked at the incredible physical risk that Austin construction workers faced every day on the job.

I worked with the committee to look at the different policy options. What policies could we develop to confront these deadly conditions and widespread legal violations at the city level? What would have to be taken on at the state (a considerably daunting cause in Texas)? What policies had worked in other parts of the country? The data collection process flowed seamlessly into planning for the next step: what big campaign could we take on and win, armed with our data? While the final touches of drafting the report took place, the construction committee began to craft its campaign strategy to make Austin construction sites much safer.

Act 3: Policy and Organizing Victories

Impact of the Study Release (Emily)

The *Building Austin, Building Injustice* report was released with national attention in mid-June 2009. Just one week before the report came out, Austin was shocked by a deadly worksite accident when a mast-climber scaffold broke and three construction workers fell eleven stories. The accident illustrated the findings of the report, and when WDP members collected and lined up 142 pairs of boots in front of city hall to represent workers who had died in construction the previous year, our members placed three new pairs of boots to remember the workers who had just died. The release was covered by local, state, and national media, and the findings sent immediate shockwaves through the industry. In the months after the report, the U.S. House Education and Workforce Committee held a special hearing on the findings in Washington, DC, OSHA moved in to do a Texas worksite blitz that found more than $2 million in safety fines in just one month, and the OSHA region opened a new office in Austin. At the city level, Austin City Council members pledged to act on a myriad of safety proposals, kicking off a stakeholder process that resulted in requiring OSHA trainings on all city of Austin sites and launched the campaign to win rest breaks for Austin construction workers.

Thirsting for Justice: The Fight for Rest Breaks

Following the release of the *Building Austin* report, the construction committee decided on a policy proposal to require rest breaks for construction workers. Riding on the momentum of the study, the committee members crafted a proposal that required a minimum ten-minute break for every four hours of uninterrupted work. Throughout the summer, committee members highlighted the risks of working in the Texas sun without rest breaks, doing interviews with Univision and Telemundo about the risks of heat illness in construction. Throughout the fall, the committee members participated in a stakeholder process alongside construction industry representatives to build consensus on safety policies that the city of Austin could adopt based on the study findings.

The city-facilitated process revealed some challenges in making policy change. The meetings dragged on with contractor associations enumerating the many reasons they couldn't afford to provide rest breaks while at the same time insisting that their contractors already provided them. After nine months of stakeholder input, the city quietly wrote OSHA ten-hour and thirty-hour safety trainings into their contracting requirements, handing off a minor victory to the workers. But city council was still unwilling to act on the issue of rest breaks. As the temperature crept upward in May 2010, WDP members were looking at another summer without a right to a rest break. They began to think about how to escalate pressure on city council. They planned a series of meetings with council members, presenting them with the study data again. Meanwhile, they contacted Univision to run a PSA on heat safety and pitched stories about workers not receiving breaks while working in the hot Texas summer. They finally got traction with a few council offices that agreed that Texas construction workers shouldn't face another summer without the right to rest, and they requested draft language for a rest break policy. The construction committee began to plan a direct action to shame the rest of council into supporting the policy; in mid-June they would hold a thirst strike in front of Austin city hall. Participants would sit outside in the heat and decline to drink water to make the point that just a few short hours in the heat could be exhausting. There would be medical professionals on hand to make sure no one became dangerously dehydrated. At sundown, the thirst strikers would break the fast with a water ceremony. Construction committee members also wrote and performed monologues describing their working conditions in construction.

The action was a resounding success, and that day the council passed a resolution directing city staff to draft a rest break ordinance by the time the council returned from summer break at the end of July. While the council was out, WDP members and organizers met with city staff and hashed out a draft policy. As an organizer, the policy-making process was transformative for me. Our members, many of whom had only a rudimentary education, pored over the first draft from the city that we translated for them. Our members identified a gaping loophole that never would have occurred to me, since I have never worked a day on a construction site. They realized that unless the policy explicitly stated that the rest breaks had to be taken separately from a lunch break, employers would just say that they were meeting the rest break requirement by giving a lunch break. Based on this, we provided language to the city that ultimately was adopted into the policy. I realized that when community members were directly involved in crafting a policy, not only was it more inclusive and reflective of community needs, but it was actually a *better* policy. On July 29, 2010, Austin City Council unanimously passed the country's first city rest break standard, over the opposition of contractor associations and industry representatives who claimed workers already got rest breaks. But data from *Building Austin, Building Injustice* proved otherwise, and council members couldn't justify inaction. The victory was a watershed moment for Texas construction workers, winning unprecedented lifesaving protections and regulating an industry in a state that is loath to regulate business.

But the Construction Worker Committee wasn't done with just a victory in Austin. In 2011, they took their fight to the Texas state capitol, using the data from the study to pass the Texas Wage Theft Act, which created criminal penalties for employers who commit wage theft under the Texas Penal Code. The enormity of a statewide victory for immigrant construction workers cannot be overstated; the Texas legislature is one of the most anti-immigrant, antiworker legislative bodies in the nation.

How was participation in a study like this transformative for academic partners? Unlike most academic work, measured in publications and student credit hours, working on *Building Austin, Building Injustice* gave me the chance to see how a truly different kind of academic work could have important implications for social justice struggles. Like students who reported that working on "real-world" problems makes the partnership more meaningful, the concrete changes to people's working lives that came out of the project made it more meaningful to me than the "purely academic" work that often consumed my days. Furthermore, it showed me how to engage students in work that furthers social justice instead of merely preaching about it. It was also work that contributed not simply to policy changes, however important those are—and they are—but to capacity building and organizing among some of the most exploited workers in the United States, work that is now transforming the struggle for immigrants' rights, as leaders and advocates from WDP's membership shift their focus in response to attacks by the Trump administration.

Conclusion

Overall, the campaign successes flowing from the research seem to validate the theory with which we entered the project: communities impacted by injustice need to play a leading role in driving the knowledge production process. Academics played an important but secondary role in helping support the construction worker community in their struggles. This process put immigrant Latino construction workers' voices at the center, countering dominant race and class dynamics that tend to marginalize and silence them. However, academics also played a strategic role in legitimizing the research, using their speaking authority to lend validity to the project. Although strategically necessary, this move might be viewed as contrary to the centering of construction workers. We are both conscious of this contradiction, but we saw the opportunity to harness the expertise and respect commanded by academics in places of power like city hall or the Texas capitol. We chose to use that to our advantage. More work is needed to challenge the status quo, where workers' voices are considered less "expert" than academics'.

The study served as a foundation for WDP members to build our organizing campaigns and strategy. It helped us make data-driven decisions about which injustices in the construction industry to take on first and what strategies we use to address them. We have repeatedly gone back to the data and findings of *Building Injustice* to make the case for local and state policies to strengthen worker protections. The study proved extremely useful in driving forward our members' policy priorities and making headway in an industry sector that had been resistant to change. So much so that WDP and the academic team reconvened in 2012 to conduct a similar study to document construction working conditions in five Texas cities. That study, *Build a Better Texas* (2013), set the tone for future local- and state-level policy fights. *Build a*

Better Texas led to passage of a state law cracking down on the misclassification of workers as independent contractors in 2013, a Dallas rest break ordinance in 2015, and other construction policy victories in central Texas requiring standards like workers' compensation coverage, safety training, living wages, training opportunities, local hiring goals, and independent worksite monitoring under WDP's Better Builder program. To date, the Better Builder program has improved working conditions on more than $2 billion worth of construction projects in central Texas.

The *Build a Better Texas* model of research and its subsequent victories gained such attention that in 2016, WDP teamed up with national partners, Partnership for Working Families, to conduct a study of construction working conditions in six southern cities (Houston, Dallas, Charlotte, Atlanta, Nashville, and Miami). The resulting study, *Build a Better South*, documented widespread safety and wage abuses across these cities. In each of the cities outside of Texas, WDP partnered with a local membership-based organization to teach the participatory methodology. In each of those cities, members played a central role in conducting the surveys and deciding how to use the resulting data. In addition to collecting a valuable data set on southern construction workers, WDP and academic partners aimed to share the methodology of participatory research with partners across the South so that they could utilize this important tool to advance their own local campaigns. By growing the base of organizations and academics who are willing to push back against the norm that knowledge must be produced and held by academics, we hope to redefine who is the expert and lend due credit to the organic intellectuals whose lived experiences and self-determined priorities should be driving our efforts to produce knowledge and fight for protections for their own communities.

References

Cox, Lauren, Emily Timm, and Cristina Tzintzún. 2009. *Building Austin Building Injustice*. Austin: Division of Diversity and Community Engagement at University of Texas at Austin.

Gramsci, Antonio. 1971. *Selections from the Prison Notebooks*. New York: International Publishers.

Part III

Language, Literacy, and Heritage

• • • • • • • • • • • • • • • • • • • •

Language is a core element in the Sociological Initiatives Foundation's (SIF) mission. This includes aid to indigenous groups seeking to preserve and expand their languages. A related goal is cultural preservation and defense of spiritual resources. The two chapters in this part are both about Native American issues, and both are situated in the same region of the United States. However, the concerns in these two pieces are similar to problems facing tribes across the United States. Native American sovereignty and rights vested in treaties upheld by nineteenth-century landmark legal decisions are under renewed pressures. Encroachment on tribal resources and denial of voting rights have been prominent news stories. Academic and civic alliances, combined with the power of research and technology, offer ways to help protect tribal rights and preserve cultural heritage.

12

Mobilizing and Organizing Nimiipuu to Protect the Environment

• •

Fighting to Protect Ancestral Lands in Idaho

LEONTINA HORMEL, JULIAN
MATTHEWS, ELLIOTT MOFFETT,
CHRIS NORDEN, AND
LUCINDA SIMPSON

Nimiipuu Protecting the Environment (NPtE) organizes cultural activities to restore cultural knowledge and build coalitions with different indigenous groups and nontribal allies. Our chapter explores these experiences and discusses the benefits we attribute to Sociological Initiatives Foundation's (SIF) community approach to funding research. NPtE has taken significant steps toward coordinating and strengthening Nimiipuu voices in environmental movements and policy. Our work seeks to build information we may communicate to ensure Nimiipuu empowerment and improve our connections with different tribe members and across different audiences. SIF helped us document Nimiipuu perspectives and experiences through interviews, surveys, and visual work. Participants' contributions illuminate Nimiipuu life experiences in northern Idaho and the close connections between their livelihoods, social relations, and environmental conditions. The research information was used in fall 2016 to substantiate our organization's and community members' views that oversized, industrial transportation—what locals call "megaloads"— should be barred from our ancestral lands.

NPtE has worked to build connections across different communities and institutions located in the ancestral lands of the Nimiipuu, a tribe commonly referred to as Nez Perce, whose ancestral lands span along the Columbia, Snake, and Clearwater Watersheds in northern Idaho and the Pacific Northwest United States. Though our backgrounds differ, all of us who are writing this chapter share a commitment to protecting these lands and Nimiipuu traditions. We work to reduce environmental harm and dismantle the structures and processes that have silenced indigenous people in decisions affecting their livelihoods.

Most of our organizing followed antimegaload protests led by the Nez Perce Tribe that started August 5, 2013—a significant moment for the region when a diverse group of people converged to form a blockade against an ExxonMobil megaload shipment destined to cross the Nez Perce Reservation and through the National Wild and Scenic Rivers System–designated U.S. Highway 12 corridor. As part of this organizing, we sought support from the Sociological Initiatives Foundation (SIF) for research and education, developed and conducted by Nimiipuu members, to do at least three things. First, to build NPtE's capacity to collect information about tribe members that could be used for tribal and state policy decision-making. Second, to build Nimiipuu community understanding of the tribe's history, place, community, and treaty rights. Third, to build regional, national, and international alliances with indigenous peoples and advocates for indigenous peoples. We stayed true to the intent of the project and, as is described by three of NPtE's founding members, NPtE has grown its efforts to protect and restore Nimiipuu culture. In the following section, we describe our different roles in this effort, from the first-person perspectives of NPtE founders and cultural educators as well as nontribal public academics.

Elliott Moffett, Nimiipuu Protecting the Environment Cofounder and Board President

I cofounded NPtE with Julian Matthews, and we are both Nez Perce Tribe members. And for those who don't know the "story" of the Nez Perce, we call ourselves Nimiipuu, which translates to the "People." We began NPtE in response to rumors—and then confirmed news—of plans for megaloads to go through our reservation on U.S. Highway 12 starting in 2013. The 1863 Nez

Perce Tribe / Nimiipuu Reservation is located in what is now north central Idaho, a diminished version of the original Treaty of 1855 reservation. Both Julian and I are currently employed by the tribe but do not in any way represent the tribal government, except in our roles as tribal employees.

Megaloads are gigantic pieces of transport equipment that largely head for the tar sands extraction areas of Canada. We knew that the particular tar sands were located in proximity to indigenous communities near Fort McMurray in Alberta. And we knew that no consultation, let alone approvals, had been obtained to mine the tar sands and negatively affect the Dene Athabascan First Nations indigenous populations there.

In our traditional ecological knowledge (TEK), we know that everything is connected. We knew, therefore, that such a thing could happen here too. No consultation had taken place with tribal members or the tribe prior to the decision to move these potentially destructive pieces of equipment through Nimiipuu territory.

The Nimiipuu are known for the Appaloosa horse and our horsemanship. And we are river people. We led the Lewis and Clark Expedition through the hills and valleys of our territory, along the Clearwater River and farther on. It was our knowledge of the region's geography that assisted that expedition, and it is that same intimate knowledge and understanding of where we live and how we live with Mother Earth that Julian and I wanted to get represented.

And it was with such knowledge that we knew that if an accident did occur on that river highway, serious environmental degradation would surely ensue. We have had cold, clean, fast-running rivers, creeks, and streams, which supported a wide diversity of life. This must be protected. We appreciated the activism of like-minded individuals who joined the four-day rolling blockade of U.S. Highway 12 in August 2013 and the tribal members and tribal government representatives who helped stop megaloads from violating Nimiipuu Territory.

What we have been taught again and again by our elders and by repeated experience is that we must be vigilant in the protection of Mother Earth. We are, therefore, active in other environmental/social movements as well, such as the recovery of the salmon and steelhead species that travel to the ocean and back to the headwaters located in Nimiipuu Territory, serving as a cornerstone of our culture and traditional diet. Activism entails encouraging others to be civic minded and to work with others to protect Mother Earth. As cofounders of NPtE, we feel we have a responsibility to youth to help educate them in matters not learned in public schools. And therefore, the mission of Nimiipuu Protecting the Environment is to help educate young Nimiipuu about TEK.

We are inclusive of intertribal and nontribal youth and appreciate diversity of ideas and cultures. We believe that with community member involvement and input, better decisions will be made. As I said, the megaloads decision was made without consultation. The voice of the Nimiipuu was not asked for or heard.

Thus we embarked on the SIF-funded study of Nimiipuu cultural and environmental values, especially for up-river Nimiipuu in the eastern part of our lands, heading toward Montana along the Upper Clearwater and Lochsa Rivers. Such a study was not conducted by any of the involved state or federal agencies prior to the megaloads decision, and still none has been done by any governmental entities that must review and approve highway uses. The Nimiipuu know the river corridors and know if one of the gargantuan pieces of equipment is tipped over in tight stream valleys, getting crane equipment to the site to lift and move such equipment may not even be possible.

And as a treaty tribe, we knew that no analysis was conducted about the impacts, potential and real, to treaty-protected rights. The Nimiipuu still hold treaty rights to mean treaty responsibilities as well. It is our responsibility as sentient beings to do our best to live in balance. And that includes protecting the environment that "houses" such species as anadromous fish and their habitat.

If an environmental disaster were to take place from the movement of megaloads, the Nimiipuu will be the most impacted; our lives and souls are tied to Mother Earth. We are continuing to plan and organize to best protect the vast Nimiipuu Territory, which stretches from Buffalo Country to the Columbia River.

Leontina Hormel, Public Sociologist

I entered this project as a public sociologist, a person balancing one role as an environmental justice activist and another as an academic researcher. Conventional wisdom in the western scientific paradigm is to avoid advocacy, since advocacy is political and may channel personal bias into the research process. I take this concern seriously, though I am among those community action researchers who argue that scientific integrity is maintained if I am honest about my political position on an issue and follow transparent steps in designing and conducting research. I work at a university located on Nimiipuu lands and for several years have followed the politics tied to the Nez Perce Tribe's treaty rights and the State of Idaho's narrow focus on economic development. I joined another public academic, Chris Norden, on August 5, 2013, to support Nimiipuu at a late-night, antimegaload blockade right at U.S. Highway 12's western entrance to the Nez Perce Reservation.

As Elliott described earlier, the August 2013 blockades against the Omega Morgan (a subsidiary of General Electric) megaload shipment on U.S. Highway 12 arose from undemocratic decision-making between the State of Idaho and corporate stakeholders (refer to Hormel 2016 for details about this case). Though the highway winds tightly through two land areas regulated by legal bodies above and outside the State of Idaho, transportation permit deals were made without their consultation and authorization. This behavior continued even after the federal district court ordered all parties to desist from megaload activity on the highway until the U.S. Forest Service (USFS) followed protocol to

1 determine if such industrial-scale transportation fit within federally mandated criteria for maintaining a "wild and scenic" river corridor,
2 conduct an ethnographic "corridor values" study of populations affected by commercial and industrial traffic along U.S. Highway 12, and
3 consult with the sovereign nation of the Nez Perce and seek the tribe's authorization.

As the Omega Morgan megaload traveled to the Nez Perce Reservation boundary in early August 2013, USFS had not completed these steps.

For Nimiipuu and anyone critical of power relations, it was evident that USFS's consultation with the Nez Perce Tribe was problematic. The executive committee members for the Nez Perce Tribe do not represent the full range of views about politics and economics in the region. Moreover, the ethnographic study of environmental values the USFS staff conducted included only a small number of Nez Perce. Of forty-six people interviewed for the USFS study, only seven were Nimiipuu, and it was unclear how USFS selected them. I could see these problems from the outside, but I was unsure how to approach Nimiipuu activists about helping conduct research, transparently collected and analyzed, that drew a more representative sample of Nimiipuu, which would provide the Nez Perce Tribe more robust data. Scientifically gathered data would help the tribe's leadership present a case when consulted about megaload shipments in their ancestral lands. As much as I wanted to advocate for Nimiipuu, I also did not want to be another university researcher who imposed an agenda that Nimiipuu did not solicit.

Nimiipuu activists like Julian Matthews, Elliott Moffett, Paulette Smith, Lucinda Simpson, and Diane Mallickan were thinking like I was, and they were determined to maintain and spread the spark of Nimiipuu resistance and self-determination that the blockades lit up among tribal community members. Tribe members, both in Nimiipuu country and across the Northwest, were inspired by the blockades. In July 2014, the year following the blockades, NPtE conducted a strategic meeting with tribal and nontribal people that set organizational goals. One key goal was developing a response to the USFS values study, one that would focus on Nimiipuu cultural and environmental connections to the area. At the meeting, I offered to apply for SIF funding to conduct a study by and for Nimiipuu. I was nervous about making the proposal, but the idea was well received and OK'd.

For the SIF grant, we proposed a photovoice project. Nimiipuu researchers would be paired—one senior with one youth—to recruit and interview Nimiipuu members. Nimiipuu research participants would photograph significant places in the region as well as culturally important activities associated with the area. Nimiipuu participants would share their perspectives while showing photos—yielding both visual and narrative accounts. This original design's complexity did not meld well with the realities of people's hectic lives and dispersed living locations. Nimiipuu researchers who were most passionate about conducting this research were also most likely to be supporting their family and the community in a variety of ways. The work of recruiting and traveling to people's homes scattered throughout Nimiipuu territory was difficult to manage given life's daily demands. In many ways, the challenges researchers faced perhaps illuminated the reasons the USFS researchers chose to limit the scope of interviews with Nimiipuu. It takes time to do this work thoughtfully and well.

Faced with these practical challenges, we broadened our research to include a survey (total completed = 187). We distributed printed surveys at major Nez Perce Tribe events (e.g., general councils and powwows), through social networks (referral sampling), via the Nez Perce Tribe electronic help desk, at Native American student centers at Lewis-Clark State College and University of Idaho, and in the Nimiipuu newspaper *Ta'c Tito'oqan News*. Most mainstream audiences and policy makers recognize survey work as credible and are familiar with how to interpret findings. In contrast, the small sample sizes characteristic of qualitative methods like photovoice often provoke challenges that the findings are not "significant." We gained footing with a broader range of interests with a larger sample size and a research tool that provided easy-to-interpret findings.

SIF's approach to funding was advantageous, and the organization's staff treated us with a great deal of trust. We received our grant funding that we split between NPtE for education programming and a research budget at my university. My university monitored my activity, but other than that, SIF did not push a short turnaround date between project launch and project closure—a limitation of government funding and many larger funding entities. We had the time and resource flexibility to adjust our methodological approach. I was able to work with passionate Nimiipuu researchers without applying external pressures to "work faster" that would have interfered with cultivating our personal relationships and could have sunk the project. I believe that research with populations that have been silenced and marginalized historically must be done slowly. Public university research work should emphasize social connection and meaningful relationships among researchers and community members. Relationships are meaningful if they are reciprocal, and they take time.

One of our major victories at the federal and state level is that USFS halted the transport of megaloads in December 2016. Part of the credit goes to our SIF-funded research, since we were armed with research data that helped us craft a report we submitted during public comment solicitation to the Idaho Transportation Department (ITD) and USFS. Further, I believe this research reflected closely the intent to conduct research by and for Nimiipuu. The purpose of my work is to learn how to decenter the university researcher's gaze and open space for Nimiipuu voices.

Lucinda Simpson, Tribal Elder and NPtE Board Member

Many of our tribal women were part of the megaloads protests in 2013. Some got their children involved but made sure they were safe. Today many American Indian women are involved with issues that affect the environment, because as tribal people, we see ourselves as keepers of the land and our Mother Earth. For example, LaDonna Brave Bull Allard is an activist and leader in the 2016 Dakota Access Pipeline protests. Allard feared that the tribe's historic sites and water supply were at risk. She founded the Sacred Stone Camp, the first camp of the #NoDAPL movement. Winona LaDuke (Anishannabe) is another American Indian woman who is highly acclaimed for her environmental and political activism. She comes from the White Earth reservation in Northern Minnesota and assisted in starting Honor the Earth and White Earth Land Recovery Project, which Winona LaDuke directed in Minnesota.

Earth Land Recovery Project

Paulette Smith is one of our Nez Perce women activists in opposition to anything that infringes upon our tribal lands, a tribal woman who brought her daughters and her grandson Nathan to the megaloads protest to show them what fighting for our Mother Earth is all about. Her grandson is my great-grandson. Paulette was arrested for megaloads protesting in August 2013 and went to jail for it. She paid for her own court costs and is still willing to do it again if the need arises.

I, as a Nez Perce tribal elder, am very proud of these women who take a stand to protect our sovereignty and treaty rights and our tribal lands and waters. I myself didn't hear about the megaloads protest until it was over, but I got involved with the public meetings and events after those first megaloads protests. As a former police officer, I used to write tickets for oversized loads like the megaloads, but the megaloads shipments changed the legal standards for being oversized. They also received escorts by Idaho State Police when traveling Idaho state routes.

In the past I have taken a stand for tribal lands in areas where I have worked or studied. While in Crownpoint, New Mexico, I became involved with Navajo tribal elders who were fighting against a mine being put on Spirit Mountain. They spoke about the younger prodevelopment tribe members who were supporting the mine because those younger Navajo could only see dollar signs in their eyes and not the aftermath of the damage to a known sacred mountain. They were also concerned about the soil and land that they had been raised near and the damage to fresh mountain spring water.

While I was living and working for American Indian tribes of Northern California in Alturas, California, the tribal people there were trying to protect another sacred site, the source of rich volcanic glass stones that had traditionally been used by those tribes to make arrowheads. Today there are signs on the mountain that protect the sacred stones from would-be collectors put up by the U.S. Forest Service. The punishment is a fine or jail time.

In recent times I am supportive of the Idaho-based group Friends of the Clearwater in their efforts to protect inland northwest waterways and land from damage to Mother Earth, and I serve on their board of directors. I also have worked to support Wild Idaho Rising Tide, especially to stop oil spills by rail shipments from North Dakota and Wyoming en route to Pacific coast terminals.

While traveling to a commemoration of Sitting Bull descendants' adoption of the Nimiipuu people, I got acquainted with some of the Lakota tribal elders. And when the #NoDAPL movement in opposition to the Dakota Access Pipeline came along, I had strong feelings for those Lakota elders and their treaty rights and water protection.

Today many of our Nez Perce have gotten an education in higher learning, including some at master and doctorate levels. This is of value as it assists Nimiipuu tribal people when it comes to educating others about our culture, traditions, language, and ecosystems. The education a tribal member achieves among tribal family, extended family, and community is a lifetime of learning. Once you are born, you learn from viewing things outside your cradle board, from being propped up or hung up indoors or outdoors to being packed on the back of your mother in your cradle board to observe the world.

When small you are given a doll dressed in tribal clothing and are taught how to take care of her. Next you learn about the sweat lodge and what it means to our people to be of clean mind, body, and soul. I was taught how to make moccasins visually by sitting beside my great-grandmother by the woodstove, observing her making moccasins until I had a sense of how to make them, a cultural/traditional teaching I can now pass along to those willing to learn. As children we learned much about respecting Mother Earth, nature and animals and birds, and other human beings. We learned how to gather foods and hunt and care for our wild game we were fed.

Today NPtE is trying to reintroduce some of our cultural/traditional arts and crafts, along with our value system of the past and present, to our people young and old. We have presenters and local teachers explaining how to be better keepers of the land through protection from oil spills to cleaning up the Hanford Nuclear Reservation on the Columbia River in the best way we can. We have learned about the bee, the monarch butterfly, and the grizzly bear, which have been on the brink of extinction. We have had discussions on how to restore and bring back some of our traditional plants and fish. We have also learned that it is good to connect with many agencies to work toward our future goals of educating people about being better keepers of Mother Earth and her inhabitants.

During the time I attended Lewis-Clark State College in Lewiston, Idaho, another Nimiipuu tribal woman named Velda Penney and I put on a first-ever Nimiipuu-language watch, as we had concerns about the possibility of a lost language. That was one attempt to bring the language back and gain awareness from our Nimiipuu tribal community. Bessie Scott was one of the tribal women in attendance at our language watch and has been teaching Nimiipuu language, from early childhood development classes on the reservation to college classes at Lewis-Clark State College.

As a part of our cultural preservation, we are working on teaching tribal members how to make canoes and canoe paddles and women's wing dresses and shawls that are a part of our traditional regalia. Some of the paddle artwork of the American Indian has been lost since the tribes lost their lands with the Western Expansion settler movement in the 1800s. Today Nimiipuu culture is being revived, along with the cultural and traditional ways of other native peoples. Some of the west coastal tribes have managed to hang on to totem and paddle carvings, much the same as we in NPtE are returning the art of paddle making and design to our people. The canoe is one way of bringing back a lost art of the Nimiipuu tribal people.

We lecture throughout our local communities about traditional ways and traditional foods such as roots and salmon, including different ways to cook and prepare these traditional foods. We also keep the tribal government abreast of what we are doing; all our environmental summit events and canoe-building workshops are open for them to observe and share their insights with our tribal people.

Julian Matthews, Nimiipuu Protecting the
Environment Cofounder and Board Member

We began the Nimiipuu Canoe Project after witnessing other tribal canoe families from the Kalispel, Duwamish, Colville, Spokane, Puyallup, Tulalip peoples during the 2016 Free the Snake Flotilla at Wawawai Landing. We discussed the issue with some tribal members and other people and arranged to harvest the cedar and white fir logs through the Nez Perce tribal executive committee, who submitted a USDA Forest Service "special-use permit." We acquired two trees but could only retrieve the white fir.

The canoe idea goes along with the movement to remove dams on the lower Snake River that impede the flow of the Snake and Columbia Rivers, leading to possible extinction of salmon runs within our treaty area. When we saw the connection between the harvest of wood from our treaty areas and the tradition of river travel to hunt, fish, gather, and visit our families and relatives, canoes took on a new importance to our group. The use of canoes goes way back in our tribal culture, as it was the most effective mode of transportation for the Nimiipuu. When we looked at the Nimiipuu canoes housed at Nez Perce National Historical Park's Spalding, Idaho, headquarters, we were even more intrigued by this history and the question of how or why canoe carving had disappeared from Nimiipuu culture.

Seeing and meditating on canoes that were more than one hundred years old further inspired us to begin this journey to carve a canoe. Bringing back the canoe tree from a traditional treaty area has as much significance as the language, dance, music, and other aspects of our Nimiipuu culture. As we saw a vast number of tribes that have just started carving canoes, along with tribes on the west side who have continued this tradition among their people, we felt that doing this was something that could bring together elders, adults, and tribal youth. Learning to carve canoes and related cultural and environmental issues—including water, land, and forest protections within our treaty areas—would also ensure that youth particularly understand how critical it is to protect traditional Treaty of 1855 areas. As we have strong ties to the land, water, and forests, the use of cedar and other tree species has been a historically important part of our Nimiipuu culture and customs.

Since we have an inherent physical and spiritual tie to Mother Earth, we felt it was an important part of our tribal sovereignty to exercise this treaty right as part of our culture. We want to continue harvesting trees for canoes as an important part of our culture, and we want to ensure that tribal youth continue this practice for carving of canoes. Since I began this canoe journey as a Nez Perce (Nimiipuu) tribe member, it has brought me pride to have about thirty mostly tribal first through fifth graders from Lapwai Elementary come every week over the last school year to work on, learn about, and experience the carving of a traditional Nez Perce dugout canoe.

We are finishing our first dugout canoe and will be able to resume traveling on the rivers and waterways for the same purposes as our ancestors. Our tribal community and our youth will be able to experience something that most of us never have in our lifetimes: to travel in a Nimiipuu-constructed dugout canoe as our people did for years prior to the installation of hydroelectric dams. The issue of the dams again affects canoe journeys in being able to go through the dam locks, a major hurdle we'll have to deal with in much the same way as do the salmon that are born up in our area of the Clearwater, Lochsa, and Selway Rivers. These fish must "fight" their way through the dams and the hydroelectric power grid as they make their way back to their homeland and birthplace or spawning grounds.

The rivers have for centuries provided us with transportation, subsistence fishing, and other opportunities up and down the rivers. As we fight to remove the four lower Snake River dams, we have joined with other tribal members, tribal canoe families, and non-Indian environmental groups to strengthen our numbers in this battle to restore the rivers and protect the salmon and other fish that inhabit the water.

When we started our Nimiipuu Protecting the Environment group, we focused on the issue of sovereignty as it applied to our tribe and for organizing grassroots efforts to expand knowledge of our Treaty of 1855 area and ensure that we push future generations to protect and preserve these critical areas. Since the inception of the Nimiipuu Canoe Project, we have had numerous visits from tribal and nontribal visitors who were interested in the tribe or the canoe project or who wanted to take pictures and videos of work on the canoe. We have made many more connections with tribal canoe families up and down the Columbia River and have good relations with groups involved in pushing for removal of lower four Snake River dams. As we continue the Treaty of 1855 protection and environmental work that we have started, use of the canoe as a "statement" of solidarity with those fish and other animals that depend on the water for their sustenance is a major aspect of our campaign. As we work with other tribes who are also fighting for restoration of the waterways to their natural state, we feel that exercising this traditional cultural activity will enhance our drive and commitment to defend the treaty rights for future generations.

Chris Norden, Friends of the Clearwater Board Member

The resistance movement that formed in anticipation of the 2013 shipment of Alberta-bound megaloads across Nez Perce Treaty of 1855 lands, including

National Wild and Scenic Rivers System–designated parts of the Nez Perce-Clearwater National Forest, raised important questions about effective collaboration between tribal and nontribal grassroots environmental organizations. In particular, the question faced by locally based nontribal ally groups like Friends of the Clearwater (FOC) and Fighting Goliath, as well as other regional groups like Save Our Wild Salmon and Idaho Rivers United, was how to most effectively support tribal protesters asserting their sovereignty and treaty rights while at the same time maintaining focus on our own mission and longer-term wildlands protection and conservation goals.

With the guidance of our three-person staff, FOC's board of directors came to understand that our effectiveness as part of a tribal/nontribal coalition hinged almost completely on relationship building, because if we lacked this, any attempts to cooperate with information sharing, strategy, logistics, and so forth would likely fail. Once the process of getting to know our tribal activist counterparts went deeper, the first realization was that we have much more in common with tribal environmental groups like NPtE than we had realized. Both groups seek to protect native ecosystems and watersheds for future generations and view these things as axiomatic and nonnegotiable goods. We also believe the current bureaucratic-political model of public land management systematically distorts, undermines, and silences the public interest and its citizen advocates.

The second realization is that federally recognized tribal treaty rights are powerful conservation tools when effectively asserted and enforced. As FOC ecosystem defense director Gary Macfarlane puts it, "Building longer-term individual relationships across cultural lines is the only antidote to the current era we're in, especially via grassroots groups like Nimiipuu Protecting the Environment and Friends of the Clearwater. Grassroots groups like FOC are more able to cooperate with grassroots tribal activists and tribal governments than their big green counterparts." This collaboration involves information sharing with NPtE as well as tribal government and various tribal agencies such as the Nez Perce Tribe's Watershed Division and Fisheries Department.

The third realization is common to virtually all social justice movements—namely, that we are stronger when we stand together. FOC membership and development director Ashley Lipscomb's observation from the August 2013 blockade and arrests speaks to this idea: "The cops [Idaho State Patrol] were absolutely trying to separate tribal from nontribal people, to eliminate that solidarity as a deliberate tactic. 'If you're not tribal, you need to get out of the road.' But physical separation doesn't separate us."

Five years after the four nights of antimegaloads blockades on U.S. 12 in August 2013, four of the eleven seats on Friends of the Clearwater's board of directors were filled by tribal activists. The current FOC board includes the three NPtE coauthors of this chapter, plus Renee Holt (Nez Perce/Dine), with whom I traveled to the third night of the U.S. 12 protests along with Renee's teenage daughter and Pat Rathmann, a local nontribal elder and activist who had twice journeyed with Renee to Fort McMurray, Alberta, for annual Tar Sands Healing Walks.

FOC's history of working with Nez Perce activists dates to the 1992–1998 campaign to protect the Cove-Mallard roadless area in central Idaho from clearcutting, as well as the 1995 Gray Wolf reintroduction, which saw the Nez Perce Tribe as designated comanager with U.S. Fish and Wildlife following the State of Idaho's refusal to participate. In the early years of that recovery project, Nez Perce activist Levi Holt joined the FOC board, to be followed in the early 2000s by fellow tribe members James Holt and Julian Matthews.

Simply put, nothing builds relationships, understanding, and respect as much as working and standing together in solidarity and protest, particularly in defense of wildlands and species and the traditional indigenous values that hold these things as supreme goods whose integrity and survival must not be sacrificed for any reason.

They have a lot at stake there; they were brave enough to stand in front of that megaload. The tribal women still had a calmness in them, the mothers with their children, in a calm but firm stance. A real lesson to be learned, the way they held their presence in the face of big corporations, and even their own tribal government, willing to bring their own family into that kind of nonviolent direct action context.

—Ashley Lipscomb

This sort of cooperation is essential because we're headed for a cliff that will take a lot of critters with us if we don't fundamentally alter our relationship with other species and create a more radical discourse.

—Gary Macfarlane

Following the 2013 megaload protests, Friends of the Clearwater's collaboration with Nimiipuu Protecting the Environment has continued along a variety of avenues, from cosponsored public education events and public policy panel discussions to forest monitoring of proposed U.S. Forest Service timber sales and water quality-based appeals of USFS management plans. Perhaps the most visible and innovative collaboration has been a series of annual Free the Snake Flotilla events featuring a multiday encampment; hundreds of canoes, kayaks, and other human-powered watercraft; and tribal elders and other speakers calling for the breaching of the four lower Snake River hydroelectric dams as part of a comprehensive program to recover the salmon and steelhead runs that the tribal people of this region have depended on for millennia as a key food source and an irreplaceable cultural cornerstone.

"Working closely with the Nimiipuu and Nimiipuu Protecting the Environment to breach the four lower Snake River dams has been an enlightening experience," says Brett Haverstick, education and outreach director for Friends of the Clearwater and flotilla organizer. "We come from different cultures and look at the world through different lenses, and yet this partnership has taught us about how much we have in common. There is incredible value in that. Breaching the four lower Snake River dams and beginning the largest wild salmon restoration project in the world is an exciting and daunting task. The Nimiipuu Protecting the Environment activists and other Nimiipuu people have taught me, however, that overcoming long odds is a way of life and something that can be done."

In twenty-first-century American Indian country, environmental activism is of a piece with defense of tribal sovereignty, treaty rights, culture, and language. Citing the United States v. Winans case (1905), Nez Perce activist Gary Dorr brings the role of tribal environmental advocacy and protest back to the fundamental question of reserved treaty rights, a recurring theme voiced by respondents to the SIF-funded Nimiipuu Cultural and Environmental Values survey project. Dorr reminds us that treaties between Native American tribes and the U.S. federal government enumerate certain rights *given by tribes* to the federal government, with all other unenumerated rights being retained as reserved treaty rights. "Everything else, we kept."[1]

Note

1   See https://radiofreemoscow.org/2016/10/20161021/.

References

Hormel, Leontina. 2016. "Nez Perce Defending Treaty Lands in Northern Idaho." *Peace Review* 28 (1): 76–83.

Hormel, Leontina, and Chris Norden. 2016a. "Coyote Challenges the Monster: Assessing Nez Perce Environment." *Practicing Anthropology* 38 (3): 17–19. http://dx.doi.org/10.17730/0888-4552-38.3.17.

———. 2016b. "Nez Perce Environmental and Cultural Values: Report of Preliminary Findings." Nimiipuu Protecting the Environment. http://www.nimiipuuprotecting.org/documents-and-archives.

13

Building Future Language Leaders in a Participatory Action Research Model

•••••••••••••••••••••

ROBERT ELLIOTT AND

JANNE UNDERRINER

The Northwest Indian Language Institute (NILI) was created in the Department of Linguistics at the University of Oregon (UO) in 1997 in response to tribal requests for Native American language teacher training. Speakers from tribes across the Pacific Northwest region met with UO linguistics faculty and graduate students to outline their teacher training, assessment, and curricular needs, which set in motion NILI's first Summer Institute in July 1998. It is important to note that this meeting and resulting institute were the outcomes of relationship building over years (since the early 1980s) with tribal language programs and speakers and linguistics faculty and students. Working collaboratively with indigenous partners requires time for relationship building.

Today, the Summer Institute remains the heart of NILI, and it is here that one feels its tribal community origins and purpose. Since 2007, when NILI became a research institute at UO, it has become a year-round program with faculty and graduate and undergraduate students serving Native American language communities locally, nationally, and internationally. NILI provides outreach services on issues of language endangerment and advocates for language revitalization issues and Native American language policy at the state, local, and national levels. It is known for its work on culture place-based learning; its development of Native American language proficiency benchmarks and assessments; the role of technology in Native American language learning, from creating e-books with youth to distance-learning classes; its documentation and material development of regional languages; its research on Native American language and culture as a foundation of wellness; and its mentoring of learners of Native American languages in communities as well as at the UO and at nearby Lane Community College.

When I (Robert Elliott) first started working with language revitalization and Native American communities in 2012, one of the first things I did was to visit a tribal language immersion program for preschool children. Many tribes that are involved in language maintenance start with the youngest learners. As a parent of young children and as a language teacher, I was very interested in what the setting would be like in a preschool designed to foster indigenous language skills, what the challenges and successes would be, and how this setting might vary from mainstream preschool programs.

One challenge I anticipated was that while the children would have strong exposure in school to the target language, outside the classroom, English would creep into nearly every domain of life. Exposure to rich language in immersion schooling is critical if the Native American tongue is to have any chance to thrive.

During that initial observation, I was impressed by so many of the school routines being handled in language: greetings during drop-off and pickup, mealtime, story and group time, and disciplining and rewarding behavior. Still one incident stood out and bothered me. I observed the children taking part in a circle time participating in activities spoken in the indigenous language. Wonderful! Then the children had free-choice time at learning stations around the room. Makes sense. Some children went to the kitchen and continued to play in language. Some went to the dress-up station and played roles such as police officer, firefighter, or chef—all while staying in language. But one group of children went to the computer station. This group was drawn to technology. They were highly engaged while playing with some of the learning games that were loaded on the computers. However, the computer interaction was conducted purely in English; consequently, the children switched back to communicate with each other in English.

Here was a missed opportunity, a chance to extend the use of language to the technology station. Yet because this was a small, endangered language, no software was available in the target language. Publishing companies rarely find it profitable to invest in developing language applications for small languages, and tribal language programs, strapped for time and money, can rarely afford to divert scarce resources toward paying to develop apps on their own.

But what message is being sent? What language ideologies are being reinforced? The message seems to be "My heritage language does not fit into the modern world. It is less important than English. It has no value. It is a thing of the past." I felt there was a need to be met, and we began to develop some ideas with our partners.

Between the fall of 2013 and spring of 2015, together, NILI and the Language Program at the Confederated Tribes of the Umatilla Indian Reservation (CTUIR) created a pilot project to look at technology and language learning. The seed for the current project grew from an earlier one at the Yakama Nation, where we looked at language and culture as protective factors to risky behavior in Native American youth (Jacob 2013; Jansen, Underriner, and Jacob 2013). The youth in this earlier project built a curriculum using their heritage language—Ichishkíin—to be used in the preschool immersion classes. What emerged from that project was the desire of youth to engage language with technology. We wanted to expand to work with other youth learning the Ichishkíin language, so we began conversations with the language program at Nixyáawii High School at CTUIR. One of the fluent speakers and instructors at the school, Thomas Morning Owl, indicated that the youth would be highly interested in working with technology. Several grants were dovetailed together, including funds from the Sociological Initiatives Foundation, to support the project and to purchase technology.

Building on the project at the Yakama Nation, we developed a plan to have high school language students at Nixyáawii Community School build multimedia language materials for the preschoolers at the Tamalut immersion school. At the time, e-books were just gaining popularity, and iBooks Author was a powerful and easy-to-use tool for creating e-books. Training for the high school youth would be needed in digital audio, images, and video and in using iBooks Author. The initial plan was that I (Robert) would visit Nixyáawii High School five times throughout the year for one-week stays, and some of the in-person training could be followed up with online training using video conferencing. Intergenerational learning would be promoted as the youth would visit the immersion class, present the e-books, and talk about the e-books with the children. Two youth participating in the project would be selected to attend the NILI Summer Institute—our annual conference that brings together fifty to seventy indigenous-language teachers and leaders from across the Pacific Northwest and entire country—on scholarship to further reinforce their budding interest in language as well as give them university experience.

But before we go into detail about the project, we would like to back up and give some context about our field, about NILI and about our CTUIR partnership.

Language Loss in the United States

A commonly stated prediction is that of the world's approximately six thousand languages, more than half will cease to be spoken before the turn of the next century (Woodbury 2013). The loss of linguistic diversity means a loss of intellectual and cultural diversity. Each language is a unique tool for analyzing and synthesizing the world and incorporating the knowledge and values of a speech community. To lose a language is to "forget" a way of constructing reality, to blot out a perspective evolved over many generations. The less variety in language, the less variety in ideas. When a language ceases to be spoken, entire bodies of knowledge about flora, fauna, medicines, cultural practices, history, and linguistic and psychological understanding are likely to vanish. For individuals from these language groups, aspects of their identity and understanding of self are lost.

Tribal communities throughout North America, including the Confederated Tribes of the Umatilla Indian Reservation, have been impacted by some of the highest rates of language loss. At the time of European contact in the 1500s, linguists estimate more than three hundred languages were spoken on the continent, with at least half being gone today, and the problem is accelerating. According to Living Tongues Institute (2007), both the Southwest and Pacific Northwest regions of the United States are among the top five "language hotspots" in the world as measured by linguistic diversity and level of endangerment or loss.

Although many factors are involved in language loss, in North America, government policy is one of the most important. While current news of family separation of immigrant children from parents may seem shocking, for Native American peoples, this is all too familiar. In the late 1800s and lasting through the mid-1970s, Native American boarding schools were used by both the United States and Canadian governments as vehicles of forced assimilation. The smothering of Native American tongues and cultures was brutally effective. Today, of the remaining 160 or so indigenous languages in the United States, all are endangered, and estimates are that only about twelve are being passed on to the next generation of children.

Language Revitalization

Language revitalization is a relatively new field within applied linguistics. People working in this area are aiming to strengthen indigenous languages in some form for their communities in schools, the home, or public places. This may mean classes at the school or community center, parents choosing to raise children in the Native American language at home, prayers and ceremonial openings used at social and religious gatherings, phrases painted on murals at the health center, or informal gatherings of language groups in the community committed to speaking and learning their heritage language.

In North America, many admire the model and successes of language revitalization in Hawaiian communities. With their *pūnana leo*, or language nests, which began in the 1970s, strongly committed families established Hawaiian immersion schools and raised children in the language at home (Aha Punana Leo 2007). On the mainland, similar efforts have been taken up. For example, Navajo immersion schools were created in the 1970s and in the 1980s; the Cutswood School in Browning, Montana, began efforts to establish immersion schooling in the Blackfeet language. Today many tribes are involved in some form of language restoration, often having an office for culture and language as a part of the tribal government. At CTUIR, language revitalization work was initiated by elders, their language program director and other speakers, and the tribal linguist in the late 1980s. A decade later, the Tamalut immersion school was established, and in the early 2000s, the charter school Nixyáawii High School was created.

People working in language revitalization come from a wide variety of backgrounds. First speakers, such as elders or others raised in the language, are of extreme value. Learners, culture bearers, language activists, teachers, and linguists are all typically involved. In contrast to teaching major languages such as Spanish, Japanese, or Arabic, where fluency is a primary requirement for becoming a teacher, the phenomenon of the "learner-teacher" (Atkins 2012) is common in language revitalization. Younger people with interest or partial fluency in language, and perhaps some training in language teaching, are put into the role of teachers; their challenge of simultaneously improving their own language skills and teaching others is unique, often requiring them to be researchers, linguists, pedagogical experts, language activists, and materials creators all at the same time. If they are lucky, they can partner with an elder fluent speaker; if unlucky, they must rely on documentation of the language, typically produced by linguists for linguists. Such documentation can be nearly impossible to interpret by nonlinguists, and such data do not lend themselves to be used for daily, conversational phrases.

Native American Language Learning, Health, and Wellness

At NILI, one area I (Janne Underriner) explore is the relationship of identity (building) through Native American language learning and wellness as fundamental precepts to Native American student health. Native American language learning within a rich cultural context shows promise as a protective factor for wellness and academic achievement of Native American students (see Lipka and McCarty 1994; Demmert and Towner 2003; McIvor, Napoleon, and Dickie 2009; Mmari, Blum, and Teufel-Shone 2010; Jansen, Underriner, and Jacob 2013; McCarty and Lee 2014).

Behavioral outcomes suggest that Native American children and youth who learn their own language are more likely to become responsible members of their community and experience a secure sense of health and well-being, with increased resiliency to addiction and fewer risky behaviors (Ngai 2006; Mmari, Blum, and Teufel-Shone 2010; Goodkind et al. 2011). Moreover, Native American language learning contributes to student's social-emotional growth, increases community engagement, and builds intergenerational support for Native American students (Demmert and Towner 2003; McIvor, Napoleon, and Dickie 2009).

In my work on Native American language as protective factors, qualitative evidence shows that high school students report learning their language increases cultural identity. One student recently shared, "Last summer I was watching my sister's nieces, so when my mom was gone, I would help them write their name because the oldest is five now, she was starting kindergarten. So I was trying to talk to her a little bit in Sahaptin [Ichishkíin]. And sometimes she'd kind of look at me, and she'd kind of try, and then sometimes afterward, she *would* say the words. So I was like, okay, I'm getting really inspired now to pass it [on]." The experience suggests she is developing an identity as a language bearer, positively influencing her younger relatives.

Our goal for the e-book project at Nixyáawii High School was for youth to build a small library of e-books to share with children at the Tamalut immersion school and the wider community. Through doing this, we hoped it would (1) increase their confidence in using language to build materials and work with children, (2) increase their sense of ownership and identity related to the language, and (3) improve their skills in technology and project management in creating the multimedia materials. We hoped the language learning and material building would serve as a protective factor, strengthen their cultural identity, and help prepare them for college.

Building the Partnership for Language Preservation and Revitalization

The partnership between NILI and CTUIR that allowed this project to occur developed over many years. The Confederated Tribes of the Umatilla Indian Reservation is located in Northeastern Oregon, near the city of Pendleton, at the base of the Blue Mountains at Nixyáawii, *the place of many springs*. For decades, the tribe has worked to preserve and revitalize the three languages of their ancestors and community—Umatilla (Southern Sahaptin) and Walla

Walla (Northeastern Sahaptin) Ichishkíin and Weyíiletpuu (a dialect of the Nez Perce language spoken by the Cayuse people).

The Confederated Tribes of the Umatilla Indian Reservation's elders and speakers were instrumental in creating NILI in 1997, but the relationship with the UO predates NILI by more than a decade. Dr. Noel Rude, a graduate of the Department of Linguistics at UO (1985) who wrote his dissertation on Nez Perce grammar and discourse, became CTUIR's linguist in the mid-1990s and worked with CTUIR elders and the language program for more than twenty years to document and revitalize all three languages. CTUIR tribal members, who are the tribe's linguists, teachers, and administrators, are graduates of UO's linguistic and education departments. Members of the language program have been Ichishkíin language instructors and consultants at NILI's Summer Institute. CTUIR is instrumental in promoting Ichishkíin language learning across the area with other Ichishkíin-speaking tribes. Perhaps the most visible aspect of this is the Language Bowl they host yearly, a challenging, inspiring, and fun competitive event at which UO Ichishkíin students and instructors assist.

Working with tribes demands institutions work collaboratively; it takes years to develop equitable relationships with tribal communities. It takes showing up at reservations and language programs and schools and participating in communities (CTUIR is approximately 365 miles from Eugene, Oregon, and NILI/UO). A tribal-university relationship based on mutual trust and respect requires and deserves time to develop, especially given the past role such institutions played in colonizing tribal families and communities. NILI's work with tribes is an example of tribal-university collaboration, and it has been and is possible only because of the time, patience, and care that we received from the people from whom we have been mentored—tribal elders, speakers, teachers, and administrators. We owe much of our learning and growing to them, and we are grateful to them. The ability to create this collaborative e-book project relied on this long-term, deep relationship.

Building Youth Leadership through E-books

In the summer of 2013, we were able to prepare for the project for the start of the new school year. We contacted Thomas Morning Owl at CTUIR and together came up with the idea of building on the project at the Yakama Nation by training youth to build multimedia e-books instead. We realized that we needed an easy-to-use yet powerful authoring tool. After researching various options, we all felt that the Apple program iBooks Author would work well: it was both powerful in its multimedia capabilities and as easy to use as PowerPoint. The iBooks Author program is "wysiwyg" (what you see is what you get), and thus the students would not need to learn code. However, Nixyáawii High School had a PC computer lab only. The biggest challenge with deciding to use iBooks Author was the proprietary nature of the program: you can neither create nor view the e-books on non-Apple products. We thus decided we needed to build a portable language lab consisting of a set of three Apple computers for the creation of the iBooks and five iPads, which would allow us to use the iBooks students made in the Tamalut immersion class.

Another challenge was my (Robert's) limited Ichishkíin language skills. Although I had a basic knowledge of Ichishkíin, I was not, nor should I have been, the expert on the language. On a parallel note, the limits of technology skills by the CTUIR language teachers was a concern for the sustainability of the project after the end of the grants and during the periods when I was not at the reservation school. What was "nice" about this particular set of challenges was that it necessitated a partnership with clearly defined roles. Teaming up closely and creatively would be required for this project to work.

During my initial site visit, I (Robert) established a working relationship with Damien Totus, a high school teacher of the Imatillim/Ichishkíin language. Damien and I knew each other only slightly, though we quickly found a comfortable working relationship. Discussions began on that first visit about logistics, including types of products needed, training times, class times, and how to decide on what students to bring into the project. The collaborative negotiation of the project at this early stage led to some critical choices that ensured later successes. In retrospect, what was important at this stage was to have some general ideas for the project but to be flexible enough so that the project could meet the specific needs and concerns of Damien and the school.

One of the project's most important decisions was determining which youth to involve. At another tribal location where a parallel project was simultaneously taking place, the decision was made to work with the entire class of eighteen language students. However, Damien suggested using a pull-out group of four to six students who were more proficient in their language learning than other classmates. The reasoning was that advanced students could create stronger projects more independently and begin to use their language for an authentic purpose while the remainder of the students could continue to catch up with the basics of the language in regular class. The project could also act as an incentive for language growth for students with less speaking proficiency. The biggest disadvantage was that the narrower project would target fewer youth. In the end, the choice to go with the pull-out group led to more successful results with fewer class management issues, more focus on the part of the youth, and more e-books produced.

There was a total of five visits through the first school year, each involving a five-and-a-half-hour drive from Eugene in Western Oregon (where NILI is located) out to CTUIR in eastern Oregon. Each visit started with a planning session after my (Robert's) arrival on Monday afternoon. Damien and I would map out goals and procedures for the upcoming visit and work that around the schedule and topics of the class. I would then work with the same four to six youth the remainder of the week during their language class on building the e-books, and Damien would help provide the critical language needed so the students could complete the work accurately.

Over time, my relationship with Damien and the youth grew close. Often I brought treats, such as fruit, bars, and smoothies, so the youth could snack during project time. Damien and I often had lunch together, talking about where to take the project next. He invited me to events outside of school, such as the Thanksgiving lunch at the government offices, a *kupen* (traditional digging stick)-making workshop, and a knife-making workshop.

During the first two visits, students at the language class received some basic training in technology skills they would need to produce the e-books. They started learning to work with digital images and were introduced to recording and editing short films. The students created introductions in language for a webpage they helped build, taking images of themselves and recording introductions in their language and in English.

After I worked with them on the foundational skills, students began to build their first e-book on the second visit. An existing children's hardcover book that had already been translated into their language was used. The youth photographed the book, added audio, and acted out the situations, making the book "come alive" with short video clips, taking advantage of the multimedia format. For example, the book was about friends doing things together and had short verbal phrases such as "jumping and laughing." The group would then film themselves jumping and laughing as well as record audio clips of the text in their own voices in the language, then edit and finally insert these clips into the e-book.

After the first book was finished, Damien and I wanted to tap into the creativity of the youth and allow them to take over the direction of future books. We ran a brainstorming session and came up with numerous ideas for possible books. We broke down what would be needed to complete each book, including what they would need to be able to say in the language, what images and video they would need to find or create, and what audio they would like to have. Over subsequent visits, we would choose one of those books from our brainstorm list to develop. I served as an aid in storyboarding and project management, while Damien helped with composing and proofreading text and accurately pronouncing the often difficult words they were recording.

The students' creative process improved with each book. By the end of the first year, six books had been created, with two books per visit as the goal. In one example, one of the last books the youth developed was about various community members introducing themselves in the language. They wanted to represent the community as widely as possible, so they recorded elders, teachers, themselves, and even some of the Tamalut children, producing short or long introductions, depending on their level of fluency, in a culturally appropriate manner. They then matched the audio with still images of the speakers they had taken to produce the multimedia e-book.

During the last visit of the first year, once a small library of books was developed, the youth felt ready to bring the books to the Tamalut children. The youth paired up and sat with three or four children, showed the books, and let the children play with the swipe and interactive features. Natural conversation in the Ichishkíin language took place between the youth and the children following the reading. The visit lasted for about one and a half hours and served as a culmination point of the project-based learning endeavor.

Several unanticipated challenges and successes occurred during the project. One problem was that the original model included working remotely with the youth group while I (Robert) was back at the university, which proved to be impossible. The technology plan was to use Skype or a similar program to "teleconference in" and follow up during off periods. However, due to the logistical limitations of technology at the school and the fact that the project was already taking time away from curriculum, Damien and I decided to keep the face-to-face component as the main work period.

Another issue was access to the preschool. During one of the early visits, we had planned an observation session of the preschool so that the youth could see what the class was like and to better know the audience for the books. However, during the times when the students' language class met, the preschoolers were involved in a regularly scheduled activity that was not easy to rearrange, so no preproject visit took place. In yet another issue, once the project was running well, students wanted to take on ambitious projects that could not be completed during the limited fifty minutes of the daily language class. Many of the youth were also involved in sports, which limited their time availability. Our solution was that students could come back to work on the project during lunch, after school, and sometimes even during other classes they were ahead in. Because of these multiple spontaneous works sessions, file labeling and organization became critical; sometimes the students misnamed or misplaced files, causing minor delays in moving projects forward. In the evening I typically had to return to the materials to organize and "clean them up."

There were a number of unexpected successes as well, with perhaps the most important one being the involvement of the resource coordinator, Michelle Van Pelt, who also serves as the college prep counselor at Nixyáawii. When Michelle learned about the project, she backed it fully and felt that those involved would have valuable college preparedness experiences by participating in the project. She became instrumental in extending the project after the original ending date, as explained later. Another success was how the youth took on specialized roles that increased their confidence in using technology. For example, one youth, initially shy about using technology, became particularly interested in digital audio. As she increased her skills, she took on all the extra recording and editing jobs and aided her peers with their digital audio. Over time, we dubbed her our "audio expert."

Measuring Success

Measuring success poses a challenge to many language revitalization projects. In a traditional language class, success is relatively straightforward: assess language proficiency before a lesson is taught (time 1), reassess after the lesson has been taught (time 2), and look for progress. However, in language revitalization, language progress might meet only one of several possible benchmarks of proficiency. Further, language goals can be difficult to attain when there are few or even no fluent speakers to practice with, when materials and even exposure to language are lacking, or when there is no community of speakers with whom to interact and practice. While building fluent speakers ready to engage with a speech community might be a long-term goal, other nonlanguage goals might be more realistic and attainable in the short term.

What are alternative measurements of success in a language revitalization project? One option as explored by my (Janne's) work mentioned earlier is well-being and health. If language is truly a protective factor, can we look at reduction or abstinence from risky behavior as indicators of success? Another possibility is identity. Do young people who know their language, culture, and history have a better sense of who they are in the world and how they fit in? In projects working with high school youth, can grades or college acceptance be considered a sign of success? Is getting young people from a tribe interested and engaged in learning more about their language a sign of success? And finally, what about self-satisfaction? Does feeling good about a project and what you did by aiding a heritage language count, such as in this case completing a set of materials for children, learning about technology tools, or increasing intergenerational interaction?

Ultimately our measurements of success were geared toward the well-being of youth, the interest in language (rather than traditional language fluency), and the bridging to college. The summer following the project's first year, two youth from Nixyáawii Community School attended the annual NILI Summer Institute. They took part in our initial youth program, which sought to inspire youth in the language revitalization movement as well as expose them to a college campus and courses. The youth attended classes in linguistics and language, a youth seminar, a class in activism, and one in technology. They lived in dorms, and they interacted with language revitalization leaders from tribes throughout the Pacific Northwest and the nation. They built three additional e-books to add to the CTUIR library. And attendance at Summer Institute helped spark future conferences for the youth, as will be discussed in the next section.

Of the original eight students who participated over the first year, seven went on to college after the end of the project. One received a Gates Scholarship and attended Stanford University, while another received a full scholarship to University of Idaho. Michelle, the high school college counselor who coached the students on their college applications and scholarship letters, encouraged them to write about their experience and skills learned in the e-book project, including technology and language skills, building e-books, and working with the preschoolers.

Conversations and reflections with students after the project's completion brought up several themes. Students reported that they felt considerably more confident using computers. Several students mentioned the specific skills of using digital audio and digital images as particularly useful. Everyone mentioned that building the books was new to them and increased their confidence in their ability to use technology for learning.

A second theme that surfaced targeted language. Four students discussed that using their Native American language to build e-book content assisted their language learning. This offered them a chance not just to learn vocabulary and phrases but to use language for an intended purpose. One student mentioned that working on the project pushed her to extend the language she knew into new areas or domains. Several said they felt more confident using language and teaching family members some of the words and phrases they had learned. And many discussed the importance of language for knowing their identity as a Native American person and better understanding their Umatilla heritage.

Damien and Michelle stated in conversations that the project succeeded in strengthening students' leadership abilities and tribal identity. They mentioned that the youth who took part had an experience making language materials for an authentic purpose. They thought that youth input into the types and direction of projects helped them build skills as leaders and team players. They also felt that the youth developed a sense of ownership and responsibility to the language during the project, that this was their heritage, and that they could be contributors in safekeeping the language for future generations.

With regard to the technology and the use of Apple products, Damien and Michelle thought it was useful to learn about using newer products, such as iPads and Apple computers. However, it was challenging to get the school to purchase these so they could continue working on video and e-books. Ideally, future projects should build in more funding for hardware that would stay with the tribe or school.

Since the end of the initial project, there have been positive effects both at the school and at NILI. The project extended on through a second year, with three more visits sponsored by NILI and the building of several more e-books for preschool children. Since the visits were fewer than in the initial project, no training occurred. Rather, I (Robert) had the returning students help several new students get up to speed with the skills, and together we continued to grow the e-book library. Since the project, more Nixyáawii High School students are showing an interest in their language and in language revitalization. In the 2017 Summer Institute, for example, four high school youth from Umatilla attended, and one hopes to study linguistics in the future at the university. Nixyáawii High School has also launched several projects independently related to the language project. For example, a film about why language is important was produced in-house, with interviews of students, teachers, and elders about the value of learning Ichishkíin/Imatillim.

Perhaps the biggest aftereffect was participation at national conferences. After the first year of the project, Michelle suggested the project should be presented at the National Indian Education Association (NIEA) conference in Anchorage in 2014 as a team, with Damien, the students, and I as presenters. Although originally there was no planning or funding for conferences, CTUIR and Nixyáawii High School pulled together some funds to help send the teacher and two students to the conference. Additional money was raised by bake sales and fund-raisers Michelle and Damien organized. Together, we presented in front of a national audience of Native American educators about the e-book project. Variations of this presentation were later done at two additional national conferences, with other students involved with the project having opportunities to present.

Benefits to the University and Institute

NILI has also been affected by the legacy of the project. At our annual NILI Summer Institute, youth presence has continued to grow. Each year the youth who attend seem even more committed to learning and using language based in part by the contact we have through collaborative projects with tribes like the e-book project. What I (Robert) personally have learned by working with the high school class at CTUIR has also strengthened me in my work at NILI and the university. I have been leading our youth outreach at NILI SI. While I was never trained in working with teens, my confidence and skills have increased in working with this age group. Further, in classes that I teach or lectures that I give, I often refer to this project and use it as a successful model.

We are also starting to see some of the youth who have been involved in our outreach programs return to the University of Oregon. These "older youth" and other university Native American students are now becoming increasingly involved with the new generation of youth who attend Summer Institute. This type of informal mentoring is increasing the public face of UO as a place that welcomes Native American students and understands and supports the important efforts of indigenous language work.

Youth outreach is an effort that makes sense for language work. A project that piques interest in young people in academics and gets them excited about learning is potentially life changing for a kid growing up on the reservation. Perhaps some see this as a cause greater than themselves, for their people, culture, and language. To successfully inspire them, we need to meet young people where they are. Given training, scaffolding, and support, young people are capable of being part of a team effort that is required for language revitalization. As a movement, we truly are in need of inspired, dedicated people, which in turn reinforces the identity and wellness of the youth. Given the right conditions, they can find a purpose and truly succeed, carving out roles as future leaders of their communities and stewards of their language.

Conclusion

We would like to reiterate the importance of relationships, collaboration, and doing the work on-site for language revitalization work to be successful. This project's successes were due in large part to the long-term relationship established between NILI and the language personnel at CTUIR, the new relationships that were built during this project, and the collaborative nature of the approach. CTUIR and NILI codeveloped the plan, modified the procedure, and shared in the extension of the project. The distance education model, which was less successful, does not provide the type of mentoring, nor relationship building, that face-to-face training does. Despite the potential time and cost savings an online model might offer, Native American people have learned by watching and doing alongside a mentor for millennia, and that remains, in our opinion, the most successful way to teach and learn.

References

Aha Punana Leo. 2007. "History." http://www.ahapunanaleo.org/index.php?/about/history/.

Atkins, Marnie. 2012. "Strategies for an Indigenous Self-Apprenticeship Language Learning Program." MA thesis, University of Oregon. http://nilirc.com/community/nili-publications.

Demmert, W. G., Jr., and J. C. Towner. 2003. *A Review of the Research Literature on the Influences of Culturally Based Education on the Academic Performance of Native American Students.* Portland, Ore.: Northwest Regional Educational Laboratory. http://

educationnorthwest.org/resources/review-research-literature-influences-culturally-based
-education-academic-performance.

Goodkind, Jessica, Kimberly Ross-Toledo, Susie John, Janie Lee Hall, Lucille Ross, Lance Freeland, Ernest Coletta, and Twila Becenti-Fundark. 2011. "Rebuilding Trust: A Community, Multi-agency, State and University Partnership to Improve Behavioral Health Care for American Indian Youth, Their Families and Communities." *Journal of Community Psychology* 39:452–477.

Jacob, M. 2013. *Yakama Rising: Indigenous Cultural Revitalization, Activism, and Healing.* Tucson: University of Arizona Press.

Jansen, Joana, Janne Underriner, and Roger Jacob. 2013. "Revitalizing Languages through Place-Based Language Curriculum." In *Language Death, Endangerment, Documentation, and Revitalization*, edited by E. Mihas, B. Perley, G. Rei-Doval, and K. Wheatley, 221–242. Amsterdam: John Benjamins.

Lipka, J., and T. L. McCarty. 1994. "Changing the Culture of Schooling: Navajo and Yup'ik Cases." *Anthropology & Education Quarterly* 25:266–284.

Living Tongues Institute. 2007. "Language Hotspots." http://livingtongues.org/language-hotspots/.

McCarty, T. L., and T. S. Lee. 2014. "Critical Culturally Sustaining/Revitalizing Pedagogy and Indigenous Education Sovereignty." *Harvard Educational Review* 84:101–124.

McIvor, O., A. Napoleon, and K. Dickie. 2009. "Language and Culture as Protective Factors for At-Risk Communities." *Journal de la santé autochtone*, November, 6–25.

Mmari, Kristin N., Robert Wm. Blum, and Nicolette Teufel-Shone. 2010. "What Increases Risk and Protection for Delinquent Behaviors among American Indian Youth?" *Youth and Society* 41:382–413.

Ngai, P. 2006. "Grassroots Suggestions for Linking Native-Language Learning, Native American Studies, and Mainstream Education in Reservation Schools with Mixed Indian and White Student Populations." *Language, Culture and Curriculum* 19:237–265.

Woodbury, Anthony. 2013. "Endangered Languages." *Linguistics Society of America*, August 9, 2013. www.linguisticsociety.org/content/endangered-languages.

14

Conclusion

● ●

Linking Research to
Social Action

PRENTICE ZINN, SUSAN D.
GREENBAUM, AND GLENN JACOBS

Since its founding in 1998, the Sociological Initiatives Foundation has provided more than $1.5 million for 164 grants to support research linked to col-
lective action. Although the cases in this volume are a small sample, they give
us a rare glimpse into projects rooted in the idea that marginalized groups can
challenge systems that treat people unfairly, build political power that is more
democratic, and produce knowledge and data that are valid, incisive, and relevant to issues of policy and justice.

Few foundations fund underserved communities to undertake strategies of
systemic change such as community organizing and advocacy (Schlegel 2016,
2–3). Even fewer support community-based research as an essential part of
citizen-based advocacy. Sociological Initiatives Foundation's (SIF) support
of the integration of these too often separate approaches offers a useful perspective on the dynamics of community research, the politics of collaborative
research, and the social production of knowledge. By sponsoring social change
through consistently funding the joint efforts of laypeople and academicians,
the foundation's insights, questions, and actions are unique in the domain of
philanthropy. It embodies a key theme of this book: the use of social science

ideas to guide investigation by community-based groups, whose findings are incorporated into action programs that facilitate social change. Our book offers a timely example for those seeking to link research to action and to bring the voices of those on the margins up to the front.

Praxis through Partnership

The accounts in this volume demonstrate how research linked with social action can be a transformative tool for social change. Their struggles can be described in the activist-social theorist Antonio Gramsci's terms under the headings of a "war of maneuver"—that is, direct confrontation or targeted direct action against repression and exploitation as opposed to the "war of position" or tactically "boring from within" the extant social structure (Gramsci 1971, 233–235, 238–239, 243). The examples in the book largely lean toward direct action but employ mixtures of both orientations. We urge the reader to reflect on the application of Gramsci's categories to these cases to the tactical matter of "policy wins."

Policy wins are a favorite yardstick for measuring success in this context, but they are a shadow of the whole story. As we have seen, most of the projects have broader and deeper outcomes than immediate legislative or policy achievements. "Wins," or the apparent results of maneuver, are based in fact on the positional strategies and tactics of fostering leadership, building organizational membership, forging alliances and trust, and enhancing organizational resources among community-based organizations. These outcomes are key reasons that the SIF supports community-based participatory research. This kind of result is seldom incorporated into the narratives and official reports of how change happens and how people build power.

How these processes influence public opinion and how they increase community dialogue or lead to further cycles of inquiry and action are critical elements that are harder to document. The preceding chapters descriptively and analytically address these issues. Our authors outline varied efforts and tactics to integrate community-based research with organizing (and vice versa), thereby opening a valuable opportunity for strategic thinking about social transformation.

Policy Change Is Not Linear

All foundations face the nagging question of whether their grants make a difference. SIF provides small grants that alone will not usually bring immediate change but sometimes have enabled key events or payments, some of which are identified here. The broad philosophy of participatory action research (PAR) and popular education is underpinned by basic values of democracy and fairness, but can that approach bring actual change? In other words, like other small nonprofit enterprises, SIF wants to know what they are getting back on investments. The groups in our chapters, like all activist organizations, operate in complex social and political environments with dynamic variables that are difficult to isolate or measure. Above all, these accounts testify to the capacity of social action organizations to look at themselves.

The path from a successful research project to a policy or program intervention can be traced through reports, interviews with staff, and other documentation and media, but the circumstances and factors associated with success and failure are interwoven and tied to uncontrollable political influences. In hostile contests, it may not be enough to have facts on your side, yet they will nearly always be needed, and data need to be defensible and correct. Even if initial efforts fail, the truth can still come out. Most projects take several years to play out, beyond the normal limits of SIF funding. Collaborative research and action are not subject to formulaic direction. Human relations, class and cultural differences, external events, and the inherently iterative nature of the process play large roles and constitute significant challenges to both projects and movements.

These cases cover a wide range both regionally and topically, but there are some notable similarities in the nature of problems confronted and in how they established and won social justice campaigns guided by evidence. The methods used in these cases are quite similar in design, logic, and sequence. Multimethod strategies are preferred. Quantitative data from records and surveys are typically combined with in-depth narratives, often supplemented with visuals that give life to results and profile human costs and problems. As noted at the outset, the epistemology of PAR, more than packaging or even the triangulation of results, is also a redefinition of expertise. The surveys and personal interviews bring the people affected by the campaign issues to the forefront and into a dialogic experience of examining and conversing about issues in their lives with others who share the same problems. Research questions arise from such conversations rather than from theoretical hypotheses. The intrinsic validity of the research begins there and ends in a forum where skeptics abound. But skepticism is a critical part of science, and the emergent value of PAR has been the capacity to deliver credible responses to predictable objections.

Collaboration Is Tough to Organize and Manage but Essential for Success

As the case studies attest, organizational coalitions are better at producing and using research to win policy campaigns than researchers or organizations working independently. SIF learned early to avoid "lone wolf" researchers or organizations working alone but also not to fetishize collaboration and coalitions. Some coalitions work; others are quiet failures. The importance of both lasting and flexible partnerships is a common theme among the contributors in this volume.

Research results are important only to the extent that they can be deployed effectively. Tireless organizing and knocking on doors at all levels of power are also critical to policy success. There is a natural division of labor between activists and academics, but consensus is needed on research. It must be truly participatory. The problems, issues, methods, and remedies should be defined collaboratively. How that works in practice varies considerably, and failures are common. Academic researchers and grassroots organizers are known to have trouble communicating, and they often confront external pressures that can divide and sow doubt. Comfortable and equitable relations are critical to success, and their absence signals likely failure.

Community-based research is not a simple matter of inserting technical skills into a researchable problem. A wide social distance typically separates ivory towers from surrounding communities. In contrast, Nobody Leaves Mid-Hudson is a group that began with the youthful ideals of Vassar students in the Occupy anti-eviction campaign, but it was voluntarily transformed with grassroots partners into an effective and durable vehicle for achieving community-determined goals. Collaborative decision-making, trust in the wisdom of participatory inquiry, and dedication to the long haul are shown to be critical in all the projects highlighted here. Most address the challenges of this work but also the satisfaction. Academic authors in several chapters discuss the impact on their own understanding of social issues they had studied in graduate school and on the relationships that formed from the research in which they were involved. They also reflect on the occasional utility of their own privilege as an element of protective coloration in strategies to secure just outcomes.

In varying degrees, all these projects to which SIF contributed have brought tangible—in some cases large—benefits to the constituencies involved. Participatory research, as well as producing knowledge, is shown to produce collateral effects that help strengthen organizations and aid in winning benefits and concessions. Restaurant workers across the country have gained new protections and wage increases resulting from the Restaurant Opportunities Center's tireless work, some of which are featured in chapter 6. Many of the chapters are about labor activism, often tied to issues of immigration and racist and sexist exploitation. Day laborers, dairy and forest workers, house cleaners, and others struggling against difficult workplace odds have forged partnerships with researchers whose credentials help open doors and gain the attention of power. In addition, two Native American organizations in the northwest, whose tribes have faced significant threats of cultural extinction and physical encroachment, used SIF funds to partner with environmental allies against damage to the forest and in a language retention program with assistance from a University of Oregon program that includes Native American students.

In all the cases, outcomes are very difficult to measure, and they vary widely in scope and intensity. In virtually all cases, SIF funds covered only a small part of the resources needed, although several authors pointed to crucial aid the foundation provided. Easier to glean and potentially more instructive are the challenges and obstacles these cases reveal.

Academic-Community Partnerships

The labor and skills of university-affiliated graduate students and faculty researchers can be very useful for community organizations in need of evidence or information. Similarly, many academics are also interested in doing social justice research. However, university partners face challenges related to timing of semesters and limitations on student involvement that do not easily align with project needs along with a raft of responsibilities that can interfere. University requirements—that is, institutional review boards (IRB)—are mainly designed to protect conventional research subjects and do not always have flexibility to understand, negotiate, and adapt to community-based research. Most of the chapters reflect academic partnerships that are long-standing and in several cases also include university-level institutes and organizations.

There remains in most universities, however, a large gap between the standard definitions of "service learning" and "community engagement" versus the types of involvement reflected in these cases. Faculty members who work with community organizations that criticize and protest local powers will sometimes find themselves in trouble with administrators and fund-raisers. Tenure is very helpful in undertaking this work, but the academic researchers in this volume reflect the whole range of faculty experience and status, including several whose dissertation research was the origin of their involvement.

Unlike the familiar "top-down" research process found in traditional academic practice, PAR calls for active involvement of community members in all phases of research, a mandate for democratic approaches to developing and sharing knowledge. Participatory frameworks are good in theory but are quite varied in practice. The examples in this book were all very serious about enacting these egalitarian goals. Nonetheless, there are limits on how much, and in what contexts, members of most of the collaborating communities could participate in meetings and other activities outside of work. In some cases for forest workers, for example, fear of retaliation inhibits open participation.

Each research group confronted such barriers, which they have addressed to a greater or lesser extent in these chapters and in other venues. Expedience and old habits can undercut good intentions to maximize participation; these issues need to be explicitly recognized and discussed as part of the larger collaboration. Several cases in this book, notably the Restaurant Opportunities Centers (ROC) and the Brazilian Workers Center, have incorporated onboard research components from the outset, enabling them to ease these barriers.[1]

Political Winds Can Change Quickly

Research and social justice organizing projects emerge at the fault lines of the policies that affect and enact social inequities in communities. The state or federal policy battleground creates the urgency of questions that might be addressed by research but can change with a vote, a stroke of a pen, or an emergent crisis. Even small shifts in public policy can reduce the political leverage of a research project under way. For example, Andy Puzder, CEO of Carl's Jr. and a prime foe of the Restaurant Opportunities Center, was suddenly nominated to be U.S. secretary of labor. Attention was immediately diverted, and with the help of a broad group of opponents, his nomination was scuttled. Immigrants, both documented and not, face enormous new challenges in the Trump era, but defending their right to be paid and to be free of extortion and abuse are long-standing projects. Over the course of many years, the work done by the Brazilian Worker Center, the Worker Center of Central New York, the Workers Justice Center of New York, the National Day Labor Organizing Network, and the Workers Defense Project, some of which has been reported in this volume, provide important sources of resistance and aid. Research that has been conducted by these collaborators into conditions and infractions helped secure rights and win allies. The need for such efforts has greatly intensified in recent years.

How Does Research Mobilization Work?

Policy outcomes and community benefits are somewhat easy to track, but we need to know more about how organizations disseminate research results and how these make a difference in the end. Approaches to dissemination range from the perfunctory and traditional to the enthusiastic and strategic. At minimum, all SIF projects produce reports and white papers that document the research findings and recommendations. A year or two later, most academic authors will have published results in academic journals. Altogether such documents typically do little to alter the problems elucidated. As accounts in this volume demonstrate, the most successful projects aggressively integrate the communication and dissemination of research results into their organizing strategy and continue to tell and retell the story that emerges from the data and project participants.

The foundation has learned from experience that organizations that have produced illustrated reports, press releases, and press conferences and hosted community forums about their research findings have attracted the most media attention and generated the most opportunities for public discussion and community engagement. The groups represented here typically have gone beyond that. The work of the Class Action group, whose mission is to focus on issues of class in social justice organizing, produced a book (Leondar-Wright 2014) and fashioned a unique book tour that took their messages and findings to a targeted audience of local activists and communities in cities across the United States. Their campaign offers important ideas for breaking the social barriers that bracket most academic publications. The San Francisco Coalition on Homelessness (COH) involves unhoused partners in all phases of their work, including serving as authors of chapter 4 and especially as participants in public presentations and meetings with officials. Their goal is to redefine expertise and to combat insulting caricatures of "homeless" people. It is noteworthy that the 2018 San Francisco election included victory for "Prop C," which taxes the rich to provide housing for low-income residents. The San Francisco COH was a major actor in the success of that campaign.

Integrating Research and Organizing

The accounts in this volume celebrate the power of combining research and organizing. Many of the research-activists in this volume offer clear examples of the efficacy of this strategy. They are strong public policy actors who are well familiar with municipal, city, and state politics and power. They lead base-building organizations that seek to expand power by developing the leadership of hundreds of members through chapters and alliances. Most exhibit the skills and affinities for the methodologies of popular education, problem-posing education, or similar forms of adult education. Their seasoned community organizers have inquiry "baked in" to their culture. They ask participants to identify the questions, name the problems, propose solutions, and take action. Some members contacted through interviews find reasons to join more actively. Activist members who do outreach for the research also bring the messages of the organization, adding to recruitment. The broadened flexibility of role requirements within these interactive processes and activities illustrates both praxis and the hybrid nature of PAR.

These observations and questions focus on the methods of linking research and action, but they also remind us to pay attention to how organizations and public institutions can become more inclusive and participatory. Racism, classism, sexism, and ethnocentrism are inimical to the goals of both research and action, but unconscious bias and thoughtless expedience can threaten research and undermine justice. The lessons of these chapters offer a starting point for asking more probing questions about contradictions within many well-meaning citizen organizations, foundations, nonprofit organizations, and academia that sustain unequal power relations even as they attempt to change them. The cases composing this volume hopefully have provided clues and probative inquiries into how idealistic students, faculty, and community activists can join together working for justice in projects that will both aid the struggle and contribute to a more balanced understanding of the reasons and remedies for societal ills.

It is important to reiterate that understanding the struggles of these groups to remove obstacles standing in their way also necessitates understanding the societal predicaments and cleavages encompassing them. Although simply appearing to be played out locally, these struggles are more far reaching in their implications with respect to the local, national, and global forces activist groups contend with. The social, political, and economic processes entailed in the playing out of these forces are what Zygmunt Bauman and others call "glocalization" (Bauman 1998; Syngedouw 2004; Roudometof 2005). Social quagmires generated by larger, seemingly more remote forces are in fact brought home to be confronted locally. In line with this, Manuel Castells asks, "Why, instead of choosing the right ones, do people insist on aiming at local targets?" His answer is that "people appear to have no other choice." In other words, "when people find themselves unable to control the world, they simply shrink the world to the size of their community." In doing so, however, they "nurture the embryos of tomorrow's social movements," and their struggles open the doors to greater and wider understanding (Castells 1983, 329, 331). Indeed, some of the organizations herein have expanded beyond their original geographic boundaries, bringing their struggles to the threshold of national significance.

In view of all of this, we hope that the readers of these accounts will come to understand that well-defined targeted collective actions and struggles can provide keys to understanding broader social conflicts in these times when the proliferation of authoritarianism is an added threat to popular justice at home and internationally. We at SIF also hope that this book can assist activist organizations to grapple more directly with these issues. Andrea Cornwall in her article on "Unpacking 'Participation'" suggests that although the rhetoric of participation is widespread, few authors spell out what it means in practice. As she puts it, "Participation as praxis is, after all, rarely a seamless process; rather, it constitutes a terrain of contestation, in which the relations of power between different actors, each with their own 'projects', shape and reshape the boundaries of action," and consequently nurtures the embryos of tomorrow's social movements (Cornwall 2008).

Note

1   Another notable example is Community Voices Heard (CVH), a former SIF grantee, founded in 1994 by a group of welfare recipients with an agenda of seeking welfare reform, improving and preserving public housing, improving community governance, and reforming back-to-work policies and programs. Speaking of such integrality, CVH notes that "while a research report is just a document that sits on a shelf, it is advocacy efforts that bring research reports off shelves and into real people's lives" (McNeil and Youdelman 2012, 69).

References

Bauman, Zygmunt. 1998. "On Glocalization: Or Globalization for Some, Localization for Some Others." *Thesis Eleven* 54:37–49.

Castells, Manuel. 1983. *The City and the Grassroots.* Berkeley: University of California Press.

Cornwall, Andrea. 2008. "Unpacking 'Participation': Models, Meanings and Practices." *Community Development Journal* 43 (3): 276.

Gramsci, Antonio. 1971. *Selections from the Prison Notebooks of Antonio Gramsci.* New York: International Publishers.

Leondar-Wright, Betsy. 2014. *Missing Class: Strengthening Social Movement Organizations by Seeing Class Cultures.* Ithaca, N.Y.: Cornell University Press.

McNeil, Lori, and Sondra Youdelman. 2012. "Building Power for Low Income New Yorkers: Community Voices Heard." In *Street Practice: Changing the Lens on Poverty and Public Assistance,* edited by Lori McNeil, 47–72. Burlington, Vt.: Ashgate.

Roudometof, V. 2005. "Transnationalism, Cosmopolitanism and Glocalization." *Current Sociology* 53 (1): 113–135.

Schlegel, Ryan. 2016. "Pennies for Progress: A Decade of Boom for Philanthropy, a Bust for Social Justice." National Committee for Responsive Philanthropy (NCRP). http://ncrp .org/publication/pennies-for-progress.

Syngedouw, E. 2004. "Globalization or 'Glocalization'? Networks, Territories and Rescaling." *Cambridge Review of International Affairs* 17 (1): 25–48.

Notes on Contributors

LISA MARIE ALATORRE, MA, is a national consultant and organizer.

PABLO ALVARADO is the executive director of the National Day Laborer Organizing Network (NDLON).

VERONICA AVILA is the strategic research associate at the Restaurant Opportunities Centers United and a 2018–2019 Data and Society fellow.

JONATHAN BIX is the executive director of Nobody Leaves Mid-Hudson.

VICTORIA BRECKWICH VÁSQUEZ is vice president of Preventive Health Services, Education and Training at Sea Mar Community Health Centers in Washington.

DIANE BUSH is a coordinator of public programs at the Labor Occupational Health Program at the University of California, Berkeley.

ROBERT ELLIOTT is associate director and senior researcher at the University of Oregon's Northwest Indian Language Institute.

CHRISTINA E. FLETES-ROMO is a Berkeley Law and Harvard Kennedy School–trained attorney and public policy advocate with an expertise in community-based research and economic equity.

CARLY FOX is the advocacy and organizing coordinator at the Worker Justice Center of New York.

JENNIFER FRIEDENBACH is the executive director of the Coalition on Homelessness.

REBECCA FUENTES is the lead organizer for the Workers' Center of Central New York.

SUSAN D. GREENBAUM is professor emerita of anthropology of the University of South Florida and a trustee of the Sociological Initiatives Foundation.

CHRIS HERRING is a PhD candidate in the Department of Sociology at the University of California, Berkeley.

RICH HEYMAN teaches urban studies in the Department of Geography and the Environment at the University of Texas at Austin.

LEONTINA HORMEL is a professor in the Department of Sociology and Anthropology and director of the Women's, Gender, and Sexuality Studies Program at University of Idaho in Moscow.

WILLIAM HOYNES is a professor of sociology at Vassar College in Poughkeepsie, New York.

GLENN JACOBS taught for thirty-nine years and retired with the rank of full professor at the University of Massachusetts, Boston. He is the author of *Charles Horton Cooley: Imagining Social Reality* (2006) and is coeditor with Jorge Capetillo and Phillip Kretsedemas of *Migrant Marginality: A Transnational Perspective* (2013). He is president of the board of the Sociological Initiatives Foundation and currently teaches graduate courses and supervises doctoral students at the Boston Graduate School of Psychoanalysis (BGSP).

T. J. JOHNSTON is a journalist based in San Francisco and assistant editor of *Street Sheet*, a publication of the Coalition on Homelessness. His work has also appeared in the *San Francisco Examiner*, *San Francisco Public Press*, the *Huffington Post*, *KQED*, the *SF Bay View*, *48 Hills*, *Center for Public Integrity*, *International Network of Street Papers*, and *Street Spirit*, among others.

PEGGY KAHN is a professor of political science at the University of Michigan–Flint.

BETSY LEONDAR-WRIGHT is an assistant professor of sociology at Lasell College and a longtime board member of Class Action, www.classism.org.

BILAL MAFUNDI ALI is a community-based human rights organizer at *Poor Magazine* in Oakland, California.

JULIAN MATTHEWS is treasurer, board member, and an enrolled member of the Nez Perce (Nimiipuu) tribe and believes in both the right to "take to the streets" and using the political process to bring about change to protect the Mother Earth.

ELLIOTT MOFFETT is president and an enrolled member of the Nez Perce (Nimiipuu) tribe and has been involved with numerous issues, working on direct action or policy changes through the political process.

CHRIS NEWMAN is the legal director and general counsel for the National Day Laborer Organizing Network (NDLON) based in its Los Angeles office.

CHRIS NORDEN is a professor of English and environmental studies at Lewis-Clark State College in Lewiston, Idaho, and has served on the board of directors for Friends of the Clearwater since the late 1990s.

FABIOLA ORTIZ VALDEZ is a PhD candidate in anthropology at the Maxwell School of Citizenship and Public Affairs at Syracuse University as well as an organizer for the New York Immigration Coalition.

GRETCHEN PURSER is an associate professor of sociology at the Maxwell School of Citizenship and Public Affairs at Syracuse University as well as the chair of the board of the Workers' Center of Central New York.

BLISS REQUA-TRAUTZ is director of Arriba Las Vegas Worker Center.

TEÓFILO L. REYES, PhD, is visiting scholar, Food Labor Research Center and Goldman School of Public Policy, University of California, Berkeley, and research director, Restaurant Opportunities Centers United.

KATHLEEN SEXSMITH is an assistant professor of rural sociology and women's, gender, and sexuality studies at Pennsylvania State University.

TIM SIEBER is a professor of anthropology at the University of Massachusetts Boston and member of the board of directors of the Brazilian Worker Center.

LUCINDA SIMPSON, MSW, CDCII, is a retired Nez Perce tribal elder. She has more than ten years of experience as a law officer, a master-level social worker, a chemical dependency manager, and a counselor.

NIK THEODORE is professor of urban planning and policy and associate dean for research and faculty affairs at the College of Urban Planning and Public Affairs at University of Illinois at Chicago.

EMILY TIMM is a cofounder of Workers Defense Project (WDP) and currently works as WDP's senior organizing director, supporting a team of organizers across Texas.

NATALICIA TRACY is the executive director of the Brazilian Worker Center (BWC). She cofounded the Massachusetts Coalition for Domestic Workers, which in 2013 introduced a Domestic Worker Bill of Rights to the Massachusetts legislature, and saw it enacted into law in June 2014.

JANNE UNDERRINER is an associate professor of research and the director of the Northwest Indian Language Institute at the University of Oregon.

CARL WILMSEN is the executive director of the Northwest Forest Worker Center, a nonprofit organization that empowers forest workers and harvesters of nontimber forest products in the Pacific Northwest to improve their lives and livelihoods.

DILARA YARBROUGH is an assistant professor of criminal justice at San Francisco State University.

PRENTICE ZINN is a director at GMA Foundations and administrator of the Sociological Initiatives Foundation.

About the Foundation

The Sociological Initiatives Foundation supports social change by funding research linked to social action. It was established in 1998 from the sale of *Sociological Abstracts* and *Language Learning and Behavior Abstracts*—printed indexes of the international literature in sociology and related disciplines.

Sociologist Leo P. Chall founded *Sociological Abstracts* in 1953. His goal was to make the breadth of social science research more accessible to the public and also share the work of international scholars that were often marginalized in the field. Chall's perspective was influenced by his close friend Dr. Alfred McClung Lee, a noted leader in progressive sociology and board member of *Sociological Abstracts*. Dr. Lee was a fierce critic of the narrow confines of the field of sociology. He was known for his insistence that sociologists escape the constraints of traditional academic research and get out into communities and help "rank-and-file" people. He insisted that such social scientists "are typically not elitist and manipulative" and "their viewpoint and working stance are not attractive to [establishment] power seekers."

Continuing the interdisciplinary and activist spirit of the organization, sociologists Glenn Jacobs and Irene Taviss-Thomson converted the non-profit organization to a foundation. Both were former staff writers and board members of *Sociological Abstracts* and worked to create a new organization that could help bridge the humanist ethos of the social sciences with community action.

The Sociological Initiatives Foundation funds public research projects that defend civil society from powerful interests. The research, often coupled with community organizing and advocacy, investigates laws, policies, institutions, regulations, and practices that limit equality in the United States. The foundation gives priority to projects that address racism, xenophobia, classism, gender bias, exploitation, or the violation of human rights and freedoms. It also supports research that furthers language learning and investigates solutions to real-life language-related problems.

Trustees

Index

language revitalization, 5, 171–172, 174–175;
    success of, 181–182, 184; youth interest in,
    183, 184
Las Vegas, Nevada, 115–117, 123
Las Vegas Metropolitan Police Department
    (LVMPD), 122, 123
Latinx, 99, 107, 123; as construction workers,
    143, 152; as dairy workers, 127; as domestic
    workers, 87; as forest workers, 97
law enforcement, 45–46, 123. *See also* police
leadership: development, 133, 142, 192; of
    directly affected communities, 33–34, 35,
    152; perspectives of, 22–23; by workers,
    69, 81, 89, 127, 131, 133, 142, 143, 148–149
leadership schools, 113
Lee, Alfred McClung, 7–8, 11; *Sociology for
    Whom?*, 8
LEP. *See* Local Emphasis Program
Lewis-Clark State College, Lewistown,
    Indiana, 162
LIHEAP. *See* Low Income Home Energy
    Assistance Program
linguistics, 171, 174, 177
lived experience, 24, 37, 56, 73, 143
Living Tongues Institute, 174
living wage, 70, 71, 87
Local Emphasis Program (LEP), 127
LOHP. *See* Labor Occupational Health
    Program
Los Angeles, California, 114
lower middle class, 29
low-income energy assistance, 59
Low Income Home Energy Assistance Pro-
    gram (LIHEAP), 55–56
low-income households, 47, 57, 58, 59, 60
LVMPD. *See* Las Vegas Metropolitan Police
    Department

marginalized groups, 38, 138–139, 162–163,
    186. *See also* subaltern groups
Marx, Karl, 9, 13n1; *The German Ideology*,
    13n1
Massachusetts Coalition for Domestic
    Workers, 83, 85, 87
matched pair audit testing, 68, 70–71
Medford, Oregon, 96–97
media: campaigns, 26, 81, 150; coverage, 57,
    58, 71, 76, 91, 133, 192; Latin American, 91,
    133, 150; transformation of, 44

megaloads, 158–161, 163–164, 167–169. *See
    also* antimegaload blockades
member-leadership model, 52
Michigan, 77
middle class, 20. *See also* lower middle class;
    progressive middle class
Migrant Justice, 133
*Milked: Immigrant Dairy Farmwork-
    ers in New York State* (WJCNY and
    WCCNY), 127, 128, 130, 132; goals of, 138;
    release of, 133; use of, 133–135
minimum wage, 18, 66, 82; raising of, 71, 72,
    73–74. *See also* subminimum wage
*Missing Class: Strengthening Social Move-
    ment Groups by Seeing Class Cultures*
    (Leondar-Wright), 17, 19, 24, 30, 192
mixed methods, 8, 19
movement building, 18, 81, 88, 89
Mujeres Unidas y Activas, 85
multimethodology, 68, 188

National Autonomous University of Mexico
    (UNAM), 134
National Day Laborers' Organizing Net-
    work (NDLON), 12–13; activism, 124;
    mission of, 112–113; research program,
    113–116, 124
National Day Laborer Survey (NDLS),
    114–115
National Domestic Workers Alliance
    (NDWA), 81, 82, 94n2; *Home Econom-
    ics*, 86
National Indian Education Association
    (NIEA), 183
National Institute of Occupational Safety
    and Health (NIOSH), 97
National Labor Relations Act, 82
National Restaurant Association (NRA),
    71–74, 75
Native Americans, 3, 5, 163–165, 170, 190;
    boarding schools and, 174; languages of,
    171–173, 176–177; wellness and, 175. *See
    also individual nations and tribes*
Navajo, 164, 175
NDLON. *See* National Day Laborers' Orga-
    nizing Network
NDLS. *See* National Day Laborer Survey
NDWA. *See* National Domestic Workers
    Alliance